Nightmares in Red,
White and Blue

LIBRARY OF CONGRESS CATALOGUING-IN-PUBLICATION DATA

Maddrey, Joseph, 1979–
   Nightmares in red, white and blue : the evolution of the American horror film / Joseph Maddrey.
       p.   cm.
   Includes filmography.
   Includes bibliographical references and index.

   ISBN 0-7864-1860-5 (softcover : 50# alkaline paper) ∞

   1. Horror films—United States—History and criticism.
I. Title.
PN1995.9.H6M24   2004
791.43'6164'0973—dc22   2004005811

British Library cataloguing data are available

©2004 Joseph Maddrey. All rights reserved

No part of this book may be reproduced or transmitted in any form or by any means, electronic or mechanical, including photocopying or recording, or by any information storage and retrieval system, without permission in writing from the publisher.

Manufactured in the United States of America

Cover design by Mark Durr

McFarland & Company, Inc., Publishers
   Box 611, Jefferson, North Carolina 28640
      www.mcfarlandpub.com

Nightmares in Red, White and Blue

The Evolution of the American Horror Film

Joseph Maddrey

McFarland & Company, Inc., Publishers
Jefferson, North Carolina, and London

Table of Contents

Preface	1
PART I: AMERICAN GOTHIC IN FILM	3
1. You Must Become Caligari: German Expressionism and the Origins of Film Gothic	7
2. A New World of Gods and Monsters: Hollywood Studio Horrors of the 1930s	11
3. Shadow Play: Hitchcock, Film Noir and the Val Lewton Cycle	21
4. Bad Kids, Big Bugs, Body Snatchers and the Bomb	30
5. The Monster Is Madness: Castle, Corman and California Gothic	39
6. Apocalypse America: The Modern Horror Film	48
7. What the Fifty Foot Woman Did to the Incredible Shrinking Man	57
8. Selling the American Dream: The Postmodern Horror Film (Part I)	68
9. Old Monsters, New Flesh: The Postmodern Horror Film (Part II)	78
10. Reality Bites: The New American Film Gothic	87

Table of Contents

PART II: AUTEURS — 95

11. Tod Browning: Sideshows — 97
12. Alfred Hitchcock: Noir Town — 104
13. Roger Corman: Counterculture and Creature Features — 112
14. George A. Romero: The Fall of Camelot — 122
15. John Carpenter: Space-Age Cowboys — 131
16. Larry Cohen: Outside in America — 141
17. David Lynch: American Beauty? — 151
18. Wes Craven: The New Myths — 162

Filmography — 173
Notes — 183
Bibliography — 187
Index — 193

Preface

I suppose an explanation is in order.

People tend to give you strange looks when you admit that you not only spend much of your time watching horror movies, but are in fact writing a book about the *cultural significance* of horror movies. Sounds pretty bloody pretentious, doesn't it? The following pages present my (admittedly concise) overview of the relationship between 20th century American history and one of the most enduring film genres. In other words: horror movies as social metaphors.... Dracula promises relief from the Great Depression; Carrie White re-balances the status quo for feminists everywhere; the Body Snatchers make good on the threats of communism. These subtexts — set forth by David J. Skal, Stephen King, and every film critic under the sun, respectively — are one way to view three classic films. These interpretations, however outrageous they might seem, offer an interesting explanation for the popularity of the genre at large.

Certain horror stories remain in the popular consciousness because they effectively tap into our most primal fears. As Siegfried Kracauer points out in his book, *From Caligari to Hitler: A Psychological History of the German Film*, popular films also often seem to reflect the desires and anxieties of the time and place in which they are made. A few years ago, with this idea in mind, and with the resources of the James Madison University library at hand, I began writing a psychological history of the American horror film — to explain the enduring appeal of the genre, and to indulge my own personal obsession with the macabre.

Over time, the films discussed in these pages began to seem to me like a single signature work of a changing country. Just as auteurs develop variations on particular themes, I realized, American filmmakers and moviegoers have developed the horror genre by continually re-imagining the most basic nightmares. Even the casual viewer can recognize the repetition of certain characters and formulas in horror films—according to one critic, they are as fixed as stations of the cross—but the monsters themselves shape-shift from decade to decade as the fears of the popular audience change. This is perhaps what has allowed the genre to thrive for so many years—it is at once timeless and firmly rooted in the world we know.

Many books and articles have been written on the subject (though only a few have had the arrogance to try to cover so much material in so little space). For my money, the most interesting writers on this subject—and those who have influenced me the most—are Bruce Kawin, David J. Skal, Gregory Waller, Tony Williams, Robin Wood, Carol J. Glover, and Stephen King. Equally intriguing are the thoughts and writings of some of the filmmakers themselves, which is why I chose to include chapters on eight directors whose work fit my thesis. I hope that this book will prompt readers to visit and revisit the films and the filmmakers.

Finally, I'd like to thank several members of the faculty at James Madison University for helping to lay the groundwork for this book: Dr. James Ruff, Dr. George Wead, Dr. Ralph Cohen, Dr. Robert Hoskins, Dr. Cameron Nickels and especially Dr. Robert Geary. Also, many thanks to Benjamin Lamb for letting me raid his extensive movie collection.

Part I

American Gothic in Film

> The history of the horror film is essentially a
> history of anxiety in the twentieth century.
> — Paul Wells, *The Horror Genre:
> From Beelzebub to Blair Witch*

Not long ago, literary critics scoffed at the term "American Gothic." By most accounts, the classic period of Gothic literature — a predominantly British genre — spans the years between the publication of Horace Walpole's *The Castle of Otranto* in 1764 and the publication of C.R. Maturin's *Melmoth the Wanderer* in 1820. In this interval, the United States of America had not existed long enough for its artists to have morbid obsessions with misdeeds of the past. Most Colonial American writers, instead, echoed the boundless hope of a seemingly prelapsarian New World. By the time that the term "American Gothic" came into popular use in the first half of the 20th century, the country and the term Gothic had changed dramatically.

One critic defines the classic Gothic genre as a pattern of "concern with the brutality, cruelty and superstition of the Middle Ages."[1] More concretely, there are a number of recurring plot devices and themes — though these vary from work to work — which include the following: haunted settings and subterranean or labyrinthine corridors, tyrannical and often tragic anti-heroes who victimize virginal damsels in distress, supernatural forces, sadomasochism, obsessions with decay, and the overwhelming influence of the past. Perhaps the most common thread is the pessimistic tone of the works, a sense that human nature is innately corrupt and transcendence inherently dangerous.[2] The classic literary genre faded, but many of its motifs survived, first diluted in the German *Schauerromane* and Victorian literature and later reincarnated in the horror genre as we know it today in America.

In the words of one critic, who regarded the genre as a "technology of subjectivity," the Gothic infiltrated the Victorian novel as "a symptomatic moment in which boundaries between good and evil, health and perversity, crime and punishment, truth and deception, inside and outside dissolve and threaten the integrity of the narrative itself."[3] The Gothic has been similarly re-defined in 20th century literature and film. Visual motifs and other elements have been subsumed into the horror genre, making the classic Gothic an elusive undercurrent in the narratives. This undercurrent has not only been transposed onto specific narratives but onto American culture at large, and the term Gothic has been redefined as a distinctly American one.

The progenitor of the American Gothic story was Charles Brockden Brown, a major influence on Edgar Allan Poe, the most well-known American horror writer of the 19th century. Poe's short stories "The Fall of the House of Usher" and "William Wilson" are great examples of the traditional Gothic. "Usher" echoes the unlikely moral of *Otranto*, that "the sins of the fathers are visited on their children to the third and fourth generation."[4] "William Wilson" was one of the first American stories to employ the idea of the "doppelganger," which dominated the Gothic literary tradition in the Victoria era (though it was a popular motif in folklore and mythology as far back as Greek Classicism) and has always punctuated the horror genre in film. Poe's stories, though the products of an American mind, have a distinct flavor of European decadence and, in his own time, Poe was better received overseas (especially in France) than in his homeland. His works sparked a debate among intellectuals as to whether or not there was any place for Gothic gloom in American art. As Carlos Clarens points out in *An Illustrated History of the Horror Films*, "horror is nourished by myth, tradition and legend — all of which require centuries of rich elaboration."[5] Today, the numerous film adaptations of Poe's works are worthy of critical attention if only because they are products of a more evolved American culture than that of the original stories. Roger Corman's adaptations, in particular, reflect a distinctly dated air of decadence, rooted in the counterculture movement of the 1960s.

Other Gothic-inspired American writers have been far more indebted to their sense of national identity. Nathaniel Hawthorne wrote haunting stories about principles of Puritanism and the sort of paranoia that surrounded the Salem Witch Trials, Colonial America's own version of the Spanish Inquisition (call it "New England Gothic"). William Faulkner and

Flannery O'Connor are the most reputable authors of Southern Gothic fiction, which resonates with feelings of religious guilt and post–Civil War decay. A more recent cultural creation is California Gothic, pioneered by author Nathanael West and filmmakers like Billy Wilder and Robert Aldrich. In his book *The American Dream: A Short History of an Idea That Shaped a Nation,* Jim Cullen traces the evolution of a catchphrase every bit as vague as the term Gothic. He explains that over the years the meaning of the phrase has reflected different cultural perceptions of "the good life." According to him, the most recent incarnation of the American Dream is a dream of the West Coast — of instant fame and fortune achieved with minimal effort. Filmmakers like Wilder and Aldrich are only too willing to remind us that, for those who have achieved this new American Dream, there is a dark side. The Gothic temperament has become an almost subliminal part of America's onscreen identity, though the infusion was a gradual process.

Early Hollywood filmmakers, many of whom were immigrants, set their films in the Old World or transplanted European characters into an American setting. Even Tod Browning, who rooted many of his macabre fantasies in the strange world of American vaudeville and traveling sideshows, supposedly drew on a thorough knowledge of classic Gothic literature.[6] The result, in films like Browning's *Dracula* (1931), James Whale's *Frankenstein* (1931) and Karl Freund's *The Mummy* (1932), is a kind of Euro-American Gothic. The visual motifs of Gothic literature — haunted castles and undead monsters — were presented to American audiences, who appreciated the novelty of seeing Old World superstitions intrude upon modern life. Most of the films served to reassure audiences; there was scarcely any realistic threat. At the end, order was restored once the thickly accented villain had been vanquished.

Movie monsters were, for the most part, held at an aesthetic distance until the 1940s, when producer Val Lewton decided to dispense with the rubber-faced creatures of yesteryear. The invading "evils" remained distinctly foreign, but were not as distinctly supernatural. Cinematic ruminations on the soul at work became examinations of the psyche at work. Whereas most horror films of the previous decade had been psychological allegories, several films in the 1940s overtly raised issues of abnormal psychology that had been lurking beneath the surface of the film genre since its creation. The monsters in these films were no different from us, our friends and neighbors.

In the 1950s, horror invaded America on numerous fronts. Post–WWII malaise, often cited as the primary cause of a gradual shift toward darker, more cynical films in Hollywood (*film noir*), was compounded with

Communist fears, space-age anxieties, nuclear panic and the apparent instability of the nuclear family. All of these things helped to create an audience ripe for exploitation. Dread was a part of everyday American life; Gothic traditions had been culturally digested and the Studio Era gave way to independent filmmakers who were unconventional by nature. By the time that *Invasion of the Body Snatchers* was released in 1956, the sort of paranoia that Sigmund Freud had identified as "un-homelike" was presented onscreen as a part of the average American home. Evil from an uncertain source was taking root, and it could not be vanquished in an hour or two of screen time.

By the 1960s, screen horrors were no longer being imported or falling from the skies—they were being bred in our backyards. The new monsters belonged to decadent California, the rural hills of the Midwest and idyllic small towns with no future. Over the next two decades, the film industry's psychological siege on American moviegoers escalated to a point of utter annihilation in films like *The Birds* (1963), *Night of the Living Dead* (1968), *The Stepford Wives* (1975), *Invasion of the Body Snatchers* (1978) and *Dawn of the Dead* (1978). The trends in horror films indicated that family, tradition, gender roles and the American Dream itself had corroded and become something barely recognizable and completely unacceptable.

In the decades since, filmmakers have responded to cultural changes with cries of the damned, new hopes and a self-consciousness that seems to blur the line between film and society, fiction and reality (thereby threatening the narrative itself). One thing is certain: Gothic fears cannot be dispelled from American life or film. The horror genre is more popular today than ever, and as America continues to evolve in the shadow of its past, audiences will continue to watch those shadows on film.

1

You Must Become Caligari: German Expressionism and the Origins of Film Gothic

> "Eyes, we must have eyes!"
> — E.T.A. Hoffman,
> "The Sandman"

For well over a century, the subject of dread has been closely associated with Germany — so much so that Edgar Allan Poe was once forced to declare that terror is not of Germany but of the soul. One reason for this association is Sigmund Freud's essay "The Uncanny," written just after the turn of the century. In it, he analyzes his own response to the macabre writings of fellow countryman E.T.A. Hoffman, grandfather of the modern ghost story, to determine the exact nature of dread-without-worldly-object. He calls the uncanny "that class of the frightening which leads back to what is known of old and long familiar"[1] and says that this "intellectual uncertainty" occurs "either when infantile complexes which have been repressed are once more revived by some impression, or when primitive beliefs which have been surmounted seem once more to be confirmed."[2]

Poe's "William Wilson" was one of the first horror stories to be translated to the new medium of film. *The Student of Prague* (1913), produced by Paul Wegener and written by Henrik Galeen, has long since been lost, but the details of the plot have survived, in part due to Wegener's own 1926 remake. In the film, a poor student named Baldwin signs a contract with a magician named Scapinelli, trading his mirror image for love and wealth. The bargain proves disastrous when Scapinelli grants Baldwin's mirror image a life of its own. Baldwin is forced to answer for his troublesome twin, who kills Baldwin's fiancée's rival suitor in a jealous rage. When Baldwin finally manages to kill his double, he finds that he has mortally wounded himself.[3] Sigfried Kracauer, author of *From Caligari to Hitler: A Psychological History of the German Film*, cites *The Student of Prague* as one of the first examples of "horror story as a case of individual psychology." As such, he says, the film was indicative of the intellectual climate at that time in Germany — not only of the advent of psychology as a science, but of a kind of political self-imprisonment suffered by the middle class.[4]

Even more firmly rooted in the culture was Wegener's subsequent film, *The Golem, or How It Came into the World* (1915). Based on an old Hebrew legend about a clay statue brought to life by the mystical Rabbi Loew, the film begins when the statue is unearthed during an archaeological dig in Prague. An antiques dealer animates the Golem, which falls in love with the dealer's daughter as it becomes more human. Her rejection spurs his wrath. A six-part series entitled *Homunculus* (1916) took the formula, reminiscent of Mary Shelley's novel *Frankenstein: A Modern Prometheus*, to greater extremes. In *Homunculus*, an inhuman monster responds to mankind's rejection of him by precipitating a world war. The monster avenges himself not only on his creator but on the entire human race. Kracauer attributes the darkness of the film to the political climate of Weimar Germany, aligning Homunculus and Adolf Hitler.[5]

Paul Wegener in the 1920 remake of *The Golem*.

Just as Kracauer draws these parallels between art and culture in post-war Germany, it is easy to make similar observations about American horror films in the 1930s. In his book *The Monster Show: A Cultural History of Horror,* David J. Skal speculates that widespread social unrest during the early part of the Great Depression may have been largely responsible for the popularity of Universal's pioneering horror films in the 1930s. By contrast, the real-life horrors of World War II may be to blame for the genre's subsequent decade of unpopularity. Paul Wells, author of *The Horror Genre: From Beelzebub to Blair Witch,* opines that "the history of the horror film is essentially a history of anxiety in the twentieth century."[6] The popular films reflect a societal need for catharsis.

The continuing success of the genre, however, cannot simply be attributed to the zeitgeist. *The Cabinet of Dr. Caligari* (1920), the definitive German Expressionist film, is indisputably a product of the time and place from which it emerged, but it also reflects the past and future of the Gothic

Caligari (Werner Krauss) poses with his unwilling henchman, Cesare (Conrad Veidt), in *The Cabinet of Dr. Caligari* (Ufa, 1920).

tradition. *Caligari* did for the horror film what Henry James did for the ghost story—it defined the horror genre in film as a technology of subjectivity. Until the final moments of the film, *Caligari* seems to be a political allegory, an outcry against dictatorship. According to screenwriter Hans Janowitz, Cesare the zombie was intended to represent "the common man who, under the pressure of compulsory military service, is drilled to kill and to be killed." The writer planned to end the film with the overthrow of the carnival somnambulist known as Caligari, but director Robert Wiene had a different vision.[7] The film ends with Cesare imprisoned in a psychiatric hospital under Caligari's care, reversing the implications of Janowitz's story. Kracauer points out, however, that the wild expressionist set designs—often interpreted as Cesare's insane view of the world—remain in the final scene, undermining the interpretation of this ending as a "return to conventional reality."[8]

The art design of *The Cabinet of Dr. Caligari* is almost certainly the most significant aspect of the film. Distorted shadows painted on the sets give the film a menacingly Kafkaesque feel, while Cesare's face paint today makes him look like a reject from the early 1980s British punk era. The audience does not know what it can take for granted, so we are uncomfortable throughout the film. In the end, even the filmmakers cannot decide what is real and what is not. Thus, *Caligari* has more in common with modern American horror films (see, for example, *Let's Scare Jessica to Death* and Oliver Stone's *Seizure*) than with the films that followed in the 1920s and 1930s.

F.W. Murnau's *Nosferatu: A Symphony of Horror* (1922)—an unofficial adaptation of Bram Stoker's novel *Dracula*—had more influence on the earliest American horror films. In *Nosferatu*, pious love vanquishes a domineering force that initially seems omnipotent. Max Schreck's vampire Orlock exerts a kind of emotional tyranny over his victims. He is a sickly creature (unlikely to inspire the kind of awe that Bela Lugosi's Count Dracula later would) and his victims seem to have no will of their own. It is not power, but rather self-sacrifice that destroys the tyrant. In the final scene, Orlock is vaporized in the light of the rising sun, leaving no trace of the former threat. *Nosferatu* displays the reassuring hope that would characterize most of the Universal horror films in the 1930s—a hope that the monsters of the day, whatever form they took, could be destroyed without turning the destroyers themselves into monsters. Most early American horror films operated on the assumption that, for every invading evil force, there is a stronger opposing force that maintains the status quo.

2

A New World of Gods and Monsters: Hollywood Studio Horrors of the 1930s

> Unusual times demand unusual pictures.
> — Tag line for *White Zombie* (1932)

Tod Browning's *Dracula* (1931) is often referred to as the first American horror film — an interesting distinction since the source novel is English, the actor in the title role Hungarian, and the film itself more indebted to theatrical conventions than cinematic ones. The financial success of *Dracula* almost single-handedly legitimized a future genre of films that "function as nightmares for the individual viewer, as diagnostic eruptions for repressive societies, and as exorcistic or transcendent pagan rituals for supposedly post-pagan cultures."[1] Browning biographer David J. Skal accounts for the film's success by saying that it "liberated the dormant irrational energies Hollywood had repressed for decades, but which were implicit in the dreamlike medium from the beginning."[2] It matters little that, in comparison to many of the German horror pictures that preceded and the American monster movies that followed, *Dracula* is surprisingly un-innovative. Despite a few impressive sets designed by Charles Hall and cinematography by the reputable Karl Freund, it fails to capture the haunting visual beauty of *Nosferatu,* Carl Theodor Dreyer's *Vampyr* (1932) — both silent films — or even producer Paul Kohner's Spanish adaptation of *Dracula,* which was filmed on the same sets as the Lugosi version. Regardless, the influence of Browning's film is unquestionable.

The film was modeled on a popular Broadway adaptation of Bram Stoker's novel which featured a little-known eccentric immigrant named Bela Lugosi as Dracula. Following the death of Lon Chaney, who was intended to star in the film, Lugosi was hired to reprise the role in Hollywood. An actor who would reside in the shadow of *Dracula* for the remainder of his career just as the character of Dracula has resided in the actor's shadow, Lugosi proved to be the most enchanting aspect of the film. The unknown foreigner exuded an air of menace and sexuality—a villainous Valentino. In the opening reel, Renfield meets the Count in his Transylvania castle. Here, Renfield is the outsider—thrust, like the hapless haunted house guests in *The Bat* (1926), *The Cat and the Canary* (1927) and *The Cat Creeps* (1930), into an anachronistic Gothic reality. Later, Dracula sweeps into high society London. Although he appears as much out of place there as Renfield did in Transylvania, Dracula is welcomed eagerly. When he meets Mina at the London Opera House, he longingly contemplates death in labored, heavily accented English: "To die ... to be really dead ... that must be glorious." Mina, like female audiences across America, is captivated. Rather than the anti–Christ of Stoker's novel, Lugosi's Dracula is a tragic figure. Significantly, America's first screen monster is a victim as much as victimizer.

To audiences of the day, he was perhaps most simply a symbol of change. Skal theorizes that "for Depression era audiences, the picture may have carried all sorts of half-conscious metaphors about people paralyzed and enervated by mysterious draining forces they could not control."[3] Still, it is only for a brief period of time that the presence of Dracula actually disrupts the lives of the heroic characters, and herein lies the catharsis. Near the end of the picture, Mina tells her beau that "it's all over, our life together, our love," but her resignation is never completely believable. Prof. Van Helsing, whose almost tyrannical presence makes Dracula appear impotent rather than omnipotent, conquers the vampire with minimal effort. Thus, order is restored, and Jonathan Harker carries his seemingly unaffected bride-to-be out of the dungeons of Carfax Abbey.

Dracula's success prompted the studio to rush more "monster movies" into production, and the vampire was quickly succeeded on screen by another famous Gothic creation. Universal's *Frankenstein* (1931) was originally the brainchild of director Robert Florey, who co-wrote an early script based on Peggy Webling's 1927 play *Frankenstein: An Adventure in the Macabre*. The directorial reigns on *Frankenstein* were handed over to Englishman James Whale, whose auteurist sensibilities played a large part in defining the film.[4] As in *Dracula,* the monster is divided into personas of victim and victimizer. Whale presented the apparent monster—a hulking subhuman composed from the remains of human corpses — as an empathetic victim. (It helped immeasurably that the role was essayed by a classically trained theater actor named William Henry Pratt, better known by his professional name Boris Karloff.) The apparent hero — Henry Frankenstein himself — is the true victimizer. Ironically, the two characters have become inextricably linked in the popular imagination — the Monster is usually called Frankenstein — as if the unholy creation must embody the sins of its creator. At the end of the film, the doctor repents his sins, vowing never again to meddle with things that man should leave alone,

The Count (Bela Lugosi) poses with a midnight snack (Helen Chandler) in this publicity still for *Dracula* (Universal, 1931).

and making the film far more complex than *Dracula*. *Frankenstein* raised questions of moral responsibility that would permeate many of Universal's subsequent horror films.

Soon after the release of *Frankenstein,* Karl Freund and Boris Karloff went to work on *The Mummy* (1932), a near-remake of *Dracula* which boasted superior visuals but a less engaging monster. Later, James Whale began production on *The Invisible Man* (1933). Based on a story by H.G. Wells, the film expanded on themes explored in the director's previous *Frankenstein*. Claude Raines stars as Jack Griffin, a chemist-turned–Nietzschean Superman. Soon after he develops a serum that makes him invisible, he begins to entertain meglomaniacal thoughts: "Suddenly, I realized the power I held — the power to rule, to make the world grovel at my feet ... power to walk into the gold vaults of the nations, into the secrets of kings, into the holy of holies. Power to make multitudes run squealing in terror at the touch of my little invisible finger." Film historian Paul Jensen explains the appeal the film had for audiences of the day: "Such a figure would naturally attract people who, boxed into a corner by the Depression, were intrigued by men who ignore the rules and take matters into their own hands, whether they be Jack Griffin, Little Caesar, or Franklin Delano Roosevelt."[5]

Neal Gabler, in his book *An Empire of Their Own: How the Jews Invented Hollywood,* went so far as to align the studio moguls who defined early Hollywood — including Universal's founder and chief executive Carl Laemmle — with the Superman personas of Jack Griffin, Count Dracula and Henry Frankenstein. "When stripped down to its basics," he says, "*Frankenstein,* adapted freely from Mary Shelley's novella, is a tale of the assertion of will — the quality Laemmle most celebrated in himself and the one to which he attributes his success."[6] Other studio heads were, naturally, eager to repeat the financial success that Laemmle had achieved with his monster movies.

In 1931, Paramount Pictures released a new adaptation of *Dr. Jekyll and Mr. Hyde* featuring Fredric March in the dual role. Like his screen peers Dracula and Frankenstein, Robert Louis Stevenson's Gothic monster is a doppelganger. The difference is that *Dr. Jekyll and Mr. Hyde* presents the "eternal struggle in human nature" within one remarkably sane human. We cringe when the abusive Mr. Hyde tells his lover that "I hurt you because I love you," because we have already identified with Dr. Jekyll — who is, in fact, the hero of the story. Jekyll is rash and impulsive, but ultimately likable — and we shudder to think that, within such a civilized man, there is a primitive beast taking control. The monstrosity is clearly identified in human nature, and the film implies — like Paul Wegener's *The Stu-*

The two faces of Fredric March in *Dr. Jekyll and Mr. Hyde* (Paramount, 1931).

dent of Prague — that death is the only way for a man to tame his "sinful" impulses.

Paramount's *Island of Lost Souls* (1933) examines the duality of human nature from a different angle. Inside every primitive beast, the film would have us believe, there is a civilized human waiting to evolve. The pompous Dr. Moreau, another scientist with a God complex, is trying to speed up the process of evolution. His experiments populate a remote island with a peculiar breed of man-beasts. He is able to maintain order on the island until a group of unassuming Americans arrive and learn that Moreau, like Mr. Kurtz in Joseph Conrad's *Heart of Darkness,* has become a beast himself while playing God to a population of "uncivilized" creatures. From the safety of his fortified island compound, he subjects his creatures to the House of Pain, a surgical ward. Once the "monsters" realize that their ruler is mortal, they become vengeful.

Tod Browning's *Freaks* (1932), distributed by MGM, has a comparable ending. The film revolves around a traveling band of circus performers, many of them deformed. When one of the "freaks," a midget named Hans, inherits a fortune, he proposes to a beautiful (full-sized) trapeze artist named Cleopatra. She marries Hans, with the intention of stealing his money and running away with circus strongman Hercules, but she is unable to hide her disgust with the freaks at a wedding feast where they claim her as "one of us." Cleo soon learns the significance of the freak code: Offend one and you offend them all. In the final act, she is stalked by the "monsters"—a transvestite, a pair of Siamese twins, an emasculated clown and a limbless "human worm" who writhes in the mud after her with a knife in his teeth. In the end, the freaks physically make her one of them — apparently by cutting off her legs, cutting out her voicebox and covering her with feathers. The horror of this film lies in the fact that real freaks were cast in the roles. It was easy for audiences to react to Browning's earlier films, with Lon Chaney in the role of deformed outcast; publicity photos reassured them that it was purely entertainment. *Freaks* was perceived as an outright assault on moral decency, and it was denounced by audiences across the globe.

At Warner Bros., director Michael Curtiz brought a more acceptable element of reality to his horror films. *Doctor X* (1932) and *Mystery of the Wax Museum* (1933) were the first horror films to be set in modern-day America, and among the first to be shot using two-strip Technicolor. Curtiz claimed that filming in color was as useful as ingenious camera angles for arousing "a feeling of surprise, of terror, of repulsion, of admiration."[7] The New York setting also elicited strong reactions; audiences were unable to dismiss the horrors as the eccentricities of backward countries across the globe. Another element of Curtiz's films that was different was the choice of main characters; both films revolve around a fast-talking, tireless urban reporter — a stock character in the studio's screwball comedies, but a rarity in horror films.

In *Doctor X*, the reporter is Lee Taylor, a quirky little man who never goes anywhere without his trusty handbuzzer. Taylor suspects that an employee of New York City's Academy of Surgical Research is the "Moon Killer" responsible for a series of recent atrocities. Dr. Xavier, the director of the academy, enlists the help of Taylor to witness an unusual experiment: He plans to identify the true killer by subjecting all of the doctors at his institute to an elaborate polygraph test. Taylor is hardly the obvious choice of hero; he seems to survive by luck alone.

In *Mystery of the Wax Museum*, the tireless reporter is Florence — played by Fay Wray, one of the genre's first scream queens. It is she who first suspects the mysterious Dr. Igor (it's pronounced eye-gore) of a series of murders in New York. By day, Igor is the crippled owner of a macabre wax museum. By night, he is a killer, sneaking through the city wearing a black cape and stealing corpses to create his wax figures. Florence becomes a targeted victim, but she is not the usual damsel in distress. Though she calls on her beau for help in catching the criminal, there is plenty of sarcasm in her voice when she tells him to hurry up in case she needs him.

In RKO's *King Kong* (1933), filmed back-to-back with *The Most Dangerous Game* (1932), Fay Wray was once again cast as the heroine. As Ann Darrow, she is chosen by producer Carl Denham to star in a Hollywood production to be filmed on a remote island. As soon as Denham's crew arrives on the island, a primitive tribe tries to turn Ann into the bride of a giant ape. Exactly what Kong is supposed to do with her is unclear, but one particularly memorable sequence finds him undressing her, one article of clothing at a time, until he is interrupted by a hungry pterodactyl. This illicit love affair leads Kong back to New York City, where Denham puts him on display. "He was a king and a God in the world he knew," Denham tells spectators "But now he comes to civilization, merely a captive — a show to gratify your curiosity." And what a show he provides: Kong escapes from his captors and wreaks havoc on New York City before holding Ann hostage at the top of the Empire State Building. The violent eruption of primitive male energy on the city might be viewed as a humorous allegory for war, a subject that increasingly haunted the horror genre in the 1930s.

In 1934, Universal captured audiences by pairing Bela Lugosi and Boris Karloff in *The Black Cat*, often regarded as the first American psychological horror film.[8] Lugosi stars as Dr. Vitus Werdegast, a psychiatrist who arrives in the Carpathian Mountains to seek revenge on war general–turned-Satanic

2. A New World of Gods and Monsters

Dr. Vitus Werdegast (Bela Lugosi) and Hjalmar Poelzig (Boris Karloff) match wits in *The Black Cat* (Universal, 1934).

architect, Herr Poelzig (Karloff). Poelzig, we learn, murdered Werdegast's wife, and keeps her body in an upright glass coffin. Caught in the middle of a duel between Poelzig and Werdegast are two young American newlyweds, who arrive to give us a comparatively sane perspective on the events. Why they chose to honeymoon in the Carpathians is unclear, but they quickly find themselves at the mercy of Poelzig in his "nice, cozy, unpretentious insane asylum" on the hill. The house is as much an "embodiment of evil" as the cats who guard the labyrinthine cellar where Black Masses are held. The filmmakers seem to have been aware of the outrageousness of it all, and indulge accordingly. Paul Wells points out that "this revenge plot is merely a vehicle by which the bigger issue of the moral, ethical and social tragedy of the First World War is addressed.... The true horror lies in humankind's refusal to take responsibility for its past, and the feeling of guilt this creates is played out in the perverse preservation and amoral violence at the mansion."[9] The combination of the two stars and the supposed inspiration of an Edgar Allan Poe short story provided Universal with its most successful film of the year,[10] and the studio immediately began planning a follow-up.

The Raven (1935) is even more outrageous than *The Black Cat*, mostly due to Lugosi's exaggerated performance as Richard Vollin, a surgeon who dwells obsessively on the writings of Poe, and uses murderous devices from various stories to avenge the death of his "lost Lenore." After he disfigures an escaped convict named Bateman (played by Karloff), he forces the newly made monster to do his bidding. Then Vollin sets his amorous sights on a dancer and begins to expound on his sadistic plans to win her heart: "When a man of genius is denied his great love, he goes mad. Instead of being clear to do his work, he is tortured. So he begins to think of torture.... The torture of those who tortured him." Vollin lures several guests and the object of his affections to his home, which — as we might expect — houses a collection of torture devices, including a pit and a pendulum. "It's as if we were all in a tomb," one guest exclaims. In the end, Bateman sacrifices himself to save the girl, thereby dispelling his own fear that ugly people must do ugly things — an apt summation of Karloff's roles within the genre if ever there was one. Vollin, of course, meets a poetic fate. The same year, Peter Lorre would tackle an equally campy role in Karl Freund's *Mad Love* — MGM's remake of Robert Wiene's *The Hands of Orlac* (1925).

Eager to repeat its earlier successes, Universal asked Karloff to reprise his most famous role. Under the direction of James Whale, *Bride of Frankenstein* (1935) is a lively exaggeration of its predecessor. This time around, there are two Nietzschean characters. Henry Frankenstein is upstaged by Dr. Pretorius, played with morbid glee by Ernest Thesiger, who had a memorable role in Whale's *The Old Dark House* (1932). Pretorius arrives to congratulate the new Baron Frankenstein on his creation, and to unveil his own creations — a set of home-grown miniature people, including an archbishop who "seems to be asleep" and a Devil who "bears a great resemblance to me." Pretorius suggests that they combine their talents to populate "a new world of gods and monsters."

Frankenstein's Monster's plight is equally exaggerated in this film. After he is nearly crucified by an angry mob, the Monster becomes a wandering nomad, tamed only briefly by the friendship of a blind hermit who teaches him to talk. Later, the Monster takes refuge in a mausoleum where he interrupts Dr. Pretorius' coffin-top dinner with the deadpan pronouncement, "I love dead, hate living." Pretorius dryly responds, "You're wise in your generation." Ultimately, it is the Monster who realizes the sanctity of life. When he sees that the mad doctors' "Bride of Frankenstein" is repulsed by him, the Monster frees his creator, then plays the part of martyr, sacrificing himself, his bride and Dr. Pretorious with the words, "We belong dead."

The irreverent tone of films like *The Black Cat, The Raven* and *Bride*

2. A New World of Gods and Monsters

Dr. Pretorius (Ernest Thesiger) and the Monster (Boris Karloff) dine in a mausoleum in *Bride of Frankenstein* (Universal, 1935).

of Frankenstein was partly responsible for the 1935 creation of a revised code of ethics that forbade Hollywood to make "any illegal or immoral life seem either possible or pleasant."[11] The horror genre, which thrived on the exploitation of such taboos, was effectively emasculated. For a few years, the genre dried up. After the successful 1938 re-release of *Dracula* and *Frankenstein* on a double bill, many of the famous monsters of the early part of the decade re-emerged in new films. By this time, however, they were parodies of themselves.

Among the best of the new films was *Son of Frankenstein* (1939), directed by Rowland V. Lee. Karloff returned as the Monster, but his character was stripped of personality. The new story focused on Wolf von Frankenstein, a staunchly rational scientist who dismisses the veiled warnings of Gothic tradition, saying, "Nothing in nature is terrifying when one understands it." The new Dr. Frankenstein's overbearingly rational outlook is indicative of the shortcomings of Universal's horror films in the early 1940s—few screenwriters were willing to take the monsters, or the supernatural, seriously. Frankenstein's Monster and Dracula continued to stalk the silver screen in *The Ghost of Frankenstein* (1942), *Son of Dracula* (1944), *Frankenstein Meets the Wolf Man* (1943), *House of Frankenstein* (1944), *House of Dracula* (1945) and *Abbott and Costello Meet Frankenstein* (1948), but their mystique was gone. Hollywood filmmakers would have to re-invent the horror film.

3

Shadow Play: Hitchcock, Film Noir and the Val Lewton Cycle

> "I like the dark.... It's friendly."
> —DeWitt Bodeen, *Cat People*

In 1938, Alfred Hitchcock began making plans for his first American film, *Rebecca*, an adaptation of Daphne du Maurier's Gothic romance novel. At the time, he told an interviewer, "I shall treat this more or less as a horror film."[1] Hitchcock's definition of horror, however, was not the popular Hollywood definition. In an earlier interview, he said: "The term, meaning originally 'extreme aversion,' has been loosely applied to films which, to supply the desired emotional jolt, exploit sadism, perversion, bestiality, and deformity. This is utterly wrong, being vicious and dangerous. It is permissible for a film to be horrific, but not horrible; and between the two there is a dividing line which is apparent to all thinking people. The forerunner of the cycle of 'horror' pictures which is now drawing to a close was the stage 'Grand Guignol' and that was merely a 'stunt,' calculated to attract a neurotic section of the public. There is a growing body of opinion, inside as well as outside the film industry, against such films, which are successful in direct ratio to their power to create *unnatural* excitement. As a matter of fact, they are bound to fail, because the public is, as a rule, healthy-minded."[2] Whether the psychological thrillers of the 1940s are more "healthy-minded" than the Guignol films of the early 1930s is debatable, but Hitchcock's prediction about the death of the old-style horror movie was well-founded.

Five days after the bombing of Pearl Harbor in December 1941, Universal released *The Wolf Man*, the latest (and, some say, the last) of the studio's classic monster movies. Lon Chaney, Jr., stars as Larry Talbot, the youngest and most Americanized member of a wealthy Welsh family of "stiff-necked, undemonstrative types." As Talbot, the imposing actor was unassuming and highly likable. Early in the film, one character remarks that "there's nothing tragic about that man." Through no fault of his own, however, Larry Talbot is marked with the curse of the werewolf. The gypsy who diagnoses his affliction offers little hope for recovery as she ceremoniously repeats an ominous rhyme: "Even a man who is pure in heart, and says his prayers at night, may become a wolf when the wolfbane blooms, and the autumn moon is bright." In the end, nothing — not even love — can save this tragic hero. The resolution of the film is not reassuring in the way that earlier Universal horror films, with their distinctly Manichean view of the world, were. Larry Talbot is not torn between forces of good and evil; he is a victim of a cruel or indifferent fate in a less comprehensible world.

Larry Talbot (Lon Chaney Jr.) on the prowl in *The Wolf Man* (Universal, 1941).

Film historian David J. Skal regards the film — and its sequels, in which the Wolf Man is pitted against Universal's other classic monsters — as an expression of the complex wartime anxieties of American audiences. He calls Universal's popular four-part Wolf Man series (*The Wolf Man, Frankenstein Meets the Wolf Man, House of Frankenstein* and *House of Dracula*) an "unconscious parable of the war effort" that revolves around one man's "crusade for eternal peace and his frustrated attempts to control irrational, violent, European forces."[3] Skal also suggests that two of Universal's other wartime monster movies, *The Ghost of Frankenstein* and *Invisible Agent*, may have been equally cathartic for American audiences in 1942. "The brute image of the [Frankenstein] monster, able to dispose of any obstacle," he writes, "may have provided a rallying point for morale-battered wartime audiences."[4] More obvious is *Invisible Agent*, which introduces us to Jack Griffin's grandson, a scientist who vows to protect the Monocaine formula, saying, "There'll never be an emergency critical enough to justify its use." The bombing of Pearl Harbor changes his mind, and Griffin soon becomes the country's most secret weapon.

By late 1942, it was clear that Universal's monsters—some of them now seeming more like defending patriots than threatening foreigners— were no longer frightening audiences. (At least, not audiences over the age of 12.) The reality of World War II crippled the shock value of Hollywood's horrors. Other studios responded by incorporating the war into the text of their film, featuring German and Japanese villains in *Black Dragons* (1942), *Revenge of the Zombies* (1943), *Ghosts on the Loose* (1943), *The Gorilla Man* (1943) and *The Mysterious Doctor* (1943). Columbia's *The Return of the Vampire* (1943) blames the war for keeping alive the monster that embodied the dark fantasies of Depression-era moviegoers. The coffin of Armand Tesla (Lugosi in his Dracula regalia) is unearthed by the London blitzkrieg, and a pair of gravediggers, believing that the stake through Tesla's heart is a piece of shrapnel, kindly remove it, reawakening the vampire.

Rather than continue to rely on the old horror genre traditions, one of the studios began to create its own traditions. RKO Radio Pictures, encouraged by the successful 1942 re-release of *King Kong* (1933), hired David O. Selznick's long-time assistant, Val Lewton, to head up a horror B-movie unit. Lewton, like his mentor, demanded complete creative control over the films—a stipulation that was allowed by the front office on the condition that he accept lurid, pre-tested titles like *I Walked with a Zombie* (1943) and *Isle of the Dead* (1945). His first picture was to be called *Cat People* (1942).

Lewton's original story used the war as a backdrop; in the opening scenes, a Balkan village of shape-shifting cat creatures are pitted against a Nazi Panzer division.[5] Ultimately, Lewton decided not to shoot this prologue, focusing the film entirely on Irena Dubrovna, a beautiful young woman who escapes the village and flees to New York City. Soon after her arrival in New York, she falls in love with a "good, plain Americano" named Oliver Reed. The two hastily get married, but the honeymoon is not what Oliver expects. Irena is haunted by the superstitions of her native country—in particular, by an ancient curse dictating that feelings of jealousy, anger or "corrupt passions" will turn her into a deadly cat-creature. (What more could a man want?) She refuses to consummate their union, and Oliver seeks solace in the arms of a female co-worker who begins to suspect that Irena really is a supernatural monster.

The plot — complete with love triangle — seems to be modeled after Universal's *The Wolf Man*, but the visual style of Lewton and director Jacques Tourneur is unique. The majority of the film takes place in shadows, and Irena's transformation occurs off-screen because Lewton believed that audiences would be more frightened by the images conjured in their own imagination than by any Hollywood special effect. Though the decision may have been motivated as much by financial concerns as artistic ones (the original proposed budget for *Cat People* was under $120,000)[6], Lewton continued to employ this theory throughout his career. He claimed that "if you make the screen dark enough, the mind's eye will read anything into it they want! We're great ones for dark patches.... The horror addicts will populate the darkness with more horrors than all the horror writers in Hollywood could think of."[7] In *Cat People*, the decision to leave the monster unseen suggests to the audience that it may be a product of Irena's imagination.

In the film, Dr. Judd vocalizes this possibility in his diagnosis of Irena, paraphrasing Freud's definition of the uncanny as "emotional residue leftover from childhood traumas, sexual repression and general guilt."[8] *Cat People* is one of the most traditionally Gothic films to be produced in Hollywood, because it dispenses with the visual motifs and adopts the psychology behind the genre. William Patrick Day argues that the Gothic genre in literature addressed radical changes in science and popular philosophy in Europe in the late 1800s. "It helped shape its readers sense of their own subjectivity," he says, and "in this way, the Gothic is part of that process by which we move from thinking of our inner life in terms of souls and thinking of it in terms of psyches."[9] Dismissing his rational jargon, Irena tells Dr. Judd, "When you speak of the soul, you mean the mind, and it is not my mind that is troubled." (One can hear echoes of *Dracula's Daughter* (1936): "There are more things in Heaven and Earth than are dreamt of in your psychology, Mr. Garth.") Partly as a result of Judd's influence, however, Irena perceives herself as incurably monstrous; she knows that the problem runs deeper than Oliver or Dr. Judd can comprehend. Thus isolated, she regards death as her only escape because, as one critic puts it, "regaining innocence before death seems ... almost as inconceivable as retrieving virginity."[10]

Opposite: Sensational one-sheet for *Cat People* (RKO, 1942) featuring Simone Simon.

Alfred Hitchcock's *Shadow of a Doubt* (1943) is an equally sophisticated musing on the end of innocence for a young woman and, by extension, America at large. At the beginning of the film, young Charlie is depressed about the inertia of her family life. "We just sort of go along and nothing happens," she complains, adding that she's "talking about *souls*." Providentially, her uncle — also named Charlie — arrives in the idyllic small town of Santa Rosa, California, to shake things up. Uncle Charlie is a world traveler who fills the house with excited energy. His niece soon learns, however, that he is also a murderer who travels under a dark cloud. While poring over a family photo from 1888, Uncle Charlie reflects, "Everybody was sweet and pretty then ... the whole world. Wonderful world. Not like the world today." Uncle Charlie's character has experienced death first-hand and, like a weary war veteran, he comes home with psychological battle scars and threatens his niece's naïvely optimistic outlook on life. "The world is a sty," he rants. "Do you know if you ripped the fronts off houses, you'd find swine? The world's a hell. What does it

The two Charlies (Joseph Cotten and Teresa Wright) reminisce in *Shadow of a Doubt* (Universal, 1943).

matter what happens in it? Wake up!" In a later interview, Hitchcock reflected on the way that the Second World War influenced the film: "I would say, you know, if we take a period [around] the turn of the century, before World War I, the world was very placid in many ways.... The sheltered life in the town of Santa Rosa, where this young girl lived, may have been her world but it wasn't *the* world. Outside there, there were many other things happening."[11]

The Gothic motifs and general pessimism in *Shadow of a Doubt* seemed to pervade many of the American studio films of the early 1940s. After the war, French critics began to review Hollywood's output between 1940 and 1945, and they noticed strong tendencies in American cinema toward heightened realism, determinism and moral ambiguity. French cineaste Nino Frank dubbed this series *film noir*. Over the years, countless critics worldwide have personalized the definition and the term itself has become more ubiquitous, like the term "Gothic." Many of those same critics also attempted to localize the sociological impetus for the series. In his influential 1972 essay on film noir, Paul Schrader also calls the series a "delayed reaction to the Thirties."[12] He argues that Hollywood filmmakers spent the previous decade operating a morale-building dream machine. After the war, filmmakers and audiences alike finally began to express their long-standing disillusionment. This vague sense of disillusionment — with people, politics, heroic conventions and gender roles — is the common thread among film noirs, and critics contend that it is conveyed as much (if not more) by the visual style of the films as by the content. The world of film noir is a shadowy nightmare alley — not unlike the prowling grounds of Lewton's *Cat People*.

Several of Lewton's subsequent horror films, like many classic examples of film noir, hinged on existential fears of death in an irrational — perhaps godless — world. His third production, *The Leopard Man* (1943), contemplates man's lack of control over his life. Dispirited by a spate of unexplained murders in a small New Mexico town, one of the characters points to a ball suspended at the top of a water fountain and remarks, "We know as little about the forces that move us and move the world around us as that empty ball does." One of the most memorable scenes in the film features a teenage girl who is walking home from the store late at night. Realizing that she is being followed, she runs, screaming, only to find the door of her house locked. Because she is perfectly innocent and the world of classic horror films is relatively just, we expect her to escape, but as her mother nonchalantly moves toward the door, the screaming stops and we see the girl's blood begin to flow under the door. Lewton biographer Edmund G. Bansak says that "wartime audiences may not have liked *Leop-*

ard's downbeat message — that the young and the innocent also die — but it was an important one for them to grasp."[13]

Lewton's next film was even more downbeat. *The Seventh Victim* (1943) focuses on a young woman named Mary Gibson, who leaves the sheltered world of a religious school to search for her worldly sister Jacqueline, missing in New York City. Mary eventually learns that Jacqueline is an outcast member of a satanic cult, and is being held hostage by cult members. With a little help, Mary rescues her sister, but Jacqueline is unable to overcome her fear that the cult will continue to hunt her until she is dead. At the end of the film, she can no longer bear the waiting; she finally retreats to a rented room that is empty except for a rope and a chair.

The heroine of Universal's *Son of Dracula,* released the same year, is equally disturbed. Kay Caldwell welcomes the attack of Count Alucard because he is the only viable cure for her debilitating fear of death. After she has been bitten, a doctor explains, "I rather believe that Miss Caldwell may have made the transition from choice.... Don't forget the girl was morbid. That often means a fear of death, and Alucard could offer her eternal life." This is a world where the victims are more afraid of fear itself than they are of death. As a result, the monsters of the horror genre appear almost like heroic deliverers. In 1943 and 1944, Universal's monsters were being reduced to comic sideshows in *Frankenstein Meets the Wolf Man* (1943) and *House of Frankenstein* (1944), while RKO was pressing Lewton to make a campy monster mash titled *They Creep by Night,* which would combine the threats of "Cat People, Zombies, Leopard Men, beast-women and bat-men, blood-curdlers by the dozen."[14] Under pressure Lewton agreed to resurrect *Cat People*. The sequel, however, was not what the front office expected.

Compared to *The Seventh Victim, The Curse of the Cat People* (1944) is a much more lighthearted rumination on death and the afterlife. It picks up several years after the original. Oliver Reed is remarried, and he and his wife, along with daughter Amy, have moved from New York City to upstate Tarrytown. Unfortunately, Oliver is no better at empathizing with his imaginative daughter than he was at understanding his first wife. At one point, frustrated by his daughter's overactive imagination, he says, "She could almost be Irena's child," and scolds her for having "too many fancies and too few friends." One afternoon, Amy wanders into a neighborhood house, where she makes a wish on a witch's ring. She wishes for a friend, and Irena answers her call from beyond the grave. When Amy recognizes her new friend in a photo that her father has kept, Oliver reluctantly tells Amy about his first wife, and tries to explain to her the reality of death. Amy, like Irena, knows that there are more things in heaven and earth.

In the same year, Paramount released *The Uninvited* (1944), one of Hollywood's first serious-minded ghost stories. Like the previous year's *A Guy Named Joe*, in which a deceased WWII pilot becomes a benevolent ghost, *The Uninvited* mines the ghost story for more than shocks. Ray Milland stars as Roderick Fitzgerald, a Londoner who moves into an old house on the "ghost shores" of England, with his sister. They immediately notice disturbances—cold drafts, unusual smells and the persistent sound of a woman crying. The disturbances become more threatening when Stella, a local girl who was born in the house, visits. As Roderick begins to fall in love with her, he realizes that something in the house — perhaps the spirit of Stella's mother — is trying to harm her. Roderick responds rationally: "If a spirit comes back, it's for a special purpose. We've got to find out what it is." Eventually, he learns that there are two spirits in the house — one bad (Stella's supposed mother) and one good (Stella's true mother, who was murdered in the house). Once the murder has been brought to light, the disturbances end, and Roderick and Stella are able to look toward a brighter future together.

The war ended on August 14, 1945, after the United States dropped atomic bombs on Hiroshima and Nagasaki. Paul Schrader points out that, immediately following the war, the film noir quickly evolved into its "most aesthetically and sociologically piercing" phase, culminating with *Kiss Me Deadly*'s replication of "a world in which The Bomb has the final say."[15] The horror genre, for the most part, fell into another quiet phase, waiting for the next generation of moviegoers, who would be living with daily fears of atomic annihilation.

4

Bad Kids, Big Bugs, Body Snatchers and the Bomb

> It may well be that the mass-media dream of horror can sometimes become a nationwide analyst's couch.
> — Stephen King, *Danse Macabre*

In May of 1948, an anti-trust lawsuit filed by the federal government against the major Hollywood studios resulted in a consent decree that effectively ended the old studio system. Granted creative freedom from the demands of studio businessmen, writers and directors rebelled against the conventions of the Hollywood dream machine and its reassuring portraits of life in America. In the late 1940s and early '50s, Hollywood films became increasingly stark and pessimistic, many of them examining widespread social ills such as the alienation of war veterans, political corruption, racism and juvenile delinquency.

The threat of an impending atomic war was the ultimate collective nightmare and, by the mid–1950s, it had already become, in the words of Stephen King, the main "national phobic pressure point" probed by the horror genre. Paul Wells argues that "the Atomic Bomb was viewed not merely [as] an agent of destruction, but also as a beacon to the Universe of an advanced technological society."[1] Realizing that audiences of the day were more afraid of the "advancements" that haunted the future than of old superstitions, filmmakers updated the monster movie. Most of the monsters in early 1950s American cinema emerged from some new frontier that man had yet to discover or to fully explore. Dracula became a blood-sucking vegetable from outer space in *The Thing from Another World*

(1951). Mr. Hyde became a body-snatching alien. The overzealous Dr. Frankenstein, meanwhile, was unknowingly populating the earth with destructive mutants. Significantly, if they were not the direct results of atomic testing, the new monsters often fell — like bombs — from the sky. Wells elaborates: "If the monsters of the 1930s and 1940s were mythic, European and of an 'old world' order, subject only to isolationist rejection, then the 1950s alien can be construed as future-oriented, unknown, and modern; often accidentally, but necessarily, invited into the agencies of American progress."[2] At the dawn of the nuclear age, monster movies came from two distinctly different camps — one that stressed the accidental and unfortunate nature of new discoveries, and one that stressed potential benefits and, in some cases, eventual necessity.

In his essay "The Mummy's Pool," film historian Bruce Kawin compares and contrasts the horror and science fiction genres by focusing on two space age monster movies, each released in 1951. Like the two genres, he says, *The Day the Earth Stood Still* (a sci-fi film) and *The Thing From Another World* (a horror film) are "comparable in that both tend to organize themselves around some confrontation between an unknown and a would-be knower."[3] In *The Day the Earth Stood Still*, directed by Val Lewton protégé Robert Wise, the alien Klaatu is a non-violent and highly intelligent being that has come to Earth to dissuade mankind from waging war. The space vampire in Howard Hawks' *The Thing From Another World* is non-verbal and destructive — not to mention ugly. Since it feeds off of human blood, the possibility of a peaceful co-existence seems highly unlikely. In both films, scientists hope to learn from the aliens, while the military plans to destroy them. Because the natures of the two aliens are different, the Army appears to be the villain in *The Day the Earth Stood Still* and the hero in *The Thing*. Kawin uses this point to illustrate the difference between the genres: "Horror emphasizes the dread of knowing, the danger of curiosity, while science fiction emphasizes the danger and irresponsibility of the closed mind."[4] Horror is obviously the more conservative of the two. Its heroes shoot first and ask questions later.

This dubious moral lesson is apparent in *The War of the Worlds* and *Invaders from Mars*, both released in 1953. *War of the Worlds* begins when what appears to be a meteor crashes outside of Los Angeles. As three curiosity seekers approach it, the meteor seems to come alive. "It's a bomb!" one of the men yells. His more perceptive buddy replies, "Wait a minute ... bombs don't unscrew." As they watch, an alien probe emerges from an escape hatch. The men try to make friends, only to be scorched by a Martian death ray. By the time the military responds, spaceships are landing in cities around the globe, and taking hostile action against anything that approaches them. The authorities quickly decide to use their ultimate weapon — an A-bomb is dropped on the Martian war machines. When this has no effect on them, the characters realize the hopelessness of their situation, and begin to pray for a miracle.

Invaders from Mars revolves around a boy named David, who sees a UFO land in a sand pit outside his bedroom window, and promptly sends his father to investigate. When he returns, David's father is not quite himself — yesterday's role model is suddenly secretive and short-tempered. David notices a peculiar mark on the back of his father's neck, but the man angrily dismisses it, claiming that he got caught on a barbed wire fence (!). The affliction spreads, and David's mother — along with several authority figures in the town of Coral Bluffs — becomes possessed. With the help of two local scientists who act as surrogate parents, David learns that his real parents are being radio-controlled by "mu-tants" from another world. The scientists, surmising that the mu-tants are planning to steal a nuclear rocket from a nearby facility, call in the military. Soldiers enter the sand

David (Jimmy Hunt) suspects his parents (Leif Erickson and Hillary Brooke) are controlled by aliens in *Invaders from Mars* (20th Century–Fox, 1953).

4. Bad Kids, Big Bugs, Body Snatchers and the Bomb 33

pit and encounter a race of moss-backed synthetic humans, led by a disembodied head with tentacles ("mankind developed to its ultimate intelligence," we're told). Their solution to the threat is simple: "You gotta hit 'em right in the puss with the grenades." After an impressive fireworks display, David wakes up, believing that it was all a dream. When he looks outside, he sees another UFO land in his backyard. The message is clear: Keep watching the skies....

Although it foreshadowed the more sophisticated *Invasion of the Body Snatchers* (1956) by introducing the idea of xenomorphs, *Invaders from Mars* hinges on a comparatively straightforward "us and them" conflict. Subsequent monster movies—many of them clearly inspired by the success of the re-release of *King Kong* in the early 1950s—were eager to present a message about mankind's culpability in his destruction. In *The Beast from 20,000 Fathoms* (1953), which showcased the stop-motion animation of a young Ray Harryhausen, an A-bomb test in the Arctic awakens a sleeping dinosaur. The creature slowly makes his way to Manhattan, where it displays an overwhelming appetite for destruction. Images of the creature ripping through buildings are intermingled with wartime newsreel footage, and one reporter proclaims, "This is a full-scale war against a terrible enemy such as modern man has never before faced." It would not be the last of its kind.

In *Them!* (1954), scientists and the military face a horde of giant ants—the results of atomic testing in the New Mexico desert. The authorities eventually trap the creatures in the Los Angeles sewer system and dispose of them, but the threat of more mutations—nature's revenge—remains. At the end of the film, one character says, "When man opened the door into the atomic age, he entered a new world. What we eventually find in that world nobody can predict." Hollywood's predictions included huge spiders (*Tarantula*, 1955; *The Incredible Shrinking Man*, 1957; *Earth vs the Spider*, 1958), a giant octopus (*It Came from Beneath the Sea*, 1955), a swarm of super-sized locusts (*Beginning of the End*, 1957), and a mammoth praying mantis (*The Deadly Mantis*, 1957). The invasion quickly became international. In postwar Japan, *Gojira* (1954) emerged as "one of the biggest ritual displays of naïve metaphor the world has ever seen."[5] The film was distributed in the United States two years later as *Godzilla, King of the Monsters!* after pseudo-documentary footage with Raymond Burr as an American reporter was added to the Japanese cut. Not long after, London was trampled by *Gorgo* (1961). Nature would continue to take its revenge on mankind over the course of the next two decades, in creature features like *The Birds* (1963), *Frogs* (1972), *Night of the Lepus* (1972), *Phase IV* (1974), *Bug* (1975), *Jaws* (1975), *Grizzly* (1976), *Squirm* (1976), *Kingdom of*

Scientists Edmund Gwenn and Joan Weldon find an unlikely scavenger in the New Mexico desert in *Them!* (Warner Bros., 1954)

the Spiders (1977), *Ants!* (1977), *Day of the Animals* (1977), *The Bees* (1978), *The Swarm* (1978) and *Prophecy* (1979).

Man himself was the subject of mutation in Roger Corman's *Day the World Ended,* distributed by the American Releasing Corporation (later AIP) in early 1956. It begins with a haughty prologue: "What you are about to see may never happen ... but to this anxious age in which we live, it presents a fearsome warning.... Our story begins with THE END!" The first image is of a mushroom cloud expanding above the horizon. It is Total Destruction Day, and God, "in His infinite wisdom," has spared only seven humans. They are a disparate bunch, nestled between lead-bearing hills in the Rocky Mountains that shield them from radiation. The survivors quickly learn that, outside the protective walls of their new civilization, flesh-hungry, mutated humans are looking for food. Corman continued to make dramatic warnings about the future of mankind in subsequent films, including *It Conquered the World* (1956), *Not of This Earth* (1957), and *Attack of the Crab Monsters* (1957). In each of these, alien creatures adopt the faces or voices of humans, blurring the line between man and monster.

4. Bad Kids, Big Bugs, Body Snatchers and the Bomb 35

The most effective use of this variation on the doppelganger motif was in Don Siegel's *Invasion of the Body Snatchers*. It begins when plastic fantastic small-town America falls under the spell of an evil that cannot be seen nor heard. The tell-tale signs of invasion are not widespread violence or destruction, but a sense of the uncanny. Dr. Miles Bennell returns home to Santa Mira, California, with a premonition that "something evil had taken possession of the town." He quickly learns that he is not the only one with such fears. Initially, Bennell — a man of science — diagnoses the problem as "epidemic mass hysteria" caused by "worry about what's going on in the world." Then he meets the horror face-to-face, and realizes that residents are being replaced by emotionless doubles — aliens with the same haunting lack of sexual and emotional impulses that characterized the alien in *The Thing from Another World*. As one might expect, Bennell has trouble making others believe his discovery. A psychiatrist casually dismisses his ranting and raving as simple psychosis. "The mind is a strange and

Dr. Miles Bennell (Kevin McCarthy) and Becky Driscoll (Dana Wynter) flee from friends and neighbors in *Invasion of the Body Snatchers* (Allied Artists & Walter Wanger, 1956).

wonderful thing," he says, "I'm not sure it will ever be able to figure itself out. Everything else maybe, from the atom to the universe, everything except itself." Bennell reflects, hopelessly, "In my practice, I've seen how some people have allowed their humanity to drain away. Only it happens slowly, not all at once. They don't seem to mind. All of us, we harden our hearts, grow callous. Only when we have to fight to stay human do we realize how precious it is."

Because of this emphasis on individualism, the film is easily (and often) analyzed in the context of 1950s American politics. The "malignant disease spreading through the whole country" is regarded as an allegory for postwar paranoia, a protest of Communism (which threatens us with rebirth "into an untroubled world where everyone's the same"), a protest of McCarthyism, and an expression of anxiety regarding gender roles. However it is interpreted, *Invasion* asserts that the monsters—and the fears they embodied—had become a part of everyday life in America. Whereas only four years before, *The Thing* had ended with a warning ("Keep watching the skies"), *Invasion* ends with desperate panic. Dr. Bennell runs out into highway traffic, screaming, "They're here already! You're next! You're next!"

Invasion of the Body Snatchers might just have easily have been written to address anxieties about the generation gap in America, which was being explored by other genre films. Some major studio releases, such as *The Bad Seed* (1956), adopted a conservative viewpoint, while independent films like those released by American International Pictures were more unwieldy. *The Bad Seed* focuses on a devoted mother whose seemingly angelic daughter turns out to be a homicidal maniac. Little Rhoda casually drowns one of her classmates after losing a penmanship award to him and then incinerates a groundskeeper who claims to know her secret. All the while, she fends off her mother's growing concern with cherubic chatter: "I have the prettiest mother in the whole world. I have the nicest mother in the whole world. That's what I tell everybody." Although Rhoda gets away with her crimes in the Maxwell Anderson play upon which the film is based, Hollywood punishes her with a bolt of lightning ... and a spanking after that, if you can believe it.

In 1957, AIP (formerly ARC) released *I Was a Teenage Werewolf*, a horror film version of *Rebel Without a Cause* (1955). Michael Landon stars as Tony, a hostile high-schooler who looks like James Dean but acts like his evil twin, angrily barking lines like "I don't like to be touched!" and "People bug me." For his girlfriend's peace of mind, he agrees to see a psychiatrist. Unfortunately, Dr. Alfred Brandon (Whit Bissell) decides to use him as a test subject for a Jekyll-Hyde serum that is intended to unleash man's most primal urges. It is unclear whether or not the doctor actually intends

4. Bad Kids, Big Bugs, Body Snatchers and the Bomb   37

to cure him. Soon after, Tony is sprouting hair in unnatural places, and attacking the girls at his high school. As the violence escalates, the doctor tries to reassure himself that there is nothing to fear: "This is America, modern America, not a hamlet in the Carpathian Mountains."

One-sheet for *I Was a Teenage Werewolf* (AIP, 1957).

Because Tony's primal impulses gave audiences as much reason to cheer as to fear, the film was a drive-in hit. It immediately spawned numerous imitations, including the follow-up, *I Was a Teenage Frankenstein* (1957), in which Whit Bissell returns as the mad scientist. This time, Bissell is a British doctor who complains about how little respect American kids have for authority. When his new "son," pieced together from the body parts of an ill-fated football team, begins to rebel, the distraught "father" realizes that he has — damn it all — created a typical American teen instead of a British one. All the same, Dr. Frankenstein believes that "only in youth is there any hope for the salvation of mankind"— a sobering thought, and not a bad marketing campaign for a film targeted at teens. In *The Blob*, released the next year, it is the teens — hastily labeled as troublemakers by their elders — that recognize the latest alien threat to mankind, and ultimately save the earth from flesh-hungry Jell-O. Knowledge of the new monsters, and the future they herald, belongs to the youth.

By the end of the decade, the horror genre had cultivated a new generation of fans. Toughened by fears of nuclear war and rebelling against suburbia's push toward normalcy, this younger audience began to demand more from a horror picture — more realism and more violence.

5

The Monster Is Madness: Castle, Corman and California Gothic

> Just keep telling yourself, it's only a movie!
> — tag line for *Strait-Jacket* (1964)

In 1955, director William Castle saw *Diabolique*, the new thriller by Henri-Georges Clouzot, already dubbed "the French Hitchcock." Apparently more astounded by the audience's reaction to the film than by the film itself, Castle later asked his wife, "Did you ever see anything like what happened tonight? Those kids wanted to be scared.... They loved it! They probably have never seen a real horror film — it's been ten years or more, in fact, since Lorre, Lugosi, or Karloff."[1] Castle immediately began planning his first "real" horror film, *Macabre* (1958). The murder-by-fright plot was modeled on *Diabolique*, but Castle quickly realized that *Macabre* didn't have "that blood-curdling quality" that *Diabolique* had.[2] Nevertheless, he believed there was an audience for this sort of picture, and he knew just how to reel them in. Throughout the 1950s, filmmakers and distributors had used technical innovations (most notably 3-D) and promotional gimmicks to lure audiences away from their televisions. Castle had quickly become the patron saint of low-budget advertising, and he promoted his latest film with a Lloyds of London insurance policy that would reward $1000 to the families of patrons who died of fright during the screenings.[3] *Macabre* was a hit, and it became clear immediately that Castle had found his niche. With the help of fellow exploitation filmmaker Roger Corman, he would keep the horror genre alive in the late 1950s with sensational, and often comically ambivalent, tales of murder and mayhem. One actor in particular would add just the right touch of class and sardonic wit to both directors' most popular films.

Vincent Price had been working as a character actor in Hollywood for more than two decades, and had appeared in several horror films, most notably *House of Wax* (1953), a 3-D remake of *Mystery of the Wax Museum* (1933), and 20th Century–Fox's widescreen production *The Fly* (1958). Castle saw Price as a Chaney or Karloff for a new generation of horror fans, and he pitched his next project to the actor during a chance encounter at a late night coffee shop: "A millionaire invites six people to spend the night in a haunted house. He chooses the people carefully and offers to pay a great deal of money to each one if they agree to spend the entire night in the haunted house.... During the night, many strange ghostly things happen ... blood dripping from the ceiling ... walls shaking ... apparitions appearing. The millionaire—the part I want you to play—has plotted to kill his wife. She plots to kill you.... It's a battle of wits."[4] Price was intrigued, and agreed to do the film.

House on Haunted Hill (1959) is a throwback to haunted house chillers of the 1920s such as *The Cat and the Canary* (1927) and Benjamin Christensen's lost film *The Haunted House* (1928). In Christensen's film, a millionaire draws up a phony will, stating that he has hidden a fortune inside his house. He then sees to it that the house is well-stocked with ghostly creatures, and waits to find out which of his potential heirs is the least greedy.[5] In *House on Haunted Hill,* Price's millionaire playboy Frederick Loren is trying to prevent his own murder, which has been plotted by his greedy young wife. Loren plans a private party in a haunted house (which we're told was built a century ago, though it looks as if it might have been designed by Frank Lloyd Wright ... and was). He promises five strangers $10,000 each if they survive until 8 A.M. The kind host also provides party favors—a handgun for each of the attendees, presumably in case they have to defend themselves from a ghost. When one of the guests points out that "these are no good against the dead, only the living," Loren simply shrugs. Under the present circumstances, he realizes, the existence of any real ghosts is irrelevant—greed will determine who survives this party.

Roger Corman's *A Bucket of Blood* (1959) is another humorous spin on a familiar conceit. Corman regular Dick Miller stars as Walter Paisley, a beatnik waiter who accidentally murders his landlady's cat. To hide his crime, he covers the cat in clay and puts it on display as a sculpture at the local coffeehouse. Like Vincent Price in *House of Wax,* Paisley begins planning murders so that he can augment his art collection. Unlike Price's

Millionare Frederick Loren (Vincent Price) dispenses unique "party favors" to his wife (Carol Ohmart) and guests in *House on Haunted Hill* (Allied Artists, 1958).

character, he has no real artistic pretensions. Walter simply wants to remain popular with the locals. Taking to heart Thomas De Quincey's theory of murder as one of the fine arts, Corman effectively mocks the pretensions of the beatnik culture. The director repeated the formula again that year, producing the now-legendary *The Little Shop of Horrors* (1960).

While Castle and Corman were producing lighthearted horror films in America, however, a series of gruesome, neo–Gothic horror movies was being imported from England's Hammer Films. Hammer had been on the brink of financial ruin in 1954 when it made *The Quatermass Xperiment* (released in the United States as *The Creeping Unknown*), the success of which heralded a "quiet cinematic revolution" in the British film industry and ensured the future of Hammer.[6] The studio immediately rushed other science fiction films, most notably *X the Unknown* and *Quatermass II* (released as *Enemy from Space* in the U.S.), into production in 1956. Both films resembled popular American films of the day — *Them!* and *Invasion of the Body Snatchers*, respectively. Later that same year, Hammer announced its first horror film, *The Curse of Frankenstein*. Critics balked, but the film ultimately broke theater attendance records in England and it soon began to play 24 hours a day across America.[7] Not long after, *Horror of Dracula* (1958) went into production. The two films upped the ante on cinematic violence and gore, and spawned imitations at home and abroad, inspiring some exploitation filmmakers to focus exclusively on the gross-out factor.

Back in the States, Roger Corman decided to orchestrate his own revival of classic Gothic material. Appropriately enough, he chose "The Fall of the House of Usher" by American writer Edgar Allan Poe as his source material. Corman pitched the idea to AIP producers Sam Arkoff and James Nicholson, asking for a bigger budget and a longer shooting schedule than they usually allowed him. There was some hesitation on the part of the producers who, after reviewing the story, asked: Where is the monster? Corman explained, "The house is the monster."[8] For Roderick Usher, of course, the house *is* the monster because it embodies the "foul thoughts and foul deeds" of his ancestors. The real monster, for the viewer, is the diseased mind of Roderick Usher. Corman wisely cast Vincent Price in the part, rationalizing that "audiences had to fear the leading man but not on a conscious, physical level based on strength.... I wanted a man whose intelligent but tormented mind works beyond the minds of others and who thus inspires a deeper fear."[9]

Even more than Corman's best pictures of the 1950s, *House of Usher* (1960) is character-driven. Corman used the theories of Sigmund Freud to interpret the anxieties of his anti-hero. In Poe's story, Roderick summons a childhood friend to his isolated New England home to comfort him while he anxiously awaits his sister's return from the grave. Corman's film, scripted by Richard Matheson, makes Roderick extremely possessive of his sister, and attributes his guilt over her death to a repressed lust for her. Significantly, in the film, it is Madeline's suitor, not Roderick's childhood friend, who comes to visit when Madeline becomes ill. Roderick watches the young lovers closely, forbidding Madeline to leave the house of Usher and spread their "diseased" blood any further. After her death, Roderick laments: "Once this land was fertile. The Earth yielded its riches at harvest time. There were trees and plant life, flowers, fields of grain. There was great beauty here.... Then a suffering swept across the land and blasted it ... and the land withered as before a plague — a plague of evil." Madeline's suitor has seen this ruin — the burned-out, post-war landscape surrounding the house (actually filmed in California after a massive forest fire), and the faded, sterile décor of the house itself. The setting is emblematic of Roderick's madness, his ultimate loss of hope. For him, "Evil is not just a word. It is reality."

5. The Monster Is Madness

The Gothic themes in *House of Usher* are equally apparent in Alfred Hitchcock's *Psycho* (1960) which fixes the nightmare on America's West Coast. The Bates house, a foreboding ruinous building that looms over the sleepy Bates Motel the way Norman's mother hovers over him, is a paradigm of California Gothic. Once, we imagine, the house on the hill was a commanding sight that caught the eye of passersby on the highway. Since then, Norman tells us, the highway has been relocated, and the house has fallen into disrepair. Though Norman habitually changes the motel linens once a week, he has left everything in the house exactly the way it was when he was a boy. When Norman is in the house, we assume, he is Mother, and in a sense the house has become a monster to Norman just as surely as Roderick Usher's house was a monster to him. For both men, there is no escape — the evil is part of them.

Psycho began as Hitchcock's attempt to make a low-budget exploitation movie. He opted to use the crew of his popular television series *Alfred Hitchcock Presents* and the television branch of Universal Pictures studios for filming.[10] His source material was a lurid novel by Robert Bloch, who

Norman Bates (Anthony Perkins) silhouetted in front of his "gingerbread Gothic" home in *Psycho* (Shamley, 1960).

loosely based his story on the crimes of Ed Gein, a Wisconsin farmer arrested in November 1957 after police found the dismembered (and, in some cases, cannibalized) bodies of 15 women in his house. Hitchcock then promoted the film the way William Castle might. He spoke directly to audiences in a promotional trailer, not unlike the introductions to *Alfred Hitchcock Presents*, giving a guided tour of the Bates Motel and the house on the hill. He also forbade theater owners to admit moviegoers after the film had begun, and encouraged audiences not to give away the surprise ending. If they were expecting a typically playful horror film, audiences were in for a shock. Joseph Stefano, who wrote the screenplay, opines that *Psycho*, like the Gein murders, re-established horror for the American public: "It was a strange and seemingly good time in the country, but it wasn't a good time at all. Most of us knew that. But if you think about where we were before *Psycho* and where we were after *Psycho*, it's almost as if *Psycho* was the robin that tells you winter is here — and it sure as hell came."[11]

One of the reasons that the film had such an impact was Hitchcock's sly manipulation of audience perceptions of events in the film. By constantly giving the camera a voyeur's gaze and by making us empathize first with a thief and later with a murderer, he ascribes guilt to the viewer. The very first shots are voyeuristic — we are a fly on the wall in a cheap Phoenix hotel room where Marion Crane and her lover, Sam Loomis, are getting dressed after a midday tryst. Marion complains that she is sick of meeting in cheap hotel rooms and asks when they can get married, but Sam replies that he doesn't have enough money to make a respectable woman of her. Disheartened, Marion returns to work. A few hours later, as fate would have it, a solution to Marion's problem presents itself. An obnoxious businessman brings $40,000 cash into her office. Marion is entrusted with the responsibility of depositing it at the bank. As if the temptation isn't great enough already, the businessman tells Marion, "I never carry more than I can afford to lose." Marion takes the money and runs.

Within 24 hours, a suspicious cop is on her — and our — trail. After she shakes the cop, Marion ends up at just the sort of cheap hotel that she is trying to escape. It is owned and operated by a curious but likable young man named Norman Bates, who seems to have been browbeaten into submission by his sickly old mother. Marion feels pity for Norman and suggests that he try to take control of his life, but Norman asserts that he will never escape from his "private trap." His confession convinces Marion to return the money and escape from her own private trap and we are, briefly, grateful to Norman, in spite of his creepiness. Soon after her conversation with Norman, however, Marion is stabbed to death in the shower by a figure that we assume to be Norman's mother. With our heroine dead, the focus of the film shifts to Norman, who looks appropriately horrified when he sees what Mother has done. We watch him clean up the bloody bathroom and, in spite of ourselves, hope that he is able to erase all traces of the crime. Norman then puts Marion's body into the trunk of her car and tries to sink it in a nearby swamp. For a moment, the car appears to be stuck in plain view. Like Norman, we hold our breath until the car finally disappears into the bog. Later, when the local sheriff explains to Sam Loomis and Marion's sister—both uninteresting hero substitutes—that Norman's mother has been dead for years, we begin to realize that Hitchcock has tricked us into empathizing with a psychopathic killer. We have become the monster.

It would be years before other Hollywood filmmakers would effectively emulate *Psycho*, and begin to make horror films that were comparably subversive. In the meantime, exploitation filmmakers continued to capitalize on the more obvious sources of shock value in Hitchcock's film. In 1961, the poor man's Hitchcock, William Castle, produced and directed *Homicidal*, a shameless rip-off of *Psycho* that added a few new twists to the formula. Roger Corman followed up *House of Usher* with another Poe adaptation, *Pit and the Pendulum* (1961), in which Vincent Price stars as Nicholas Medina, another "spawn of depraved blood," haunted by the role of his sadistic father in the Spanish Inquisition and the recent death of his late wife Elizabeth. After seeing her ghost roam the halls of his castle, he becomes convinced that she was buried alive, and resolves to exhume her body. Nicholas and his physician descend into the family crypt and begin digging. When they find Elizabeth's body, her rotted face is frozen, wide-eyed, in a scream of horror. It is a moment comparable in terms of visual shock value to the climactic scene in *Psycho*, where Mrs. Bates stares at us accusingly from empty eye sockets. Nicholas' worst fears confirmed, he suffers a complete mental collapse. Afterwards, the audience learns that Elizabeth is still alive, and has plotted with her lover, the physician, to drive Nicholas mad. In our own lust for revenge, we cheer on the now-insane Nicholas as he adopts the personality of his father and gleefully subjects his wife and her lover to the "pendulum of fate." Corman continued to adapt Poe (*The Premature Burial* and *Tales of Terror* were released in 1962, *The Raven* and *The Haunted Palace* in 1963, *The Masque of the Red Death* in 1964 and *The Tomb of Ligeia* in 1965), while other filmmakers transplanted the Gothic onto modern-day settings.

In 1962, director Robert Aldrich exposed more dark secrets on Sunset Boulevard in *What Ever Happened to Baby Jane?* Bette Davis stars as Jane Hudson, a former vaudeville performer who lives in envy of her more successful sister Blanche, played by Joan Crawford. Blanche's career as a film actress was cut short by a crippling car accident caused by her sister, and she is now dependent on Jane, who delights in exerting her authority. Through the course of the film, Jane's jealousy and guilt over the accident begin to drive her mad. She even cooks Blanche's pet bird and serves it to her for dinner, cackling as her sister screams. As Jane loses touch with reality, she nurses dreams of a career revival, and begins rehearsing the song-and-dance routines she performed in vaudeville as a child. It is difficult not to cringe as the old woman distorts her sour, pancake-battered face into a clown-like grin and sings "I've Written a Letter to Daddy." Baby Jane is a new kind of freak, one of Hollywood's lost souls—desperate, unnatural, addicted and out of control. When Jane's only supporter abandons her, she descends into hopelessness, repeating miserably, "He hates me" (rather like Frankenstein's Monster after being rebuked by his disenchanted Bride). In a final desperate attempt to return to her youth, Jane takes Blanche from the dingy confines of their run-down old mansion to a California beach. There, the two sisters become freak sideshows

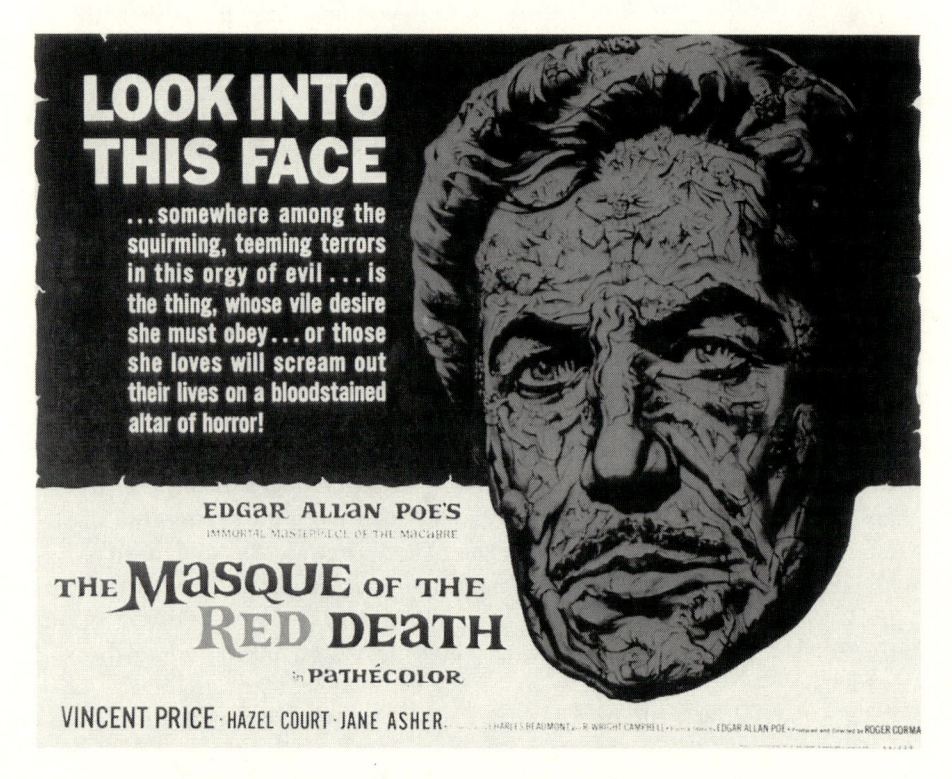

One-sheet for *The Masque of the Red Death* (AIP, 1964) with Vincent Price.

for tourists. Jane performs her vaudeville song-and-dance routine for one final audience before being carted off to the nuthouse.

The two stars, experiencing ironic career revivals, followed up with films in a similar vein. Bette Davis starred in Aldrich's pseudo-sequel *Hush, Hush ... Sweet Charlotte* (1964), as an aged Southern belle whose vindictive cousin allows her to believe that she is responsible for an ax murder. Joan Crawford went on to make William Castle's *Strait-Jacket* (1964), starring as a repentant ax murderess whose daughter is trying to drive her mad. Buoyed by his work with an A-list star, Castle set his sights on more ambitious projects, and eventually produced *Rosemary's Baby* (1968), in which he makes a brief Hitchcock-style cameo.

Corman was also gaining respectability; critics were particularly quick to praise *The Masque of the Red Death*, one of his later entries in the Poe cycle, as one of his best. The ever-reliable Vincent Price stars as Prince Prospero, a Satanist who harbors a select group of aristocrats in his castle while a plague (the Red Death) sweeps the countryside. Among his guests is an innocent village girl named Francesca, whose faith in a benevolent God rivals his own faith in Satan. Prospero takes her on a tour of human corruption—showing her how foolish, desperate and cruel the people under his care can be. Finally, he asks, "Can you look around at this world and believe in the goodness of a God who rules it? Famine, pestilence, war, disease and death ... they rule this world. If a God of love and life did ever exist, he is long since dead. Someone or some *thing* rules in his place." Satan, he says, is the only source of order in the universe: "If we lost our power, chaos would engulf the world."

In the final reel, Prospero and his subjects are finally killed by the Red Death. Only Francesca and her pious lover are saved, but it is uncertain what lies ahead for them as they flee into the desolate, unpopulated wasteland outside the castle walls.

6

Apocalypse America: The Modern Horror Film

> "And the road leads to nowhere…"
> — David Hess, *The Last House on the Left*

While there is considerable debate over which film inaugurated the modern era of the horror film, *Psycho* (1960) is among the earliest candidates. Paul Wells credits Hitchcock with giving the horror genre "the moment when the monster, as a metaphor or myth, is conflated with the reality of the modern world."[1] In *Psycho*, we recognize the monster's world as our own, and the monster as an inherent part of it. For several years, Hitchcock's nightmarish vision of America went unanswered — horror filmmakers responded to audiences' increased appetite for violence and gore with ham-handed exploitation films like *Dementia 13* and *Blood Feast* (both 1963), but serious horror pictures were few and far between. Realizing that he would have to top his own masterpiece, Hitchcock followed up with *The Birds* (1963).

The film begins as a character-driven melodrama (and not a particularly engaging one), then suddenly turns apocalyptic when feathered fiends begin dive-bombing the coastal town of Bodega Bay, and our heroes become trapped together in a house. After one of them is seriously wounded in a subsequent attack, the survivors resolve to escape and carefully make their way to a parked car. Once inside, the film abruptly ends. It is uncertain where they will go or what they will find when they get there. Hitchcock offers no foreseeable end to the crisis and no comforting explanation of this resident madness — only the town drunk's prophetic words: "It's the end of the world."

Melanie Daniels ("Tippi" Hedren) under attack in *The Birds* (Universal, 1963).

In 1968 — not coincidentally, the year that the Hollywood censorship code was lifted and the MPAA instituted its ratings system — two horror films, *Rosemary's Baby* and *Night of the Living Dead*, finally picked up Hitchcock's mantle. *Rosemary's Baby*, an Ira Levin novel about a young woman who is impregnated by the Devil, was optioned by William Castle shortly before publication. He later paired up with director Roman Polanski to produce the film for Paramount. Polanski was already regarded as something of a wunderkind in Hollywood; his first English-language film, *Repulsion* (1965), had drawn numerous comparisons to *Psycho* because both present a haunting picture of psychic instability in a secular world. Polanski's secular worldview also influenced his adaptation of *Rosemary's Baby*: "I no more believed in Satan as evil incarnate than I believed in a personal god; the whole idea conflicted with my rational view of the world. For credibility's sake, I decided that there would have to be a loophole: the possibility that Rosemary's supernatural experiences were figments of her imagination."[2] Although the film, unlike Levin's novel, fails to confirm the existence of a supernatural hierarchy, our overwhelming empathy with Rosemary throughout the film practically ensures our belief in her fears. We leave the film with a strong sense that the film has "validated the heroine's vision of a 'plot,'" and exposed a "diabolical universe."[3]

Potentially far more disturbing than the diabolical universe of *Rosemary's Baby* is the spiritual void of George A. Romero's *Night of the Living Dead*, an independent film made far from the lights of Hollywood. The film is mostly set in a rural farmhouse near Pittsburgh, Pennsylvania, where seven strangers seek refuge from an army of reanimated corpses that are roaming the countryside. As in *The Birds*, the monsters in Romero's film are emblematic of secular chaos rather than Evil. Hitchcock biographer Donald Spoto suggests that Hitchcock intended for the Judgment Day in *The Birds* to "exteriorize the failure of human relations."[4] Romero brings this same failure to light in his film. "The most frightening thing is that nobody communicates," the director says, "Everybody is isolated and alone with their own version of the world. They're all kinda insane."[5] The characters are never united by any kind of authority, either social or supernatural, that offers a solution. Religion is conspicuously

Pittsburgh locals amble on the location of *Night of the Living Dead* (Image Ten, 1968).

absent from the film. Neither the politicians nor the media are able to offer any decisive answers (though there is brief mention of an exploded space probe that may be to blame). Eventually, the bond between the survivors — even within the nuclear family — disintegrates, and each individual faces the monster alone.

Because *Night of the Living Dead* was filmed guerilla-style in black-and-white, with the unflinching authority of a wartime newsreel, it seems as much like a documentary on the loss of social stability as an exploitation film. Battle lines are drawn: black versus white, children versus parents, the un-silent minority versus the silent majority. Romero's microcosm shows us a mood of "America devouring itself."[6] Though the director says that he was never conscious of any elaborate allegories while making the film, he claims that the message of almost all of his pictures is "the longing for a better world, for a higher plane of existence, for people to get together."[7] *Night of the Living Dead* might be called hippie Gothic — it suggests that America is too disjointed to survive a violent crisis like the Vietnam War. By morning, all of the major characters are dead, and a posse of gun-toting vigilantes is surveying the remains. They seem to be in control of the situation, for better or (more likely) worse. In the final moments of the film, a reporter attempts to interview one of them, hoping to gain some insight on what is happening. The man seems unable to think rationally about the situation and says, simply, "They're dead, they're all messed up," then returns to war. Romero leaves us numb.

Equally nihilistic is *The Last House on the Left* (1972), a collaboration between producer Sean S. Cunningham and director Wes Craven. An exploitative version of Ingmar Bergman's *The Virgin Spring* (1960) set in modern-day New England, *Last House* achieved cult status for its unflinching depictions of violence. The film begins as two girls, 16-year-old Mari and her more worldly friend, Phyllis, leave for the city to see a band called Blood Lust (presumably the Manson family's answer to Woodstock). "All that blood and violence," Mary's mother quips. "I thought you were supposed to be the Love Generation." Krug, Weasel, Junior and Sadie intercept the girls and take them hostage. What follows are a series of painfully drawn-out rape and torture scenes — the symbolic deflowering of the love generation. Craven maintains that the graphic nature of these scenes (which were reputedly even more gruesome in the director's first cut) underpins his reason for making the film. "There was an initial stage in horror cinema," he says, "during which *Last House on the Left* was made, where gore stood for everything that was hidden in society.... The notion was to have that sort of war correspondent's unblinking eye and show what happens after the camera fades to black."[8] Like *Night of the Living*

Dead, the director's goal was to go "too far" and see where he ended up. In the second half of the film, the four killers—through some miracle of chance—arrive at the home of Mari's parents. Once the parents learn what has happened, they extract a revenge that is every bit as brutal as their daughter's murder. Mom seduces and castrates Weasel, then slits Sadie's throat; Dad carves up Krug with a chainsaw.

Robin Wood has interpreted the film as Craven's protest of the Vietnam War and, he points out, it resonates as a social criticism because it humanizes the monsters as well as the victims: "The film offers no easily identifiable parallels to Vietnam.... Instead, it analyzes the nature and conditions of violence and sees them as inherent in the American situation. Craven sees to it that the audience cannot escape the implications. We are spared nothing in the protracted tormenting of the two girls—our having to share the length of their ordeal is part of the point—and we cannot possibly enjoy it. They are *us*. Yet we also cannot disengage ourselves from their tormentors: *They* are us, too."[9]

The success of *Night of the Living Dead* and *The Last House on the Left*, in spite of critical backlash, prompted major Hollywood studios to take the horror genre more seriously. In 1973, Warner Brothers released *The Exorcist*, a big-budget adaptation of William Peter Blatty's immensely popular neo–Gothic novel. The book and the film focus on a broken family—actress Chris McNeil and her adolescent daughter Regan—that is targeted by the Devil. When Regan first begins to exhibit uncharacteristic behavior, her mother turns to modern science for an explanation. Regan is subjected to the tests of nearly every medical doctor and psychologist under the sun, and she doesn't simply confound them; she curses them, vomits on them, literally goes straight for their balls. As she becomes increasingly violent, her mother finally admits that she may be possessed, and turns to the Catholic church for help.

Some critics have suggested that *The Exorcist*, like *Night of the Living Dead* and *The Last House on the Left*, was an indication of an ideological crisis in America. Allison Graham attaches particular significance to the scene in which Regan tells Father Karras that she is "no one." This answer, she hypothesizes, illustrates the storytellers' intuitive understanding that "what is inside her is exactly what is inside her society: a spiritual and imaginative void."[10] Author Blatty, however, interprets the impact of the story as an indication of firmly held spiritual beliefs in the public at large: "I just never anticipated the dementia that grew up around the experience of reading the book or seeing the film. And the closest I've been able to come to explaining it is that there is a deep-seated belief in the core of many people that a malevolent and intelligent foce of evil personified does exist."[11]

6. Apocalypse America   53

Other critics offered simpler readings of the film, calling it a commentary on the effects of a collapse in traditional family values, and noting similarities to films like *The Bad Seed*. In both films, a prepubescent girl with no apparent father figure begins to rebel against conventional morality. In the years between these two films, the family had become an increasingly common focus in horror films, resulting in what Tony Williams refers to as a portrait of "the American Dream in reverse."[12] In 1974, Larry Cohen expanded on this idea in *It's Alive*, which consciously patterns itself on Universal's *Frankenstein* (1931). The film begins when a mutant baby is born into a seemingly normal, nuclear family. After killing the doctor who delivered it, the baby disappears in Los Angeles, leaving a trail of bodies in its wake. While the authorities hunt the little devil, the media turns its gaze on Frank Davies, the father, whose name — like the mad doctor in *Son of Frankenstein* (1939) — becomes synonymous with the monster in the minds of the locals. Tormented by his association with the creature, Davies makes an effort to publicly disown the child, saying, "Why does everybody look at me as if it's my own flesh and blood? It's no relation to me.... I've got an 11-year-old boy no different from anyone else!"

Killer mutant baby, on the loose in *It's Alive* (Larco, 1974).

After he learns that a pharmaceutical company is most likely responsible for the mutation, his outlook changes—he no longer views the child as a monster, but as a product of a diseased society. He then resolves to rescue the baby from the authorities. Tony Williams writes, "*It's Alive* develops the premises of the *Frankenstein* saga to their most logical conclusions by affirming solidarity between creator and monster against the real enemy—institutional forces of law, medicine and family."[13] Cohen takes the idea even further with *It Lives Again* (1978), in which Frank Davies becomes a crusader for mutant baby rights, thwarting government-funded infanticide SWAT teams. In effect, Cohen's film revolts against the time-honored horror genre tradition of labeling anything different as "monstrous," and identifies America's "monogamous heterosexual bourgeois patriarchal capitalist" society as the real aberration.[14]

In Tobe Hooper's *The Texas Chain Saw Massacre* (1974), Robin Wood argues, there is a conflict between traditional American values and the values of the hippie generation, represented by the disenfranchised cannibal family and their carefree, self-involved victims, respectively. The film opens with a foreboding disclaimer that what you are about to see is a true story (and, insofar as the film is loosely based on the Ed Gein murders, we can take the disclaimer somewhat literally), set in the here and now: August 18, 1973. A radio news broadcaster tells us, and the traveling teenagers, about a series of grave robberies in rural Texas, firmly setting the scene and the foreboding tone that makes the film so effective. Around the same time, the teenagers pick up a hitchhiker, who explains that his family used to work at the local slaughterhouse, until they were replaced by machines. Since then, we later learn, the family has resorted to cannibalism, and the teenagers are soon to become their next meal. A series of powerful images—of the slaughterhouse, a blazing sun, a dried-up swimming hole and a pocketwatch with a nail driven through it—convey the plight of the younger generation of characters. They are cattle trapped in a kind of pressure cooker, and their time has run out. The multi-generational family is in control, and their motive is madness. Wood says the backwoods family are the victims "of capitalism—*our* victims, in fact," and their resort to cannibalism is simply "the logical end of human relations under capitalism."[15] In essense, this is another example of "America devouring itself."

In support of Wood's argument, Christopher Sharrett points out that Hooper fills the screen with images and ideas associated with the American landscape and way of life—"the family home, the annual vacation trip, the town church and cemetery, the fascination with strange hobbies and cultish beliefs, the culling of childhood memories, the squabbling among siblings, the allusion to professions and industries long entrenched in the American economy."[16] Hooper seems determined to prove to us that this is not *just a movie*, but a reflection of the "pressure cooker" mentality in modern-day America; the stars and stripes are flying high over a family barbecue in the seventh circle of Hell. The final scene effectively sums up the message of modern horror film. Only one survivor has escaped — though some miracle of chance — but she is almost surely insane. Leatherface remains in plain view, wielding his chainsaw wildly and aimlessly in the first light of a new dawn.

Wes Craven's *The Hills Have Eyes* (1977) makes some of the conflicts that are apparent in *Texas Chain Saw* even more explicit. The film follows a "civilized" city family into the New Mexico desert, where they encounter a clan of cannibalistic hill-dwellers. The ensuing battle between the two families is an obvious allegory of primitive man versus civilized man, "an older system of social economy" versus a newer one.[17] From the very beginning, it seems, Craven's story was intended to address the question of how America would resolve its identity crisis. "The original draft," he says, "had the family leaving New York in 1984. This was done in 1975, so it was set 10 years in the future. New York was uninhabitable and you had to have a passport to travel between states because states had become very territorial. The family was supposed to be stationed in Sun Valley, but they didn't have a passport to get into California, so they were trying to sneak in through the desert."[18]

In the filmed version, the family is passing through the desert in search of a silver mine that they have inherited. There they meet Papa Jupiter, who hatefully admonishes his rival father-figure: "I'll see the wind blow your dried-up seeds away. I'll eat the heart of your stinking memory. I'll eat the brains of your kids' kids. I'm in! You're out!" In the course of defending themselves, the civilized family

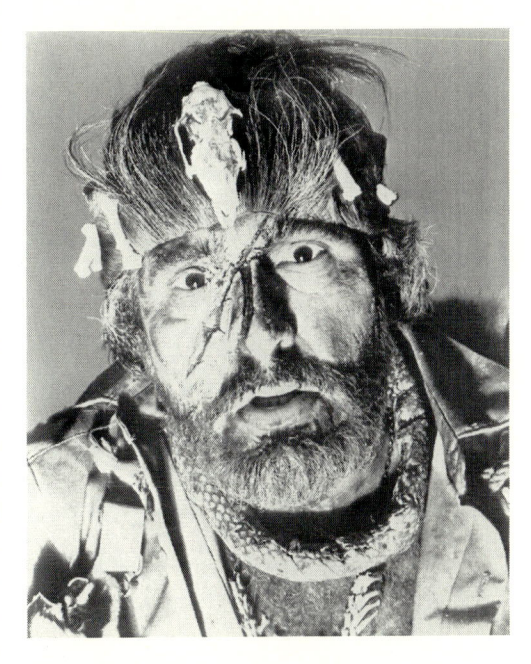

Papa Jupiter (James Whitworth) in *The Hills Have Eyes* (Blood Relations, 1977).

becomes just as barbaric as the hill-dwellers, indicating — like *The Last House on the Left*—that there is no escape from the self-destructive impulses inherent in American culture. Craven says that the film embodied "a feeling like, well, this is the last days of American civilization, the decline and fall of Western civilization. What's going to come out of it? Will the generation that had to deal with the remnants of it be able to survive? Will they survive with their savageness and conquer, or will we just sort of go back into a dark ages?"[19] The film ends abruptly on an image of Doug, one of the "civilized" family members, who has just committed a particularly brutal murder in order to rescue his infant daughter. He appears absolutely maniacal as we fade to red. "In a very real sense," one critic suggests, this final image is the "signifier of an ideological stalemate which marks not the triumph and reaffirmation of a culture, but its internal disintegration."[20]

7

What the Fifty Foot Woman Did to the Incredible Shrinking Man

"Your body is a battleground."
— Feminist slogan

Since the inception of the horror film, women have routinely been cast in the role of the persecuted. (If this does not go without saying for any reader, I sincerely hope you will enjoy your first horror film.) Robin Wood proposes two simple explanations: (1) Filmmakers assume that audiences will be more afraid when women — traditionally "the weaker sex" — are placed in danger, and will then more readily identify with the hero / protector, (2) Filmmakers are providing the predominantly male audience with a particular kind of catharsis. Wood theorizes: "As men in patriarchal society have set women up on (compensatory) pedestals and, thereby, constructed them as oppressive and restrictive figures, they have developed a strong desire to knock them down again."[1]

This idea may also partially explain why, as early as the 1930s, horror films began featuring women as monsters — diverging from the stereotypical Gothic portrayal of women as helpless victims. *Dracula* (1931) and *Dracula's Daughter* (1936) were among the first horror films to treat female characters as monstrous threats to normality, and there was a growing tendency toward women-as-monsters during the following decades, which produced classics such as *Cat People* (1942), *Weird Woman* (1944) and *Attack of the 50 Foot Woman* (1958). In the late 1960s, the socio-political implications of America's sexual liberation and the feminist movement profoundly influenced the genre's popular subtext. The ensuing onscreen "battle of the sexes" has been a subject of intense critical analysis, resulting in some compelling arguments that the horror genre offers some of "the most significant documents in America's public debate over the status of the independent woman in a society still dominated by men."[2]

Pioneering examples of the female-centered modern horror film include *Rosemary's Baby*, on one level an allegory of the invasion anxieties of pregnant women, and *The Exorcist*, interpreted by at least one critic as "a male nightmare of female puberty."[3] Like these films, Brian DePalma's *Sisters* (1973) — which Wood calls the definitive feminist horror film — identifies its central female character, Danielle Breton, as both victim and monster. At the beginning of the film, Danielle brings a new acquaintance back to her Staten Island apartment for a night of casual sex. The following morning, her wild-eyed twin sister Dominique brutally stabs him to death. Grace Collier, a local newspaper columnist, witnesses the murder and calls police, but before they arrive, Danielle secretes the body inside the living room couch. Later, while police are searching the apartment, Grace finds proof that Danielle has a twin sister named Dominique, but uncovers no proof of a murder. Upon further investigation, Grace and the audience learn that Dominique died a year earlier, and that schizophrenic Danielle is the real murderer. Grace hires a private investigator to track the dead man's body while she follows Danielle and her ex-husband / psychiatrist to a private mental hospital. There, the doctor hypnotizes Grace, forcing her to forget everything she knows about the murder. He then turns his attention to Danielle, hoping to convince her, once and for all, that her sister is dead. "Dominique" responds by slashing his groin with a scalpel, causing a fatal wound. Later, when Danielle is interviewed at the scene of the crime by an investigator, she says, in all honesty, "I have never hurt anyone in my life."

Similarities to Alfred Hitchcock's *Psycho* are obvious, but Robin Wood argues that the subtext is very different. The schizophrenic character in *Sisters* reveals a conflict of sexual identity — Danielle is, at once, sexually liberated (as Danielle) and repressed (as Dominique), and the conflict leads to insanity and murder, as it did in Polanski's *Repulsion*. Wood says that the conflict between the liberation and repression of women in American society is central to the film, not just to one character. Grace is also tormented by her identity as an independent woman — she is patronized by her employer, by the cops and, in one particularly telling scene, by her mother, who makes reference to Grace's profession as a "little job," then begins speculating on when her daughter will "settle down."

7. What the Fifty Foot Woman Did to the Shrinking Man   59

Not coincidentally, she also talks about an article she read in the local newspaper on an "experimental madhouse" where patients are allowed to roam free. "The whole idea," she explains, "is that instead of locking them up, they let them live in a house and the doctors make a home for them, and it's sort of a family situation just like real people." Eventually, Grace ends up at this hospital, becoming part of a warped "family" where the father uses hypnosis to enforce his concept of healthy normality on the children. DePalma makes it clear that the normality here is anything but desirable, indicating that "traditional normality no longer exists ... as actuality but only as ideology."[4] The director obviously takes pleasure in cutting off the fatherly head and revealing the irony that the doctor himself has freed Danielle from guilt over his murder. Since there are no remaining witnesses to either of the murders in the film, the "monster" wins—defeating the institutional forces of repression and reaffirming her independence.

The Stepford Wives (1975), a sly variation on *Invasion of the Body Snatchers*, satirically proposes a means of avoiding a society-wide descent

Katharine Ross—the perfect woman?—in *The Stepford Wives* (Fadsin & Palomar, 1975).

into murder and madness: men literally program women to be submissive homemakers, thereby avoiding any kind of power struggle. Katharine Ross stars as Joanna Everhart, an independent city girl whose ambitions as a photographer have been compromised ever since her comparatively dull husband convinced her to move to the sleepy community of Stepford. Despite the fact that everyone is willing to testify to Stepford's good schools, low taxes and clean air, Joanna is unnerved by the sexual politics of the the town — the women are mindless zombies and all decisions are made by the "sexually archaic" and "downright creepy" Men's Association. Her sense that something is wrong in Stepford is confirmed at a party thrown by Association president Diz (so named for his ominous history with Disneyland robots), where one of the wives blows a gasket and keeps repeating "I'll just die if I don't get this recipe." In the film's most chilling scene, Joanna stabs her best friend with a butcher knife to see if she bleeds, thereby confirming her suspicions that the Stepford wives are not human. Soon after, she comes face to face with her own double — an exact physical duplicate, except for shining black eyeballs, who'll "cook and clean like crazy, but she won't take pictures and she won't be me." When she wonders aloud why men would accept such a reality, Diz responds, "Because we can. Think of it the other way around. Wouldn't you like some perfect stud, waiting on you around the house, whispering how your sagging flesh was beautiful no matter how you looked?" In the final moments of the film, we see Joanna cruising the aisles of a local supermarket, and realize that she is no longer human. The men have won this round.

A deeply rooted fear of independent women also informs DePalma's *Carrie* (1976), described by Pauline Kael as "a film noir in red."[5] Stephen King, who wrote the source novel, says, "If *The Stepford Wives* concerns itself with what men want from women, then *Carrie* is largely about how women find their own channels of power, and what men fear about women and women's sexuality."[6] What is interesting about DePalma's adaptation, compared to King's novel, is that the victim / monster, Carrie White, is persecuted almost exclusively by women. The men in the film version of *Carrie* are, in terms of the narrative, practically impotent. King points out that, in the film, Tommy Ross and Billy Nolan are simply acting on the whims of their girlfriends. DePalma, he says, "sees this suburban white kids' high school as a kind of matriarchy. No matter where you look, there are girls behind the scenes, pulling invisible wires, rigging elections, using their boyfriends as stalking horses. Against such a backdrop, Carrie becomes doubly pitiful, because she is unable to do any of these things."[7] In essence, the real struggle in the film is between women who use their sexuality to control men, and then use men to exert power over each other.

7. What the Fifty Foot Woman Did to the Shrinking Man 61

Only Carrie is independent, and she uses her powers of telekinesis — brought on by an initiation to womanhood that is equally repugnant to her peers and her puritanical mother, all of whom seem to share Carrie's embarrassment over the "curse of blood" — to literally bring the house down. Her "coming out party" is everything that men fear. At her high

Sissy Spacek's prom-night bloodbath in *Carrie* (Redbank, 1976).

school prom, the femme fatale — covered in blood for the second time in the film — unleashes the sublime fury of a woman scorned, orchestrating the violent collapse of the mini-society that has no place for her.

Though DePalma has been labeled a misogynist by some critics, films like *Sisters* and *Carrie* provide a much more complex treatment of female characters than that of many mainstream horror films in the late 1970s and early 1980s — particularly the slasher subgenre. *Psycho* has been deemed responsible for several decades of films which revolve around the bodily mutilation of women (call it "axploitation") — ranging from the splatter films of Herschell Gordon Lewis to the Italian gialli of Mario Bava and Dario Argento. The real watershed film in this vein was John Carpenter's *Halloween* (1978), a blood relative of Hitchcock's masterpiece.* The film stars Jamie Lee Curtis, the real-life daughter of Janet Leigh (*Psycho*'s Marion Crane), as Laurie Strode. Unlike Marion, Laurie is shy, independent and, apparently, a virgin. The only man in her life is her psychopathic stalker. (Interestingly, Carpenter transplants the name of Marion Crane's lover, Sam Loomis, onto the eccentric old doctor in *Halloween*, who tries to save Laurie from the menace.) Unlike her friends, who are too preoccupied with sex and gossip to anticipate the danger, Laurie is not only able see the killer, but is able to fight back — precisely because, according to co-writer Debra Hill, she is not sexually liberated. "The one girl who is the most sexually uptight," she says, "just keeps stabbing this guy with a long knife. She's the most sexually frustrated. She's the one that's killed him ... because all that repressed sexual energy starts coming out."[8]

Some critics and other filmmakers interpreted the film as an indictment of promiscuous suburban teens — noting that three of the victims in the film are murdered post-coitus. Once *Halloween* became a blockbuster, theaters were glutted with imitations that followed the "sex = death" formula. In many of these films, the heroine and the killer (as well as the occasional prophetic drunk) are the only ones who can "see" what is going on. The audience often shares the viewpoints of these two characters, alternating between the camera's first-person association with the punisher and the victim. As the *Halloween* formula became more diluted in imitation slasher films — *Prom Night* (1980), *Terror Train* (1980), *Friday the 13th* (1980), *My Bloody Valentine* (1980), *The Prowler* (1981), *He Knows You're Alone* (1981), *Hell Night* (1981), *Graduation Day* (1981), *Night School* (1981) *Happy Birthday to Me* (1981) et al. — the apparent moral judgment of the teenage victims became outright contempt under the "sex = death" for-

---

*Equally influential were Mario Bava's *Twitch of the Death Nerve* (1972) and Bob Clark's *Black Christmas* (1974).

7. What the Fifty Foot Woman Did to the Shrinking Man 63

"The Shape" (Nick Castle) hunts Annie Brackett (Nancy Loomis) in *Halloween* (Compass International, 1978).

mula. The increasingly stereotypical victims existed only to incur the wrath of a faceless, unstoppable force from the past, and since neither the killer nor the victims in most of these films had any real identity (the killer is usually masked, the victims always dumb), audiences responded primarily to the destruction, often cheering the killer on. Critic Vera Dika proposes that Reagan-era audiences (the new "moral majority"?) embraced the onscreen violence as a call for sexual responsibility in a more conservative decade. In her estimation, the popularity of this cycle was due to the "psychological and sociological relevance" that it held for teenagers who related to an "ongoing process that tended to reverse the ideals, aspirations, and attitudes of the 1960s."[9]

Brian DePalma's infamous *Dressed to Kill* (1980) offered one of the most complex (and artistically rendered) reflections of America's changing sexual politics in the early 1980s. Like *Carrie*, it begins with a voyeuristic shower scene in which a woman's pleasure is interrupted by signs of violence; bored Manhattan housewife Kate Miller fantasizes that she is being physically attacked in the shower while her husband looks on. Later that morning, Kate confesses to her psychiatrist that her sex life is unfulfilling. She propositions him, but he coldly reminds her of society's ideals about family integrity. Afterwards, Kate goes to a local museum, still prowling for some kind of sexual deliverance from the monotony of her life, and begins following a mysterious stranger through the labyrinthine building. She is easily lured by the stranger to his nearby apartment, where she learns — too late — that he has recently been diagnosed with a venereal disease. Fearing the worst, she runs out on him, only to be murdered moments later by a razor-wielding woman in a trenchcoat.

At this point, the narrative shifts its focus onto four potential "detective" characters — Liz, a call girl who witnessed the murder; Peter, Kate's precocious teenage son; Marino, a misogynist detective; and Dr. Elliott, Kate's psychiatrist, who suspects that a former patient may have carried out the murder. The most empathetic characters are Liz and Peter, who never judge Kate's lifestyle, and initiate a plan to use Liz's sexuality to identify the murderer. While Peter watches through a nearby window, Liz attempts to seduce Dr. Elliott in order to get the name of the killer. She confesses to him that she has been having a recurring dream about being raped by a razor-wielding maniac, insinuating that what she really wants is a man who will exert his authority over her. Elliott is only too happy to oblige, but not in the way she expects. Instead of simply getting information from the doctor, she releases his hidden personality, and reveals him as the killer.

No doubt critics like Linda Williams — who dismisses slasher films like *Dressed to Kill* as shamelessly sexist attempts to "demonstrate how monstrous female desire can be"[10] — based their charges of sexism and misogyny on Liz's "confession" that she is aroused by violence, and on the crude suggestion of Detective Marino that Kate Miller was suicidal and self-loathing. Charles Derry, however, points out that one must consider these examples within the context of the film. Liz, an experienced seductress, only makes her confession in an effort to titillate the doctor and get what she really wants — information. Her confession is simply acknowledgment of an understanding that some men are aroused by violence against women. Marino's character is DePalma's acknowledgment of an understanding that *some* women — like Kate — are more easily victimized. Derry argues that, since the film identifies the doctor as a criminal psychopath, while clearly distinguishing between the characters of Kate (the victim) and Liz (the heroine) — neither of which are meant to represent an Everywoman — there is no reason to label the film misogynist.[11] *Dressed to Kill* ends with a second shower scene, featuring Liz as the victim of a

7. What the Fifty Foot Woman Did to the Shrinking Man 65

sudden attack. This time, the familiar scenario is part of a nightmare rather than a daydream, and Liz wakes up screaming — a final haunting scene that reveals her new perception of herself as a potential victim.

Some slasher films — most notably *Ms. 45: Angel of Vengeance* (1981) and *I Spit on Your Grave* (1978) — actually served as angry reactions to the formula of the typical slasher, which left the surviving heroine in a state of helpless shock. *Ms. 45* focuses on Anna, a mute seamstress working in the fashion industry in Manhattan. After she is raped twice — that's two *isolated* incidents — in the space of five minutes, she suffers a nervous breakdown that leads first to nightmares, and then to violence. Armed with a rapist's gun, she mounts a kind of preemptive strike, shooting every man who makes a pass at her. More deplorable is *I Spit on Your Grave* (re-released in 1981) — also known as *Day of the Woman* — in which a city girl named Jenny moves to the country, where she is raped by a group of *Deliverance*-type hillbillies. She later confronts her rapists individually and, using her sexuality to manipulate them, exacts her revenge. One hanging, one ax murder and one castration later, Jenny turns on the final rapist, who has unwisely positioned himself next to a motorboat blade, and quips, "Suck it, bitch!"

By 1986, the slasher cycle had mostly played itself out, and the horror film heroine had emerged more resourceful than before. With *The Texas Chain Saw Massacre Part 2*, Tobe Hooper chronicled the transformation of the traditional Gothic damsel in distress into avenger / monster. In an essay on the original *Texas Chain Saw Massacre*, Robin Wood noted that the horror emanated from an all-male family. "The absence of Woman (conceived of as a civilizing, humanizing influence)," he writes, "deprives the family of its social sense and social meaning while leaving its strength of primitive loyalties largely untouched.... It is striking that no suggestion exists anywhere that Sally is the object of an overtly sexual threat: she is to be tormented, killed, dismembered, eaten, but not raped."[12] In the sequel, a female disc jockey named Stretch essentially becomes part of the Sawyer family, thanks to Leatherface's growing interest in the birds and the bees. Though Drayton tries to warn his brother about the danger of women ("Sex ... nobody knows. But the saw is family"), Leatherface proceeds to woo her with a mask made from the flesh of her dead boyfriend's face and a gentle chain saw massage to the groin. Realizing that sex may be her only means of survival, she leads him on, suggestively asking, "How good are you?" Later, driven (at least temporarily) insane by Leatherface's advances and Choptop's ... er ... ribbing, she rips a chain saw from the rotted corpse of "grandma," the long-forgotten matriarch of the clan, and turns the table on her captors. In the final shot of the film, Stretch stands atop the ruins of the Sawyers' underground carnival, screaming maniacally with a chain saw raised above her head. In the process of destroying the monsters, she has become a monster herself.

Judith Halberstam gleefully says that "female power in *TCM2* is channeled through the perfect antidote to the hapless, aristocratic, lethargic Gothic heroine — a white trash bitch with a chain saw." She elaborates on Carol J. Glover's sentiments that the female heroine in slasher films is defined as both masculine and feminine (essentially an evolved, "all-encompassing gender"),[13] saying that "the final girl ... represents not boyishness or girlishness but monstrous gender, a gender that splatters, rips at the seams, and then is sutured together again as something much messier than male or female."[14] Unlike *Sisters*, *The Texas Chain Saw Massacre Part 2* presents this monstrous evolution as a necessity for survival.

As Paul Wells points out, the *Alien* series (1979–97) is perhaps the most convenient model of the evolution of the horror film heroine in the last two decades. Lt. Ellen Ripley is the only survivor of the original 1979 film, in which the crew of a space freighter is decimated by a phallic alien creature with a nasty drooling habit. The film ends when Ripley, supremely vulnerable in a T-shirt and panties, traps the monster in an air-locked hangar, then jettisons it into space like an aborted fetus. Her power, it seems, is directly linked to her femininity. In *Aliens* (1986), Ripley is more aggressive, and even more overtly defined by her femininity — the female Rambo's personal war is an effort to protect Newt, her surrogate daughter, from the monsters.

Alien 3 (1992) immedi-

"The bitch is back!"— Ripley (Sigourney Weaver) with Newt (Carrie Henn) in ***Aliens*** (20th Century–Fox & Redwine, 1986).

ately destroys the mother-daughter connection that was central to *Aliens*, leaving Ripley alone again. This time, she finds herself stranded in a prison colony for male rapists and murderers—where her gender alone guarantees that her life is in danger. Halfway through the film, Ripley learns that she has been impregnated with a queen alien. In effect, the heroine and the monster have been assimilated, now sharing the same body, and the only way Ripley can destroy the monster is by destroying herself. This third film lends itself most readily to accusations of misogyny, but it is not the final word. The assimilation of victim / heroine and monster is the starting point of *Alien Resurrection* (1997). The heroine, dedicated to the destruction of the alien species, is a genetic combination of the dead Lt. Ripley and the alien baby that she was carrying at the time of her death. The horror film heroine has now been completely assimilated with the monster, but the internal conflict remains.

8

Selling the American Dream: The Postmodern Horror Film (Part I)

In the late 1960s and early 1970s, when American society seemed to be undergoing a revolution in all things sacred, the horror film genre reached a high water mark, earning the respect of film academics who recognized the most popular films as emblems of chaotic times. As the Vietnam era gave way to the Watergate era, the sense of nihilism in the national cinema faded into cynicism and even a kind of reassuring nostalgia for the prelapsarian American Dream, leading the horror genre into a post-apocalyptic era.

In 1975, one year after the utter despair of Tobe Hooper's *The Texas Chain Saw Massacre*, Steven Spielberg's *Jaws* was a return to the comparatively conservative formula of classic monster movies. *Jaws* is set in an idyllic New England resort town, where every day is sunny and everyone seems to be on a permanent vacation. One critic calls the town of Amity an archetype of "an America that does not exist and never did, but one the audience recognizes nonetheless."[1] Behind this commercial-friendly silver lining, however, there is a dark cloud: The dream is shattered when a Great White shark starts eating the tourists.

After the first attack, Police Chief Martin Brody plans to close the beaches until a greedy politician heads him off, worried that the ensuing panic will ruin the town's commerce. We can practically see the mayor drooling over tourist dollars as he reassures a reporter that there is no danger, and cheekily reminds viewers that the word Amity means friendship.

8. Selling the American Dream

After a second attack, involving his own children, Brody takes to the sea, to hunt the shark with oceanographer Matt Hooper and an Ahab-like fisherman named Quint.

As a cop and a devoted father, Brody is the consummate American hero—at once independent and connected to the social institutions of family and government—and it is, not coincidentally, Brody's efforts that finally destroy the monster and firmly reestablish order to the ideal American landscape.

Spielberg's film is ultimately reassuring; all of the characters' problems are caused by the monster, and the destruction of the monster is decisive ... at least until the studio execs started drooling over ticket sales and began planning the sequels.

In 1978, director Philip Kaufman and writer W.D. Richter began making preparations for a film that would examine a more pervasive threat to the American way of life. Richter set his remake of *Invasion of the Body Snatchers* in San Francisco, rationalizing that "if long ago we thought the

Chief Brody (Roy Scheider) and Matt Hooper (Richard Dreyfuss) argue with the Amity mayor (Murray Hamilton) in *Jaws* (Universal, 1975).

communists were taking over the heart of America, our small towns, then if we had fears today it had more to do with how we were losing the center of our civilization, because our cities were starting to seem strange. They weren't necessarily representative of the best of us, but maybe the worst of us."[2] Tracey Knight proposes that "the film's setting in time (the cusp between the counterculture era and the 'me decade') and place (San Francisco, where flowers in the hair, if not the nervous system, were encouraged)" lend it to interpretation as an allegory of the power struggle between the counterculture and "Establishment America."[3]

The remake begins when a meteor disperses space seeds in San Francisco, producing deadly plants that call to mind another memorable horror film, *The Day of the Triffids* (1963). The morning after Elizabeth brings one of the alien pods into her house, her lazy boyfriend Geoffrey begins exhibiting strange behavior — he dresses better, emotes less and (gasp) gives away Warriors tickets. When she tells her friend Matthew about the changes, he jokingly speculates that Geoffrey could be cheating on her or, worse still, have become a Republican. Elizabeth gradually becomes convinced that she is not imagining things and turns to pop psychologist Dr. David Kibner for an explanation. Kibner calmly dismisses her fears as part of a "hallucinatory flu" that seems to be going around — resulting, he says, from a society-wide breakdown in trust. Later, when Elizabeth and Matthew find conclusive proof that the city is being overrun with pod people, it is too late. They turn to the police and then to the feds, only to learn that the aliens have taken over the government. (Was there ever any doubt?) They are finally entrapped by Matthew's trusted friend, Dr. Kibner, who prepares them for rebirth into a new life with the "same life, same clothes, same car," but none of the emotional handicaps. The two heroes continue to struggle, but it is a lost cause and they are eventually subsumed into the community of yuppie zombies.

George Romero's *Dawn of the Dead* (1978), a sequel to *Night of the Living Dead*, may be read as a variation on this idea. *Dawn* begins in a Pittsburgh television station, where technicians (including Romero himself) are desperately working to maintain emergency broadcasts in the days following the first film's apocalypse. The whole world, it seems, has lapsed into chaos. In a final desperate response, the government begins a quarantine, which promises to strip citizens of every personal freedom. Realizing that the quarantine is inevitable, four friends hijack a helicopter and escape in search of a place where they can reestablish their normal lives. The quartet stop to rest at an abandoned mall, where the three men are able to live out their consumer fantasies and ignore the reality that exists outside. They decide to stay, despite the protests of Fran, who quickly sees through their perfect world. "It's so bright and neatly wrapped," she tells them, "you don't see that it's a prison too." Eventually, the men grow bored with the creature comforts of the mall, and the aimless zombies begin to inspire melancholy rather than fear. It is then that they realize Fran is right — their existence has no more purpose than that of the zombies. (As Barbara would later say in Tom Savini's 1990 remake of *Night of the Living Dead*, "We're them and they're us.")

Nevertheless, when a gang of outlaw bikers invades the mall — destroying the illusion of normalcy for the second time — the group aggressively defends their home, still clinging desperately to the remains of the past. Once the mall has been completely overrun by bikers and zombies, Peter reaches a point of utter despair, unwilling to start over. It is only in the final seconds that he impulsively decides to escape with Fran; they climb to the roof of the mall and take off in the helicopter, with no plan for the future. "How much gas do we have?" Peter asks. "Not much," Fran answers.

Based on this reluctantly hopeful ending, Robin Wood argues that "*Dawn* is perhaps the first horror film to suggest — albeit very tentatively — the possibility of moving beyond apocalypse."[4] Generally speaking, however, America's popular cinematic horrors during the next decade were far more trivial than Romero's nightmarish vision of modern society. *Day of the Dead* completed his "waste land" trilogy, but the film was out of step with audiences in 1985. Around the turn of the decade, horror films concentrated mostly on small-scale crises of confidence that erupted behind a façade of middle-class normalcy, à la *Jaws*.

The year after *Halloween* thrashed the illusion of safety in suburbia, *The Amityville Horror* painted a portrait of a family tormented by questions of economic viability. Stephen King suggests that the film "might well have been subtitled *The Horror of the Shrinking Bank Account*."[5] The horror begins when widower George Lutz impulsively marries a divorcee with three kids, then sinks all of his money into a Long Island dream house. Friends tell him he's crazy and, as the financial burdens of George's new life begin to fray his nerves, he starts spending more and more quality time with his trusty ax and their words begin to seem prophetic. King suggests that this ghost story is more about a family's "economic unease" than about ghosts, pointing out that the film ends not in murder but in bankruptcy. The Lutz finally family flees in the middle of the night as their home and all of their belongings are liquidated — the entire house bleeds out into a thick, gooey black bile.

Amityville was adapted from a bestselling novel by Jay Anson, who based his story on real-life events. The "horror" began in 1974, when 22-

The Lutzes (James Brolin and Margot Kidder) stand in front of their dream house in *The Amityville Horror* (AIP, 1979).

year-old Ronald DeFeo killed his parents and siblings, then claimed that voices inside their ominous-looking Dutch Colonial house told him to do it.* A year later, a nearly-bankrupt couple ("the Lutzes") made a down payment on the house and moved in, only to flee after 28 days, spinning tales about strange supernatural occurrences. Less than two years after that, the novel was published.[6] The Lutzes are, presumably, living comfortably off of the proceeds, having found a way to turn their financial nightmare into Hollywood's version of the American Dream—fame and prosperity for minimal effort.

The Steven Spielberg–produced *Poltergeist* (1982) is another haunted house story that offers dark shades of the American Dream. It begins during the witching hour, in the cozy suburban California home of Steven and Diane Freeling. Steven has fallen asleep in front of the living room television just as the local station goes off the air, ending the night's broadcast with a poignant rendition of "The Star Spangled Banner." The rest of his family is sleeping soundly, with the exception of Carol Ann—the youngest of the three Freeling children—who is awakened by ghostly whispers. She follows the sound to the living room, where she plants herself

---

The "real life" story is fictionalized in Amityville, II: The Possession *(1980).*

in front of the television set and instructs the voices to talk louder. When Carol Ann finally concludes her one-sided conversation with the TV, her family is gathered around her, wondering who, or what, she is talking to.

Soon after, the haunting begins—electricity goes haywire, tables and chairs begin moving by themselves, and Carol Ann's brother is nearly ingested by an old oak tree. Before the family can escape, Carol Ann is abducted by monsters in her closet and held hostage in a kind of otherworldly dimension surrounding the house. The Freeling family remains in the house, able to communicate with their missing daughter only through the television. Eventually, Steven learns that his own employers are responsible for the haunting—a greedy real estate developer built the neighborhood on top of an old cemetery, without removing the bodies. Thus, the skeletons in their closets (not to mention their swimming pool) are, quite literally, skeletons. The family is held hostage by the past until a psychic named Tangina arrives. Tangina explains that the strongest weapon the family has against the ghosts of the past is their love for each other, and she promptly sends Diane into the closet to retrieve her daughter. Eventually, mother and daughter are reborn through a metaphysical gateway, pulled from the fourth dimension by Steven. With the family reunited, Tangina prematurely pronounces the house clean, but the ghosts retaliate, imploding the suburban funhouse before the eyes of the greedy developer.

At the beginning of *Poltergeist II: The Other Side* (1986), Steven and Diane are faced with the practical problem of reestablishing themselves financially. They go to live with Diane's mother while fighting the insurance company over the disappearance of their house. The insurance agent claims, "If the house disappeared, then technically it's only missing." Unemployed and unable to provide for his family, Steven begins to drink. As his feelings of inadequacy begin to unravel the family, the Freelings again become vulnerable to attacks from the undead—this time, in the form of Reverend Kane, a Jonestown-type father figure. Tangina sends a mystic Native American named Taylor to live with the family and help Steven rediscover his "manhood." This time, it is the father who must cross over to "the other side" to save Carol Ann. By reestablishing his role as protector, Steven is able to reestablish the strength of the family itself, allowing them to defeat the ghosts again.

The family continued to be the locus of horror throughout the decade. In Stanley Kubrick's adaptation of Stephen King's novel *The Shining*, ghosts use the emotionally unstable Jack Torrence as a weapon against his wife and son. The film's most genuinely unnerving moment comes when, on

Dysfunctional father Jack Torrence (Jack Nicholson) and son Danny (Danny Lloyd) in *The Shining* (Warner Bros., 1980).

the brink of a homicidal rampage, Jack cradles his adolescent son in his arms and coos, "I would never do anything to hurt you." The maniacal gleam in his eye tells a different story, and soon Jack is pursuing Danny down the endless halls of the Overlook Hotel with an ax. At the end of King's novel, Jack's deep-rooted love for his wife and son allows them to escape the hotel. In the film, Kubrick reveals that Jack was one of the ghosts all along. Based on this misinterpretation of the father as monster, King considers the film a failure, and has accused Kubrick of producing a domestic tragedy rather than a "genuine horror film."[7]

In King's stories, "evil" is never inherent in the family, or in the hearts of God-fearing, law-abiding American citizens. Generally, the threat is some ancient, otherworldly power, released and amplified by vulnerable and / or corruptible characters or agencies. Though King's heroes are rarely able to completely eradicate the source of the evil, they are usually able to dispel it and return to normalcy. Mark Edmundson suggests that King's work was popular because it was ultimately reassuring. King, he says, invites readers "to relive their childhoods with him, to take a self-righteous vacation away from their day-to-day immersion in the adult world."[8] His most popular stories—*'Salem's Lot, The Dead Zone, Christine, Cujo,*

Firestarter et al.—acknowledged the existence of dangerous, corrupting forces (be they vampires or crooked politicians, ghosts or government agencies), but reassured readers that evil could never get a permanent foothold in American life. Asked in 1986 what he thought of America, King replied, "I think it's fantastic. We're killing ourselves; we're fiddling while Rome burns. I mean, while we've got enough explosives to turn planet earth into the second asteroid belt, the largest weekly magazine in the country is talking about where celebrities shop, and why people in Hollywood don't want to serve finger foods anymore. It all seems really ridiculous to me, but I love it."[9] In King's imagination, even a Romero-esque apocalypse could lead to a relatively happy ending (see *The Stand*), and this was a message that the moviegoing public wanted to hear.

Throughout the decade, King's novels topped best-seller lists, and many of his stories were adapted to the screen by prominent genre filmmakers, including Brian DePalma, Stanley Kubrick, Tobe Hooper (*Salem's Lot*, 1979), George Romero (*Creepshow*, 1982), David Cronenberg (*The Dead Zone*, 1983), Lewis Teague (*Cujo*, 1983, *Cat's Eye*, 1985) and John Carpenter (*Christine*, 1983). Carpenter, in particular, seemed to understand that King's liberal approach to the horror genre was partly rooted in the concept of a historical "innocent time" in America. *Christine* is a male-oriented version of *Carrie* that focuses on two 1950s–era emblems of male coming-of-age: hot wheels and rock n roll. King says, "For me, rock 'n' roll was the rise of consciousness ... I don't have any bad memories of the Fifties. Everything was asleep. There was stuff going on, there was uneasiness about the bomb, but on the whole, I'd have to say that people in the Fifties were pretty loose."[10]

Just as weirdly nostalgic is Joseph Ruben's *The Stepfather* (1987), a horrific spin on *Father Knows Best*. The titular character is Jerry Blake, a real estate agent who believes wholeheartedly that he is "selling the American Dream." In fact, Jerry has spent his entire life in pursuit of the elusive ideal—a nuclear family existing in perfect harmony behind a white picket fence. His latest stepdaughter, Stephanie, complains, "He has this whole fantasy thing, like we should be like the families on TV and grin and laugh and have fewer cavities ... I swear to God it's like having Ward Cleaver for a dad." She gradually begins to realize that Jerry is a little *too* dedicated to the ideal—he has already wiped out several surrogate families that didn't live up to his expectations. What distinguishes this film from earlier films about horror within the American family is that the horror stems not from conflicts within the family, but from the incompatibility of the real and the ideal. Rather than an allegory about the breakdown of traditional values, *The Stepfather* is a tongue-in-cheek examination of America's potentially destructive focus on unrealistic "traditional values."

David Lynch achieves a perfect synthesis of the real and the ideal American in his film *Blue Velvet* (1986). It begins with an elaborate depiction of the Jerry Blake fantasy: The camera pans down from a cloudless blue sky onto the sleepy northwestern town of Lumberton. Roses are in full bloom behind a white picket fence. An old model fire truck passes us in slow motion. (The firemen are, presumably, on their way to rescue a cat that is stuck in a tree.) Mr. Beaumont watches the truck pass, while watering the lawn and watching his dog playfully run circles around him. Mrs. Beaumont sits peacefully on the couch inside their home, watching her soaps on TV. She is oblivious when her husband suddenly collapses on the lawn, the victim of a massive stroke. The camera pans down, below his inanimate body, into the earth, where bugs are writhing in the darkness. For Lynch, the scene is symbolic of his childhood in the 1950s: "It was a really hopeful time, and things were going up instead of going down.

Jeffery Beaumont (Kyle McLachlan) makes a gruesome discovery in *Blue Velvet* (DeLaurentiis, 1986).

8. Selling the American Dream

You got the feeling you could do anything. The future was bright. Little did we know we were laying the groundwork then for a disastrous future. All the problems were there, but it was somehow glossed over. And then the gloss broke, or rotted, and it all came oozing out."[11]

Blue Velvet is the coming-of-age story of Jeffrey Beaumont, a naïve, all–American boy whose curiosity leads him into the twisted world of a sexually deviant lounge singer and a drug-addled, psychopathic criminal. By transferring the sadistic and masochistic impulses of these characters onto Jeffrey, Lynch subtly integrates darkness into the American Dream, creating what Pauline Kael calls a distinctly "American darkness—darkness in color."[12] What makes the film stand out above the horror films of the 1980s is Jeffrey's sense of wonder at the end of the film — he is able to embrace the complexity of his new world, without sinking into nihilism or repressing the horrible things that have happened. In its failure to reestablish "normalcy," Lynch's film is the type of progressive horror film that Paul Wells says can prove that "audiences have come to terms with the darkness at the heart of contemporary civilization and can endure its less palatable outcomes."[13]

9

Old Monsters, New Flesh: The Postmodern Horror Film (Part II)

> "Back from the grave and ready to party."
> — tag line for *Return of the Living Dead*

In 1978, George Romero wrote and directed *Martin*, an independent feature about a Pittsburgh teenager who may or may not be an 84-year-old vampire. The title character is a shy, sexually inexperienced kid who subdues female victims with drugs and razor blades, then drinks their blood. Martin is, by all rational accounts, a sociopath rather than a supernatural monster; he himself claims that "there is no real magic." Nevertheless, he fantasizes that he is a traditional Hollywood vampire — omnipotent, aristocratic and desired by women — and the fantasy has become a support system, reinforcing his belief that he can fulfill his need for human intimacy only through violent means. He replaces the "sexy stuff" with ritual bloodletting.

Romero says that *Martin* originally came to him as a "middle-of-the-night idea" — "basically a vampire would have a hard time today! Nobody would pay him a lot of attention or get particularly shook up."[1] The idea of transplanting an Old World vampire into contemporary America was nothing new,* but Romero wanted to make a film that transcended, rather

---

*See *Son of Dracula* (1943), *Blood of Dracula* (1957), *The Return of Dracula* (1958), *Count Yorga: Vampire* (1970), and *Blacula* (1972).

9. Old Monsters, New Flesh 79

than parodied, the classic monster movies. Robin Wood says that "one can sense throughout the film a hesitation on Romero's part as to whether he wanted to make a horror film at all."² *Martin* is closer to a realist drama than a traditional horror film, in part because the usual conflict between the forces of Good and Evil is replaced with a conflict between an empathetic sociopath and a contemptible hero. Martin's "evil" is cured by a compassionate sexual relationship with a neighborhood woman, but his fanatically religious cousin Cuda kills him anyway, by driving a stake through his heart. This final scene, which lingers on the teenager's violated body for a painfully long time (presumably to show that he is not going to turn to dust), proves to the audience that Cuda's belief in the vampire mythology is just as dangerous as his cousin's. By focusing on the concept of the vampire fantasy-as-monster instead of simply spinning a fantastic tale about vampires, Romero made *Martin* one of the first intelligently reflexive horror films. In the words of one critic, it "forces us to become a more informed, wary, self-conscious audience — an audience that realizes that movies can be about movies and movie-going even when they are not literally about filmmaking."³

In the following decades, more and more horror films adopted this mode of self-consciousness, attempting to rise above the recognizable formulas and cliches of the genre by acknowledging them in the text. Tobe Hooper's *The Funhouse* (1981) added a more whimsical tone to the reflexive postmodern horror film. The opening sequence is an obvious parody of both *Halloween* (1978) and *Psycho* (1960): The camera adopts the gaze of a mischievous young boy, who dons a clown mask and attacks his teenage sister in the shower with a rubber knife. Amy, our virginal heroine, vows revenge and unintentionally gets it the next next night, when she and her friends go to a carnival with little Joey in tow. For Amy's friends, the carnival is a convenient backdrop for sex and drug use, and they decide to spend the night in a funhouse full of mechanical monsters, unaware that at least one of the monsters is real. After the carnival has shut down for the night, they witness a murder committed by a man in a Frankenstein mask. No longer amused by the horrors of the funhouse, they try to escape, only to be trapped by the killer. Just as things get really ugly, one of the victims realizes the irony of their situation and recounts an incident from his childhood: "When I was a kid, I once tried to spook my older brother by hiding in his closet and, while I was in there, waiting to jump out and scare him, a weird thought came into my head. What if he knew? What if he knew I was in there and he was standing just outside the closet door, waiting to jump out and scare me?" Fear is no longer fun. When the monster finally jumps out, the teens are not just being punished for sexual promiscuity (as is apparently the case in most slasher films), but for the morbid curiosity that led them to the funhouse in the first place. When Amy escapes the following morning, she looks 20 years older, owing to her new awareness that the monsters are sometimes real.

The Howling (1981), written by John Sayles and directed by Corman alum Joe Dante, sets out to prove the same thing to its audience. The premise is that werewolves do exist, but we don't believe in them because they have been the subject of decades of hokey horror movies. As Professor Van Helsing said of Dracula, their greatest strength lies in our disbelief. In *The Howling*, the secret is guarded by Dr. George Waggner, a psychiatrist who has organized a colony of werewolves in Northern California. After a television news reporter, Karen White, is attacked in Los Angeles by one of the members, Dr. Waggner decides to keep her under observation to make sure she doesn't discover the truth. Eventually, Karen not only learns the secret, but becomes a part of it — she is bitten, and therefore cursed, while trying to escape. Back in L.A., she transforms herself into a werewolf on the nightly news, to warn the world about the impending danger. Ironically, most of the viewers shrug it off, dismissing the transformation as particularly good special effects. For the viewer of *The Howling*, the film's "warning" is undercut not only by the heavy

Karen White (Dee Wallace) begins her on-air transformation in *The Howling* (AVCO Embassy, 1981).

emphasis on special effects, but by constant reminders that we are watching a film. The reminders include characters named after old horror movie directors (George Waggner, Terry Fisher, Fred Francis, Erle Kenton and Lew Landers), noteworthy performances and cameos by genre legends (Roger Corman, Dick Miller, Kenneth Tobey, Kevin McCarthy, Slim Pickens and John Carradine), and a recurring movie within a movie (*The Wolf Man*). Like *Piranha* (1978), an earlier collaboration of Dante and Sayles under the creative guidance of Roger Corman, *The Howling* knowingly deposits us in a postmodern funhouse where smoke and mirrors are the main attraction.

With more and more films adopting a lighthearted approach to the old horrors, the genre entered its most commercially successful phase. The most popular films were often variations on familiar stories— Brian DePalma was continually reinventing Hitchcock, *The Texas Chain Saw Massacre* (1974) was spoofed by *Motel Hell* (1980) while *Alone in the Dark* (1982) parodied *Halloween* (1978), and *An American Werewolf in London* (1981) and *Q: The Winged Serpent* (1982) paid homage to the classic monster movies. Eager to capitalize on the mainstream popularity of the genre, major Hollywood studios bankrolled big-budget remakes (*Invasion of the Body Snatchers,* 1978; *Dracula,* 1979; *The Thing,* 1982; *Cat People,* 1982; *Twilight Zone: The Movie,* 1983) and family-friendly horror shows like *Gremlins* (1984), *Ghostbusters* (1984), *Fright Night* (1985) and *Teen Wolf* (1985). On the other end of the spectrum, independent filmmakers were making more concerted efforts to push the envelope on screen violence (see *The Evil Dead,* 1981; *Basket Case,* 1982; *Re-Animator,* 1985), appealing to the cult audience. In 1985, Dan O'Bannon's *Return of the Living Dead* set the tone for the decade by transforming George Romero's nightmare vision of America into a gruesome but hilarious monster mash. It all but eclipsed *Day of the Dead,* Romero's bleak finale to his zombie trilogy, released the same year.

The advent of home video— which promised unlimited access to such films— revitalized an unending debate about the influence of cinematic violence on the public. David Cronenberg, a frequent target for such censorship, was quick to respond to the debate in his 1983 film *Videodrome,* in which the medium of television literally becomes the message of conservative thinkers who want to eliminate America's "social climate of violence and sexual malaise." By imbedding cancer-carrying signals in a snuff porn telecast called "Videodrome," the conservatives are able to induce a fatal tumor into the brain of morally bankrupt producer Max Renn. The tumor acts as a kind of mind control device, allowing them to use Renn to target a mass audience— the "unhealthy" portion of society, in their view—that absorbs sex and violence as entertainment Later, Renn is reprogrammed by the opposition, who are led by media guru Brian O'Blivion (a thinly disguised Marshall McLuhan), to assassinate those who would prevent the public's potential to reach a higher level of consciousness through television. By committing suicide, Renn finally frees himself from an existence in which he has lost all identity and power, and reconstitutes himself in the "new flesh" of the video world, where there are no laws of objective reality.

Videodrome is particularly difficult to interpret because it treats Renn's perception of events as its objective reality, leaving the viewer unable to distinguish between the real world and the video world. This technique of manipulating the audience's perception of events is one of the strengths of the horror film, and it is the crux of what was arguably the most influential film of the decade. In Wes Craven's *A Nightmare on Elm Street* (1984), serial killer Freddy Krueger haunts the dreams of a group of teens in suburban Illinois. The teens quickly learn that death in the dream means death in reality. As the Elm Street kids start dying in spectacularly gruesome ways, Nancy Thompson tries to explain that a scarred madman with a knives for fingers is behind the murders, but her alcoholic mother and stubborn father refuse to listen. Eventually, she learns the identity of her stalker: He was a child murderer, burned alive by the outraged parents of Elm Street several years before. After Nancy confronts her mother with the truth, the woman turns their suburban tract house into a prison — putting bars on the window to keep her daughter safe. Freddy, of course, is already inside, and nobody is safe.

In the sequels, the adults on Elm Street continued to ignore the warnings of their children, and Freddy essentially replaced the parents of Elm Street as a surrogate authority figure. At the end of *A Nightmare on Elm Street Part 2: Freddy's Revenge* (1985), he crashes a backyard barbecue, hovers over the teens and quips, "You are all my children now." In *A Nightmare on Elm Street Part 3: Dream Warriors* (1987), the doctors in a psychiatric hospital refuse to acknowledge the "mass delusion" of the last remaining Elm Street kids; only their murderer takes the time to understand them. He then dismantles each one through their individual hobbies, obsessions and addictions— appearing in an ex-junkie's dream with syringes for fingers (crooning "Let's get high!"), attacking an aspiring starlet through the TV set ("Welcome to prime time, bitch!") and snaring one of the more shy teens by growing breasts and engaging in a rousing game of tonsil hockey ("What's wrong, Joey? Feeling tongue-tied?"). By the third film, as Ian Conrich points out, Freddy had been transformed from a boogeyman to a comedian who performs for the filmgoing audi-

Freddy (Robert Englund) gets chummy with Dick Cavett and Zsa Zsa Gabor in *A Nightmare on Elm Street 3: Dream Warriors* (New Line, 1987).

ence (the subject). As Freddy, Robert Englund "seduces the subject through a combination of his power and personality and supporting series of clever images and stimulating visuals."[4]

According to Craven, it was New Line Cinema producer Robert Shaye who decided to market Freddy as an anti-hero in the sequels, making him a pop culture icon — a wicked stepfather for moviegoing teens across America.[5] Freddy's name and image were associated with a wide variety of products, including books and comics, clothes (most notably, a plastic glove which boasts that "you too can become the bastard son of a thousand maniacs"), key rings, dolls, board games, model kits, watches and alarm clocks, Christmas tree ornaments, amusement park rides and MTV videos.[6] In 1988, Freddy even became the host of his own cable television series, *Freddy's Nightmares*. By the end of the decade, Freddy's power to cross over from dreams to reality had translated into an ability to cross over from the video world to the real world. In effect, he had become pop culture's premier urban legend.

After Freddy was supposedly killed off in the fifth *Nightmare* sequel, a new horror anti-hero emerged from the mind of bestselling horror novelist Clive Barker. *Candyman* (1992) tells the story of a University of Chicago grad student named Helen Lyle who, while researching a thesis on urban legends, helps to empower an undead murderer. Candyman, an

The Sawyers mimic *The Breakfast Club* in this promotional still for the postmodern *The Texas Chainsaw Massacre Part 2* (Cannon, 1986).

ex-slave who was tortured to death centuries earlier, now thrives on the fear of the residents of Chicago's infamous Cabrini-Green housing project. When Helen begins interviewing the locals and encouraging their disbelief in the myth ("Candyman isn't real," she says, "He's just a story ... like Dracula or Frankenstein"), the killer appears to her. In a deep, seductive — and strikingly polite — whisper, he confesses, "Your disbelief destroyed the faith of my congregation. Without them, I am nothing, so I was obliged to come." In their essay on the film, Aviva Briefel and Sianne Ngai point out that the murders are caused by Helen's curiosity. Unlike Freddy Krueger, who exercises a diabolic will of his own, Candyman appears only because Helen has summoned him, and murders only to maintain his existence. The film deviates from the slasher formula, they say, "by claiming that such myths can no longer naturally and effortlessly intrude into a community."[7] The victim and the audience are responsible for empowering the monster.

The same validation from his audience brings Freddy Krueger back to life in *Wes Craven's New Nightmare* (1994). In the film, the real life creators of Freddy (Craven, Shaye, Englund and actors Heather Langenkamp and John Saxon) are being stalked by the dream killer. Craven explains to

Langenkamp that Freddy is a new incarnation of an ancient evil that cannot be destroyed. For whatever reason, that evil likes its current form and has decided, now that Hollywood has discarded the dream master, to enter the real world as Freddy. Mark Edmundson argues that the cinematic monster's "freedom" represents changes in contemporary American society. He says, "We find ourselves in a culture where the Gothic idiom has slipped over from fiction and begun to shape and regulate our perception of reality, thrusting us into a world in which crazy militiamen, deranged priests, panoptic power, bizarre molesters, Freddy, Jason and Leatherface constitute reality. They are — to more and more of us — what's out there."[8]

In *New Nightmare*, Langenkamp's son, Dylan, is particularly affected by this cultural shift toward the Gothic. When he begins acting suicidal, L.A. doctors speculate that it is because he has seen his mother's films (conveniently overlooking his father's recent death). Only the inner-circle of filmmakers—standing in for the teenage victims of the earlier *Nightmare* films—know that the real threat is Freddy, now a flesh-and-blood monster in the everyday world. The fictional films, *New Nightmare* suggests, allow us to cope with the existence of such monsters. Once Dylan has been rescued from the depths of Freddy-Hell, his mother lulls him to sleep by reading to him from the *New Nightmare* script.

John Carpenter's *In the Mouth of Madness* (1995) addresses the same question about the Gothic saturation of American culture, and its effects on the public. Sam Neill stars as John Trent, an insurance claims investigator who is hired to locate Sutter Cane, a bestselling horror author who has recently gone missing. Trent travels with Cane's editor, Linda Stiles, to New England, where they magically end up in Cane's fictional town of Hobbs End. When they find Cane, he explains that the world of his imagination has been constituted as reality by the audience's belief in it. More people, he points out, believe in his fiction than in the Bible and, though no one's "ever believed religion enough to make it real, the same cannot be said of my work." This prompts Stiles to ask, "What if reality shared Cane's point of view?" Because Cane's fiction exists in a Lovecraftian world of ancient demons and even more demonic humans, Trent returns to New York after the publication of Cane's latest book and finds the world in chaos. Cane's publisher (Charlton Heston) delivers the coup de grace, pointing out that the few survivors who haven't been driven mad by reading the book will be corrupted by the film adaptation, coming soon to a theater near you.

John Kenneth Muir attributes the commercial failure of *In the Mouth of Madness* to its inaccessability to mainstream audiences. "Its success," he says, "depends largely on an audience's knowledge of the genre, and it

The kids aren't all right: Billy (Skeet Ulrich), Randy (Jamie Kennedy) and Stu (Matthew Lillard) in *Scream* (Dimension, 1996).

demands that one bring this knowledge to any reading of it."[9] Nevertheless, Wes Craven and screenwriter Kevin Williamson were able to draw a huge audience to the theaters with *Scream* (1996), the final word in reflexive horror. The film, like *In the Mouth of Madness*, served as a cautionary tale — warning that impressionable teens could be turned into killers by too much TV. Of course, it also demonstrated that potential victims could be trained by survive. In the final moments of the film, the heroine is warned that "this is the moment when the supposedly dead killer comes back to life for one last scare." When the inevitable happens, she promptly shoots him in the head, point blank, and says, "Not in my movie." It seems likely that *Scream* succeeded because it was neither preachy nor patronizing. At the same time, as Paul Wells points out, it wasn't very horrifying either, because it invokes only "the obvious strategies to create predictable sensations in an audience." He adds: "It is at this point when the horror genre, despite its supposed extremes, becomes highly conservative and reassuring."[10]

10

Reality Bites: The New American Film Gothic

"This is not an exit."
— Bret Easton Ellis, *American Psycho*

Like Dracula himself, the vampire film appears ageless, spanning the history of the horror genre with unremitting popularity. Alain Silver and James Ursini point out that, over the years, the silver screen's most persistent monster has "acquired new powers and new weaknesses, new desires and new anguishes. There have been vampire dogs and moths, vampire turkey men and trees. They have come from outer space, from Shangri-La, from Burbank, and to Kobe to make beautiful women."[1] Originally a product of Victorian literature, the vampire has crossed boundaries of gender, race and species, proving adaptable to any time and place, as well as any body. His / her defining characteristics — superhuman power (oftentimes intellectual and social, as well as physical) and an insatiable lust for life — have universal appeal for moviegoers in any culture, and the seductively amorphous nature of the monster is particularly well-suited to the dream-like medium of film. Thus, the cinematic vampire has remained in vogue for almost a century. As one of the characters in *The Understudy: Graveyard Shift 2* (1988) says, the vampire is "the perfect movie star — its shape changes, it lives forever in the dark, it feeds on our imagination."

The most obvious source of the vampire mystique is Bram Stoker's novel *Dracula*, which was first adapted to the screen by German filmmaker F.W. Murnau in 1921 as *Nosferatu*. Unlike Stoker's creation, *Nosferatu*'s vampire Count is human neither in appearance nor in motivation — Orlock is simply a waking nightmare. Less than a decade later, Dracula was cleaned up for his simultaneous American and Spanish film debuts—both set in modern-day London. Almost three decades after that, English filmmakers appropriated Stoker's creation, placing him in historical settings. David Pirie says that *Horror of Dracula* (1958) returned the monster "to the tradition in which he was created—the tradition of English (as opposed to European) Gothic; the villain again becomes what he was always meant to be, the charming, intelligent and irresistible host who is on the point of turning the cosy Victorian world upside down by transforming women into ravening sexual animals."[2] In the following years in Europe, screen vampires became even more overtly sexual.* American filmmakers, however, mostly treated the monster as an absurd anachronism in farces such as *The Return of Dracula* (1958), *Count Yorga: Vampire* (1970), *Blacula* (1972), *Scream Blacula Scream* (1973) and *Love at First Bite* (1979).

Love at First Bite features George Hamilton in the role of a comically melodramatic vampire from the Old World, who claims that "in a world without romance, it's better to be dead." John Badham's adaptation of *Dracula*, released the same year, more seriously explores this idea, reinventing the monster as a Romantic anti-hero for contemporary audiences. The film begins with the arrival of the Demeter, Dracula's ship, on the shores of England. The suave, overtly sexual Count—played by Frank Langella—immediately sinks his teeth into Lucy Harker, and sets his sights on Mina Van Helsing. After Lucy's death, Mina's father, Professor Abraham Van Helsing, arrives in London just in time to witness her resurrection as a vampire. He then vows to destroy Dracula in order to protect his daughter from the same fate, eliciting protests from Mina. "You dare try to confuse me," she says, "tormenting him who is the saddest and kindest of all!" Despite her loyalty to the Count, Van Helsing and Jonathan Harker track Dracula to his crypt, prepared to destroy him in the customary way. At the last minute, however, Mina awakens the vampire, who promptly drives a stake through Van Helsing's heart, then transforms into a bat and flies off in broad daylight. Mina looks positively radiant. Badham's film set the stage for the postmodern American vampire film, which often champions the monster and revels in the stylized destruction that follows him/her.

The American film vampire was re-imagined by Tony Scott's *The Hunger* (1983), which also redefined the aesthetics of the horror film for

---

*See Hammer's lesbian vampire trilogy (The Vampire Lovers, *1970*; Twins of Evil, *1971*; Lust for a Vampire, *1971*) Jess Franco's *Vampyros Lesbos* (1970) *and* Andy Warhol's Dracula *(1974)*.

the MTV generation. The film begins at a New Wave nightclub in the early 1980s, where bloodsuckers Miriam and John Blalock pick up two unsuspecting victims, then take them back to a posh apartment and seductively violate them. The director uses every element of this opening sequence — sets, lighting, wardrobe, music and especially editing — to brand the murderers as fascinating creatures rather than horrifying monsters. (One can almost hear Lugosi swooning over the "children of the night ... what music they make" as Bauhaus performs "Bela Lugosi's Dead" in the neo–Gothic atmosphere of the nightclub.) The choice of cast contributes to this effect — Catherine Deneuve and David Bowie are as sexy as any screen vampires have ever been. Like the two pop culture icons themselves, John and Miriam Blalock represent a contemporary kind of American aristocracy. Cynthia Freeland points out that Miriam's superiority over her victims is demonstrated by her surroundings. Her commodities—from her liquor cabinet to her wardrobe to the Egyptian ankh she uses as a murder weapon—"are not so much an accumulation of wealth as an accumulation of *taste*. They suit this wise, learned woman who has devoted her particular immortality to the pursuit of art and beauty."[3] Like Dracula, this contemporary American vampire is charming, sophisticated, mysterious and irresistible. As a result, we idolize the monsters and envy the victims.

John (David Bowie) and Miriam Blalock (Catherine Deneuve) on the prowl in *The Hunger* (MGM, 1983).

Anne Rice illuminated this shift of loyalty from victim to victimizer with her hugely successful 1974 novel *Interview with the Vampire*, followed in 1985 by *The Vampire Lestat*. Katherine Ramsland says that the neo–Gothic mythology popularized by Rice and her peers drew "sensitive, alienated kids who seek mystery, magic, and a distraction from the dullness of mundane life, and who resonate to death images"—just the type who frequent the New Wave nightclub in *The Hunger*. Many of them, Ramsland says, "respond to the image of a vampire as the ultimate Gothic icon."[4] Like George Romero's vampire Martin, they seek a connection to the world and the people around them; the vampire mythology presents itself.

In 1987, the influence of the Gothic monster on youth culture in America was captured by *The Lost Boys*, which equated the bloodsuckers with James Dean, Jim Morrison and Tony Manero. In the film, brothers Sam and Michael Emerson move with their mother to the quiet town of Santa Carla, California. Soon after their arrival, they realize that Santa Carla is not like other towns. Michael is initiated into a gang of teenage bikers who sleep all day and party all night. When Sam realizes that his older brother is being turned into a vampire ("My own brother, a goddamn shit-sucking vampire. You wait 'til Mom finds out!"), he seeks help in the most unlikely of places—a comic book store. Like Peter Vincent in *Fright Night* (1985), vampire hunters Edgar and Alex have learned their trade from movies that trivialize the real threat of monsters in our midst. Realizing that Santa Carla is a breeding ground for the undead, the brothers stockpile holy water, garlic and wooden stakes and prepare for a war in the name of "truth, justice and the American way." The irony, of course, is that *The Lost Boys* also trivializes the vampire myth, and lacks the punch of films like *The Hunger* and *Near Dark* (1987).

In 1988, Thomas Harris's novel *The Silence of the Lambs* introduced audiences to real-life vampires and vampire hunters. The novel revolves around Clarice Starling, a student at the FBI Academy who is sent on an unlikely errand for the Bureau's Behavioral Science Unit. BSU Chief Jack Crawford asks her to interview convicted serial killer Hannibal "The Cannibal" Lecter, in the hope that she can gain insight into the mind of an active serial killer nicknamed Buffalo Bill. In his book *Whoever Fights Monsters*, former FBI profiler Robert Ressler, who coined the term "serial killer" in the late 1970s, explains that he met with Harris prior to the publication of *Red Dragon*, the 1981 novel that introduced Lecter. Ressler implies that the Lecter may have been based on serial killers Edmund Kemper and Richard Trenton Chase, otherwise known as the Sacramento "Vampire Killer," and that the interview scenario between Lecter and Starling may have been based Ressler's own interviews of Kemper.[5]

10. Reality Bites

The immensely popular 1991 film adaptation of *The Silence of the Lambs* begins with Starling's visit to Dr. Lecter's cell. Clarice is told to expect a monster, pure and simple, but the doctor is not the type of monster she expects. He does not rant and rave like the other prisoners. Instead, Lecter calmly asks to see her credentials, then offers her a chair, smiling the whole time. As they begin to talk, he remains dignified, well-spoken and surprisingly courteous. ("Discourtesy," he tells her, "is unspeakably ugly to me.") Clarice quickly learns that Dr. Lecter is unusually sophisticated and hauntingly perceptive. Taking clues from her accent, her clothes and her smell, he creates a psychological profile of her, calling her "a well-scrubbed, hustling rube." She fights back: "You see a lot, doctor. But are you strong enough to point that high-powered perception at yourself? Or maybe you're afraid?" Lecter's polite demeanor disappears briefly when he is patronized, but he responds without compromising his cultured manner: "A census taker once tried to test me. I ate his liver with some fava beans and a nice Chianti."

Lecter is, at once, a combination of real-life killers and Anne Rice's aristocratic monsters. Appropriately, a wave of vampire films followed the critical and commercial success of *The Silence of the Lambs*. Anthony Hopkins, who essayed the role of Dr. Lecter, was cast as Van Helsing in Francis Ford Coppola's romantic adaptation, *Bram Stoker's Dracula* (1992). The film turned the vampire hunter into a crude Exorcist — during a ritual exorcism, the demon vomits blood, rather than pea soup, on him — and Stoker's anti–Christ into love's greatest martyr. The Count weeps and moans at the thought of damning the soul of his beloved. "I love you too much to condemn you," he says, prompting Mina to beg him for release "from all this death." Alain Silver and James Ursini credit the film with single-handedly revitalizing the vampire film.[6] Without a doubt, it encouraged filmmakers to capitalize on renewed interest in the Gothic myth. Soon after, Full Moon Entertainment released direct-to-video sequels to *Subspecies* (1991), the first vampire film shot entirely in Romania; Roger Corman's production company churned out *Dracula Rising* (1993) and *To Sleep with a Vampire* (1993); and David Lynch served as executive producer on *Nadja* (1994).

In 1994, Anne Rice's anti-heroes, Louis and Lestat, finally made their way to the silver screen in a big-budget adaptation of *Interview with the Vampire*, featuring superstar heartthrobs Brad Pitt and Tom Cruise in the lead roles. The film begins with Louis' offer to tell his life-in-death story to a reporter, so that he can warn humans about the existence of vampires. As he recounts his tale, Louis tries to convince us that vampirism is the most horrible of curses, but even the interviewer is not convinced. At the end, the reporter begs him to share his "gift." Louis, frustrated, disappears, and it is the more irreverent, fun-loving Lestat who obliges, instantly dismissing Louis's cautionary tale: "Louis, Louis, Louis. Always *whining*, Louis!" He turns to the bitten reporter and adds, "I've had to listen to that for *centuries!*" We, of course, identify with Lestat, who becomes a rock star and the unlikely hero of humanity in the sequel, *Queen of the Damned* (2002) — an adaptation of Rice's first two follow-up novels.

One of the most telling scenes in *Interview with the Vampire* (1994) is Louis' first meeting with Armand, the oldest living vampire. Armand calls Louis the spirit of "the new age." Louis retorts, "I'm not the spirit of any age. I'm at odds with everything," to which Armand replies, "Louis, don't you see? That is the very spirit of your age." In her book *Piercing the Darkness: Undercover with Vampires in America Today*, Katherine Ramsland argues that this is precisely why the vampire myth has become so popular in contemporary American culture — it fills a spiritual void in the lives of many Generation X-ers. Ramsland interviewed several supposed real-life vampires, one of whom explained to her that "the advent of postmodernism heralded the official dissolution of absolute truth within the religious community." He told her that "to be spiritual in the postmodern age is to be whatever one wants to be."[7] Another interviewee claimed that, despite his willingness to concede the existence of objective reality, the vampire fantasy is more real to him than life.[8]

Former FBI profiler Robert Ressler senses danger in the willingness of a mass audience to identify with onscreen monsters. Responding to the success of *The Silence of the Lambs*, he says, "As a society, we seem to be flying too close to the flame, looking for stimulation — we are bored audiences more attuned to fantasy than to reality, in danger of falling completely into the abyss about which Nietzsche warned us."[9]

Abel Ferrara takes up this alarming sentiment in his 1995 film *The Addiction*. The central character is Katherine, an NYU grad student-turned-vampire, who uses the writings of Friedrich Nietzsche, Jean-Paul Sartre, Samuel Beckett and William Burroughs to explain and control her thirst for destruction. Resolving to live according to Nietzsche's belief in master morality, Katherine proves her doctorate thesis through murder. Ultimately, however, she is unable to use philosophy to escape her human addiction to sin and guilt, and she finally gorges herself to the point of utmost suffering. On her deathbed, she regains her humanity by asking God to forgive her inherent weakness. The film itself adopts a tone of resignation: We are the monsters and our own victims. We could not — would not — have it any other way.

Perhaps for this reason, we have made the vampire — in Freudian terms, the embodiment of Id — our cinematic hero, often relying on the

10. Reality Bites 93

filmmakers to play the role of our Ego. We embrace the vampire hero of *Blade* (1998), a superhuman devil-with-a-soul who loathes his own kind and wages a seemingly endless war against corporate vampires. We even embrace Hannibal Lecter, who — after his escape from custody, and perhaps owing to his connection with Clarice — acts according a peculiar understanding of justice. At the end of *Silence*, he targets the obnoxious prison warden who delighted in tormenting him. In *Hannibal* (2001), he attacks only those who attack him, and eats only those who threaten to destroy Clarice's idealism. As characters in the latter film point out, he only eats the "free range rude" and commits murder as a form of "public service." We embrace Lestat, that resilient opportunist who realizes the American Dream of wealth, fame and power, and ultimately saves the human race — if only so that he'll have something to eat later. In his speculations on the transfusion of the Gothic into contemporary American culture, Mark Edmundson suggests that there may be "something to gain in accepting the harsh belief that the world is infested with evil, that all power is corrupt, all humanity debased, and that there is nothing we can do about it. With the turn to contemporary Gothic — no-fault, dead-end, politically impotent though it may be — we recover a horizon of ultimate meaning."[10]

Wesley Snipes makes a grand entrance as the vampire hero in *Blade* (New Line, 1998).

Count Orlock (Max Schreck) rises from below deck in *Nosferatu* (Ufa, 1921).

In an essay on the modern horror film, Robin Wood asked, "Can the genre survive the recognition that the monster is its real hero?"[11] These recent examples prove that the American horror film has survived by transforming the nonconformist values often attributed to the "monster" into necessary virtues. Thus, the horror film has survived, like a vampire, by redefining itself for a new time period.

In *Shadow of the Vampire* (2000), which fictionalizes the making of the 1921 film *Nosferatu*, director F.W. Murnau expounds on the power of film to grant immortality. Murnau's lead actor, Max Schreck, is a genuine vampire, and therefore uninterested in being preserved on film, which causes constant conflicts on the production. Finally, Schreck grows tired of filming, and proceeds to eat the crew while Murnau cranks his camera. At one point, he stops to reprimand Schreck for being off his mark: "Frankly, Count, I find this composition unworkable.... If it's not in frame, it doesn't exist." Murnau's own life is spared by the coming of the dawn, which dissolves the monster, relegating him to the eternal memory of film. Murnau, pleased with the results, says, "I think we have it."

Part II

Auteurs

In the January 1954 issue of *Cahiers du Cinema*, Francois Truffaut espoused his influential theory that certain directors contribute a unique personal vision to their collective bodies of work. For some critics, the idea that any one person should be recognized as the "author" of any film is practically absurd; film, after all, is a collaborative art form. Nevertheless, the auteur theory has been championed in America over the past half-century. In 1962, Andrew Sarris wrote the first English-language essay on the subject, identifying three main premises of the auteur theory: (1) the technical competence of a director as a criterion of value, (2) the distinguishable personality of the director as a criterion of value, and (3) concern with "interior meaning."[1] The writings of Truffaut and Sarris helped to canonize several studio-era directors, and to encourage future filmmakers to indulge their most personal artistic visions, and their darkest obsessions. The works of these eight filmmakers—who have, to varying degrees, been associated with the horror genre—reveal not only interior meaning "extrapolated from the tension between a director's personality and his material,"[2] but also changing views of life in America over the course of the twentieth century.

11

Tod Browning: Sideshows

Tod Browning is widely regarded as the father of the American horror film not just because he directed *Dracula* (1931), but because he was the genre's first auteur. To be sure, many of his peers—particularly James Whale and Karl Freund—deserve equal recognition but, as Andrew Sarris puts it, "Browning's career is more meaningful ... in terms of a personal obsession."[1] The director's biographers, David J. Skal and Elias Savada, point out that Browning's thorough knowledge of Gothic literature informed many of his films.[2] Though his preoccupation with the macabre was unusual among filmmakers in the 1920s, he understood that he was not an anomaly among American moviegoers. "Ninety percent of the people are morbid-minded," the director said. "I am not sure that the average should not go higher. O. Henry once remarked that more people would gather to look at a dead horse in the street than would assemble to watch the finest coach pass by, and this homely observation comes very close to representing the actual fact."[3]

According to Skal and Savada, the wayward path that the director took to Hollywood inspired his morbid fascinations. Browning claimed to have run away with the circus at age 12, and spent his teen years in the vaudeville circuit, headlining as a "Living Corpse," before being hired as a motion picture actor by D.W. Griffith. In 1915, Browning began directing one-reelers for Reliance-Mutual and in 1917 graduated to feature-length pictures. Two years later, he was paired for the first time with actor Lon Chaney on a film called *The Wicked Darling*. Working well together, the two were quickly re-teamed on another crime picture, distributed by Universal Film Manufacturing Company. Chaney, already established as a versatile actor with an uncanny ability to change his appearance, played two roles in *Outside the Law* (1920) — villain "Black Mike" Sylva and Ah Wing, a Chinese servant. As Sylva, Chaney was a man that audiences loved to hate — an opportunist gangster whose criminal activities revealed the dark side of free enterprise.

The commercial success of *Outside the Law* prompted Universal to announce that Browning and Chaney would collaborate again, on an adaptation of Victor Hugo's *The Hunchback of Notre Dame*.[4] In 1923, the film was made under the direction of Wallace Worsley. Chaney received overwhelming praise for his portrayal of Quasimodo but, as his star rose, Browning fell into a downward spiral. Years later, he told an interviewer, "[I] suddenly got sick of pictures, work, people, life, everything — and most of all myself. I didn't care what became of me.... I would write feverishly — the melos I'd always wanted to write, with strange characters in unusual situations. Then, in a fit of despair, I would throw them in the waste basket."[5] When Browning emerged from a long bout with alcohol addiction, Irving Thalberg, the Hollywood wunderkind who had produced *The Hunchback of Notre Dame* for Universal, was waiting for him. Now at MGM, Thalberg was eager to reunite Browning and Chaney, believing that the two men brought out the best in each other.[6] Browning already had a project in mind.

Among his melodramas "with strange characters in unusual situations" was one based on a story by Tod Robbins. *The Unholy Three* (1925) featured Chaney as Professor Echo, a "velvet-voiced ventriloquist" who plans the perfect heist. Echo disguises himself as an elderly woman named Mrs. O'Grady, who — with the help of circus performers Hercules (a strongman) and Tweedledee (a midget disguised as an infant) — cons his way into the homes of unsuspecting society types and steals their valuables. Echo's scam is foiled when his accomplices impulsively murder one of the victims. The professor skips town, but he is unable to escape the repercussions of his crimes: The disappearance of Mrs. O'Grady casts suspicion on Hector, the beau of the woman Echo loves. Overcoming his jealousy, Echo appears at Hector's murder trial, clearing his name and allowing Hector and Rosie to live happily ever after. Afterwards, he returns to the carnival and poignantly greets his audience, "That's all there is to life, friends ... a little laughter ... a little tear."

Browning later recalled that he had been told "You can't make an audience seriously believe in a crook dressed up as an old woman and dwarf disguised as a baby ... the stuff's comedy. Mack Sennett might use it and get a million laughs, but for the mystery drama — impossible."[7] The director proved otherwise, and effectively channeled his fascination with the shadowy circus world of thieves and freaks into a commercially viable

11. Tod Browning

melodrama. Browning and Chaney followed up with another unusual crime picture employing Gothic themes. *The Black Bird* (1926) features Chaney as Dan Tate, a career criminal who is able to hide from the authorities in London's Limehouse district by posing as his own twin brother, a crippled Bishop. As in *The Unholy Three*, the criminal's downfall is a woman. Tate falls in love with Fifi, who has also won the affections of a high society thief named West End Bertie. When Bertie attempts to give up his criminal life to demonstrate his love for Rosie, Tate frames him for the murder of a Scotland Yard inspector, then attempts to convince Fifi to marry him instead. The plan is working until the cops get a tip that Tate himself committed the murder, and come looking for him at the Bishop's apartment. In a frantic attempt to change into the Bishop's clothes, Tate falls and breaks his back, ending his life as a genuine cripple.

The Black Bird and was among superstar Chaney's highest grossing films at MGM,[8] and it encouraged the studio to grant Browning the creative freedom to indulge increasingly "morbid" fantasies. *The Unknown*

Lon Chaney as Alonzo the Armless in *The Unknown* (MGM, 1927).

(1927) is perhaps the duo's most perverse melodrama. It tells the story of Alonzo, a murderous member of a traveling gypsy circus. He falls in love with the ringmaster's daughter, Nanon, who has an irrational phobia of men's "beastly hands." This would seem to make Alonzo and Nanon the perfect match, but we soon learn that Alonzo is not really crippled — he keeps his arms pinned to his back to conceal a deformity in one of his hands that would identify him as a killer. Afraid that she will hate him if she learns his secret, Alonzo arranges to have his arms amputated. As he is recovering from the surgery, Nanon overcomes her fear and falls in love with circus strongman Malabar. When Alonzo realizes what has happened, he devises a plan to tear Malabar's arms from his body, but the plan backfires, killing Alonzo himself.

Chaney biographer Michael F. Blake suggests that Alonzo's story is tragic because he is a realistic character placed in realistic surroundings, and is therefore sympathetic. This, Blake says, is what distinguishes Browning's films with Chaney (the melodramas) from his later work (the horror films).[9] The duo's next collaboration, *London After Midnight* (1927), featured Chaney as a razor-toothed vampire who moves into a London home exactly one year after the previous owner's murder. His gangling appearance unnerves the locals, who blame him for a series of strange occurrences. At the end of the picture, the "vampire" is revealed to be a theater actor hired by a Scotland Yard investigator (also played by Chaney) to entrap the real murderer.

London After Midnight is an obvious precursor to the film version of *Dracula*; David J. Skal speculates that it may have actually been inspired by the Broadway theatrical production of *Dracula*, which Browning had considered adapting to the screen as early as 1927.[10] Universal studio head Carl Laemmle had refused the idea, saying that it was too morbid for American audiences. Browning disagreed, and eventually convinced Laemmle that it could be made if Chaney agreed to play the lead role.[11] In 1929, however, it became clear that Chaney would not be able to take the role. After a long illness, Chaney succumbed to throat cancer on August 26, 1930, and the role of the silver screen's most famous vampire went to Bela Lugosi.

Dracula was Browning's first foray into supernatural horror. It utilized the type of Gothic set dressings that were prevalent in earlier Hollywood thrillers — most notably, the haunted house films of Paul Leni — but, in Browning's film, the monster is real. The film opens on an exotic Transylvanian setting, where nervous locals warn a traveler to stay away from Dracula's castle. Mr. Renfield dismisses the warnings as ridiculous superstitions, but he soon becomes nervous when his carriage driver appears to turn into a bat. Things are stranger still when he arrives at the castle, where Count Dracula lives among cobwebs and armadillos. Despite his eccentricities, it is only after Dracula leaves the Gothic trappings of his home and visits the drawing rooms of modern-day London that we are presented with proof of his supernatural abilities. Professor Van Helsing notices that the vampire casts no reflection. David J. Skal says that "throughout the twenties, the appearance of magical events, ghosts, or monsters would almost always be 'explained away' as the materialistic machinations of some master criminal, a plot to steal an inheritance, etc. It was Tod Browning who ... would push the envelope."[12] Van Helsing warns us, "The superstition of yesterday can become the scientific reality of today," and this seems to be Browning's message as well. *Dracula* served as "proof" that there are horrible things going on in our everyday world that we cannot understand.

Browning's next film focused on a real-life microcosm of Depression-era America. Carnivals had served as a backdrops in earlier horror films like *The Cabinet of Dr. Caligari* (1920) and Paul Leni's *Waxworks* (1924), as well as Browning's *The Unholy Three* and *The Unknown*. In his seminal work on the sociological implications of early German cinema, Sigfried Kracauer describes the carnival in *Caligari* as "an enclave of anarchy in the sphere of entertainment.... For adults, it is a regression into childhood days, in which games and serious affairs are identical, real and imagined things mingle, and anarchical desires aimlessly test infinite possibilities."[13] Browning's carnival in *Freaks* (1932) is a horrifying world where the performers are neither children nor adults; they exist entirely outside the sphere of normalcy. Browning drops us into a closed community of freaks who cannot relate — physically or emotionally — with polite society. The nightmare begins when this community is breached by outsiders. Because the stars of the film were genuine carnival sideshow performers, audiences could not help feeling guilty for invading the closed community. The most guilt-inducing moment comes when Hans turns on Cleopatra, and us, snarling, "Dirty ... slimy ... freak."

Freaks was a financial disaster for MGM and, following a second commercial failure, it was years before the director could get assigned to a new project. Browning's return to the genre was, unfortunately, a return to the type of melodrama that had been produced before *Dracula* popularized had been the horror genre. No doubt *Mark of the Vampire* (1935) seemed like a safe bet to the brass at MGM; it recycles the plot of the hugely successful *London After Midnight* and typecasts Bela Lugosi as a vampire. Unfortunately, in post-*Dracula* Hollywood, the revelation that Lugosi and his vampire daughter are actors and not real vampires made the film hugely anticli-

The real-life "carnies" of Tod Browning's *Freaks* (MGM, 1932).

mactic for audiences. *Mark of the Vampire* was only a moderate success and Browning would have only one more opportunity to indulge his morbid curiosity.

The Devil-Doll (1936) is perhaps the director's most personal and most accomplished film, recycling elements of several of Browning's earlier films. Lionel Barrymore stars as Paul Lavond, an escaped prisoner who has sworn to avenge himself on the men who framed him for theft. He assumes the identity of an old woman named Madame Mandelip and travels to Paris with a set of unique organic toys—human beings who have been shrunken to one-sixth their original size and, in the process, robbed of their willpower. Lavond orders his "little people" to invade the homes of the three men who framed him, and exact his revenge.

The "us and them" scenario—little people versus the wealthy, dishonest normals—conveys Browning's increasing bitterness, but *The Devil-Doll* also reveals the director's sentimental side. We learn that Lavond is not only motivated by revenge, but by a desire to clear his name so that his daughter can live in peace. His scheme eventually forces a public confession from the third man, after which Lavond arranges to meet with his daughter one last time. Disguised as Madame Mandelip, he introduces himself to her at the top of the Eiffel Tower, and delivers a message from her father: "He told me to tell you not to forget him, to find happiness and keep it, to marry and give your children all the love you might have given him if he hadn't been taken away from you."

The scene is every bit as poignant as Chaney's final scene in *The Unholy Three*. Lavond is obviously disappointed that things have worked out this way, but he seems satisfied with this resolution. As Lavond prepares to descend the Eiffel Tower, he says to his daughter, "Better be going — Sun's almost down." She reassures him, "It'll be up again tomorrow." With a haunted smile, Lavond responds, "Will it? I wonder." Like Lavond, Browning was planning his escape into obscurity; after a few more years, he would abandon the film industry completely.

Feature Films Directed by Browning, Starring Lon Chaney

The Wicked Darling (1919)
Outside the Law (1920)
The Unholy Three (1925)
The Black Bird (1926)
The Road to Mandalay (1926)
The Unknown (1927)
London After Midnight (1927)
West of Zanzibar (1928)
Where East is East (1929)

Feature Films Directed by Browning, 1929–1939

The Thirteenth Chair (1929)
Outside the Law (1930)
Dracula (1931)
Iron Man (1931)
Freaks (1932)
Fast Workers (1933)
Mark of the Vampire (1935)
The Devil-Doll (1936)
Miracles for Sale (1939)

12

Alfred Hitchcock: Noir Town

Though Alfred Hitchcock's thrillers are practically a genre unto themselves, the director has been justifiably called the "father of the modern horror film" on the basis of several of his pictures, including *Shadow of a Doubt, Psycho, The Birds* and *Marnie*.[1] Perhaps more than any other single filmmaker, Hitchcock Americanized Gothic horror, firmly planting the themes of the British literary genre in the American landscape.

Hitchcock began his filmmaking career in London during the silent era, but later confessed that he always had his sights set on Hollywood. "I certainly was deeply entrenched in American cinema," he told Francois Truffaut in 1962. "This dates back to the time when I was reading the film trade papers at the age of sixteen.... I did regard their moviemaking as truly professional and very much in advance of that of the other countries."[2] American filmmakers, he believed, were particularly good at "capitalizing the unusual and achieving freshness by contrast and variety."[3] In 1934, he expressed his disgust with the staid middle-class characters and drawing-room settings of most British pictures, asking an interviewer, "Have you ever considered what an interesting film might be written around, say, the engineer of the Tower Bridge who lets the bridge up and down? If the Americans had such material at their disposal they would have made a film about it years ago. The engineer as the central character, the river craft and docks for atmospheric background — and you can bet your life they would have managed to make their way up to Piccadilly for a little more atmosphere before the film was over!"[4] With *The Thirty Nine Steps* (1935), in which a Canadian tourist is framed for murder in the UK, Hitch-

Hitch poses with a feathered friend in this promotional still for *The Birds* (Universal, 1963).

cock achieved the contrast and variety that he so admired in American films, following the wrongfully accused hero all the way from London to the Scottish Highlands. The film bears more than a passing resemblance to Frank Capra's *It Happened One Night* (1934), an American screwball comedy in which a blue-collar reporter and a high-society woman fight and fall in love as they travel across the country.*

The Thirty Nine Steps secured Hitchcock's international reputation as cinema's master of suspense, encouraging producer David O. Selznick to summon him to Hollywood in 1940. Hitchcock's first American film was an adaptation of Daphne du Maurier's English Gothic novel *Rebecca*. Though the director admitted that the film was a "completely British picture," he attempted to give it an "American stylization." Part of this stylization, he says, is apparent in the setting: "Let us assume that we had made *Rebecca* in England. The house would not have been so isolated because we'd have been tempted to show the countryside and the lanes leading to the house. But if the scene had been more realistic, and the place of arrival geographically situated, we would have lost the sense of

---

Hitch made his own American screwball comedy, Mr. and Mrs. Smith, *in 1941.*

isolation."[5] In later films, Hitchcock would achieve the same sense of isolation in some rather unlikely settings throughout the United States.

Saboteur (1942), the first of Hitchcock's American chase pictures, is a wartime thriller about a Los Angeles factor worker falsely accused of being a Nazi spy. After being branded a terrorist, he flees from sea to shining sea in pursuit of the real culprit. Hitchcock confesses that the film was conceived to fulfill "a desire to cover various parts of America in the same way that *The Thirty Nine Steps* traveled across England and Scotland."[6] Along the way, the accused takes shelter in Tod Browning's America — hiding in a sleeping car with a traveling band of circus freaks from the Midwest. Bones, the troupe's human skeleton, empathizes with the persecuted stranger, remarking solemnly that "the normal are normally coldhearted." The hero also finds himself in peril beside the Hoover Dam, a testament to American ingenuity, and on top of the Statue of Liberty, the most recognizable symbol of freedom and democracy in the world. By staging acts of sabotage and murder in such locations, Hitchcock conveyed a message to audiences that there was more at stake in the war overseas than the lives of a few innocent men; the American way of life was in jeopardy. (He presented the same idea to Cold War audiences in *North by Northwest*, which finds Cary Grant fleeing from international spies across the faces of Mount Rushmore.)

Hitchcock's next film, *Shadow of a Doubt* (1943), places the threat to the American Dream in an equally unassuming location — the idyllic small town of Santa Rosa, California. At the beginning of the film, Uncle Charlie, a jaded world traveler, arrives in Santa Rosa to visit his sister and her family; the locals never entertain the thought that he is not like them. As it turns out, Uncle Charlie is a murderer, but not, Hitchcock points out, "a murderer in the sense of a fiction murderer, where the tendency would be to make him look sinister and you'd be scared of him.... He has to be charming, attractive. If he weren't he'd never get near one of his victims."[7] (Hitchcock had already tested this theory the previous year, casting Cary Grant as a homicidal playboy in *Suspicion*.) Charlie's niece all but worships him until she learns his secret, and realizes how deceiving appearances can be. Robin Wood compares the film to Frank Capra's *It's a Wonderful Life* (1946), noting that "both films have as a central ideological project the reaffirmation of family and small-town values that the action has called into question. In Capra's film this reaffirmation is magnificently convincing ... in Hitchcock's, it is completely hollow."[8]

Hitchcock biographer Donald Spoto calls *Shadow of a Doubt* "the first spiritually autobiographical film" of the director's career and argues that it serves as a "handbook of all the literary and cultural influences on his own life."⁹ The Gothic theme of the double, used here with Uncle Charlie and niece Charlie — representing experience and innocence, respectively — would be employed again in several of the director's films, most obviously *Strangers on a Train* (1951) and *Psycho* (1960). It seemed to express not only the director's perception of himself, but his vision of America as well.

The conflict between well-meaning Americans and the corrupting influences of a war-torn world was even more obvious in the director's next film. *Lifeboat* (1944) is set entirely in one claustrophobic location (implied by the title), where a group of castaways — eight Americans and one German — are bound together in a struggle for survival. It soon becomes apparent that the Nazi, who seems smarter and stronger than the others, is in control of their fates. Some critics misinterpreted the film as un–American, prompting Hitchcock to clarify that the film was intended as a warning: "We wanted to show that at that moment there were two world forces confronting each other, the democracies and the Nazis, and while the democracies were completely disorganized, all of the Germans were clearly headed in the same direction. So here was a statement telling the democracies to put their differences aside temporarily and to gather their forces to concentrate on the common enemy, whose strength was precisely derived from a spirit of unity."¹⁰

After World War II, Hitchcock revisited one of the prevalent ideas in *Lifeboat*— that of Nietzsche's philosophy of the "superman" (*ubermensch*), whose exertion of his own will on the world partly constitutes his moral superiority — in *Rope* (1948). This time, the willful villains are two ambiguously gay American college students, who strangle a classmate and then invite his parents and girlfriend over for dinner. For the duration of the film, both the murderers and the body remain in a cozy New York apartment — a setting that reinforces Hitchcock's belief that murder can happen anywhere, that no place is safe. Looking back on his thrillers in a 1948 interview, Hitchcock points out that "in none of these was the house filled with shadows, the weather dull and stormy throughout, the moor windswept, and the doors creaky."¹¹ The horror exists right under the noses of the characters.

In *Rope*, only the murderers' philosophy professor — played by Jimmy Stewart, the all–American hero of Frank Capra's populist fantasy *Mr. Smith Goes to Washington* (1939) and *It's a Wonderful Life* (1946) — realizes what they have done. He also realizes that his teachings are partly to blame. In future films, Hitchcock would transform Stewart's onscreen persona into an increasingly disillusioned American hero. In *Rear Window* (1954), Stewart stars as invalid reporter L.B. Jeffries, who becomes convinced that a murder has taken place in the Greenwich Village apartment across the alley from his own. Rather than contact the police, Jeffries continues to spy on his neighbor, Mr. Thorwald, and eventually convinces his girlfriend to break into Thorwald's apartment and search for evidence. Together, they decide that Thorwald has secreted the body of his dead wife in a trunk in his apartment.

"Sure, he's a snooper," Hitchcock says of Stewart's character, "but aren't we all?"[12] The question is rhetorical — at least, Hitchcock implies, for American audiences. In a 1957 *New York Times* interview, he argues that such a murder would have gone unnoticed in his native country. In England, he says, "If Mr. Jones' wife suddenly disappears, instead of being the subject of back-fence talk the next morning, it may be months before someone says: 'Err, don't mean to pry at all, old boy, but it seems a deuced long time since we've had the pleasure of Mrs. Jones' appearance.'"[13] By contrast, Jeffries, his girlfriend and even his nurse casually speculate on the horrors that have taken place in Thorwald's apartment, reveling in sordid details. "Where do you suppose he cut her up?" Jeffries asks the nurse. After a moment's pause, he eagerly answers his own question, "Of course — the bathtub!" She adds, "He better get that trunk out of there before it starts to leak."

In the following years, Hitchcock found it increasingly difficult to dream up sensational thrillers for the silver screen, believing that the reality of life in America was often more sensational than fiction. "Where can you get movie stories that are better than today's headlines?" he asked in 1951. "Government officials turn crooked, planes go up to 1500 miles an hour, the world waits for days to learn whether a war will end, diplomats disappear. How can you top that for drama and suspense?"[14] Five years later, he made *The Wrong Man* (1956), a docu-drama ripped from the headlines. At the beginning of the film, Hitchcock appears onscreen in silhouette to inform us that "this is a true story, every word of it, and yet it contains elements that are stranger than all of the fiction that has gone into all the thrillers that I have made before."

The Wrong Man begins on January 14, 1953, when family man Christopher Emanuel Balestrero is mistakenly identified as a bank robber. "Manny" is spun through the wheels of justice, but his situation only worsens. After being charged with a series of robberies in New York, he is unable to find the three men who can provide him with an alibi. Subsequently, his wife goes mad, convinced that a higher power is "stacking the cards" against them. "No matter what you do," she says, "they've got it fixed so that it goes against you. No matter how innocent you are or how hard you try, they'll find you guilty." The tone of the film — its documentary realism, cynicism and stylistic use of light and shadow — make this Hitchcock's most obvious example of film noir. This time, branding an innocent man as a criminal has revealed the Gothic double in everyday America.

In his next film, *Vertigo* (1958), Hitchcock delved deeper into the psychology of the Gothic. Jimmy Stewart stars as retired detective Scottie Ferguson, who is hired by an old college buddy to follow his wife, Madeline Elster. Scottie quickly deduces that Madeline is suffering from a kind of schizophrenia, having convinced herself that she is the reincarnation of an ancestor who committed suicide. As Scottie falls in love with her, he becomes obsessed with his own role as her savior, and follows her to an old Spanish mission in southern California, where she tries to reenact the ancestor's suicide. Because of Scottie's own fear of heights, he is unable to stop her from leaping to her death. Afterwards, he falls into a deep depression. For years, he is unable to shake his guilt over the incident, and returns to life only when he meets Judy, a woman bearing a striking resemblance to Madeline. Eventually, Scottie learns that Judy is in fact the woman he fell in love with — hired by Madeline's husband as a decoy; the real Madeline was in fact killed by her husband. In an effort to cure himself, Scottie takes Judy back to the Spanish mission — where, in a fateful accident, she falls to her death.

Unlike the heroes of Hitchcock's previous films, Scottie is a failed romantic hero. Whereas L.B. Jeffries' obsessive voyeurism in *Rear Window* solves a murder, Scottie's voyeuristic obsession causes only death and depression. Laura Mulvey uses the latter film to illustrate her point about a tendency in cinema to associate the camera's authoritative point of view with male characters and to treat female characters as the passive objects of their gaze. She says that *Vertigo* "focuses on the implications of the active / looking, passive / looked-at split in terms of sexual difference and the power of the male symbolic encapsulated in the hero."[15] The audience, therefore, identifies with the male, though he is less and less empathetic as the film progresses; at the end, we are as guilty as he is. This manipulation of the audience is even more apparent in *Psycho*, in which Norman Bates — the voyeur whose gaze is shared by the audience — is revealed as an insane murderer. The object of Norman's gaze is also the subject of his — and, by association, our — violence. As the killer promises, "We *all* go a little mad sometimes."

After the overwhelming commercial success of *Psycho*, Hitchcock delved even deeper into his audience's lust for sex and crime. In 1962, he announced that he would direct Grace Kelly in an adaptation of Winston Graham's *Marnie*, about a compulsive thief who can't bear to be touched, and the sexually deviant man who loves her for it.[16] Kelly eventually backed out of the project, leaving Hitchcock to find a new leading lady. *Marnie* was shelved for two years, while the director filmed *The Birds* with newcomer "Tippi" Hedren in the lead role.

As ill-reputed prankster Melanie Daniels, Hedren bore the brunt of the on-screen (and off-screen*) violence in *The Birds*. The film begins when Melanie meets Mitch Brenner, an arrogant lawyer, in a San Francisco pet shop. Feeling slighted and challenged by him in their first encounter, Melanie later tracks him to his weekend house, intending to deliver a pair of love birds in the hope that they will "do something" for his acidic personality. She arrives just in time to witness a series of attacks by flocks of seagulls, sparrows and blackbirds. As the chaos swells, one of the locals angrily points out that the attacks began when Melanie arrived in town. "I think you're the cause of all this!" she screams, "I think you're evil!" Because Melanie is the main character in the film, the accusation must just as well be leveled against the viewing audience. The film, however, never clearly identifies the cause of the attacks.

In a newspaper ad for *The Birds*, Hitchcock said, "I have, in my time, produced many films whose major intent was to mystify and astonish their viewers. Inasmuch as such stories often brought much pleasure, they fulfilled their requirements. This time, however, I have introduced serious purpose beneath the pleasure. There is a terrifying meaning lurking right underneath the surface shock and suspense of *The Birds*. When you discover it, your pleasure will be more than doubled."[17] The director never explained this "terrifying meaning" (and one suspects that this ad may have been the real cause of Hitchcock's own apparent pleasure), but Robin Wood suggests that the birds are "a concrete embodiment of the arbitrary and the unpredictable, of whatever makes human life and human relationships precarious, a reminder of fragility and instability that cannot be ignored or evaded and, beyond that, of the possibility that life is meaningless and absurd."[18] Significantly, the film is left open-ended, without any reassuring romance.

"We don't know how they are going to come out," Hitchcock says. "For the ordinary public, they got away to San Francisco—but I toyed with the idea of lap-dissolving on them in the car—looking—and there is the Golden Gate Bridge—covered with birds!"[19] The director left future filmmakers to address his nightmare vision of Judgment Day. After the commercial failure of *Marnie*, his films were far less personal—the only exception being *Frenzy* (1972), by far his ugliest film dealing with the victimization of female characters.

*See Spoto pp. 458–60.

12. Alfred Hitchcock

One may argue that Hitchcock's treatment of "the look" in terms of sexual politics and the attending violence has been his biggest contribution to the modern horror film. (It laid the groundwork for the slasher films of the early 1980s.) Brian DePalma picked up where Hitchcock left off after *Marnie*, spending the first decade of his career emulating the master of suspense in *Sisters* (1973), *Phantom of the Paradise* (1974), *Obsession* (1976), *Dressed to Kill* (1980) and *Body Double* (1984). Hitchcock's influence is also apparent in the thrillers of countless other filmmakers of the past and present, including George Cukor (*Gaslight*, 1944), Otto Preminger (*Laura*, 1944), Robert Siodmak (*The Spiral Staircase*, 1946), William Castle, Stanley Donen (*Charade*, 1963), George Romero, Tobe Hooper, Larry Cohen, Dario Argento (*Deep Red*, 1975) and John Carpenter. Undoubtedly, his films will continue to haunt future generations.

Feature Films Directed by Hitchcock, 1940–1976

Rebecca (1940)
Foreign Correspondent (1940)
Mr. and Mrs. Smith (1941)
Suspicion (1941)
Saboteur (1942)
Shadow of a Doubt (1943)
Lifeboat (1944)
Spellbound (1945)
Notorious (1946)
The Paradine Case (1947)
Rope (1948)
Under Capricorn (1949)
Stage Fright (1950)
Strangers on a Train (1951)
I Confess (1953)
Dial "M" for Murder (1954)
Rear Window (1954)
To Catch a Thief (1955)
The Trouble With Harry (1955)
The Man Who Knew Too Much (1956)
The Wrong Man (1956)
Vertigo (1958)
North by Northwest (1959)
Psycho (1960)
The Birds (1963)
Marnie (1964)
Torn Curtain (1966)
Topaz (1969)
Frenzy (1972)
Family Plot (1976)

13

Roger Corman: Counterculture and Creature Features

Today, the name Roger Corman is synonymous with low-budget, independent filmmaking. After almost 50 years of filmmaking, the "King of the B-Movies" is recognized across the globe as a major force in the industry. There is also an ongoing debate about his status as an auteur. In 1968, Andrew Sarris dismissed Corman's artistry with the following sentence: "It is quite possible that he is miscast, like [Joseph] Mankiewicz, [William] Wyler, and [Robert] Wise, as a director, when he would be much more effective as a producer."[1] In his 1990 autobiography *How I Made a Hundred Movies in Hollywood and Never Lost a Dime,* Corman makes his own case for auteur status, claiming that he was the driving creative force behind many of his pictures. "Is the producer/director an auteur?" he asks, self-referentially. "I believe he is, if he is the one whose passion for a story brings it to the screen. Are his movies projections of his personality, his fears, dreams, obsessions? I tend to believe they are, because we work from both the conscious and unconscious levels of the mind. The very selection of themes and stories tips your hat somewhat."[2]

There is a tendency among auteurs to continually revisit certain themes and obsessions and, for that reason, become associated with a particular genre. Corman's early work as a director spanned several genres — Westerns (*Five Guns West, Apache Woman, The Oklahoma Woman, Gunslinger*), rebellious youth pictures (*Rock All Night, Sorority Girl, Teenage Doll*), gangster films (*Machine-Gun Kelly, I Mobster, The St. Valen-

Roger Corman on the set of *The Wild Angels* (AIP, 1966) with Bruce Dern and Peter Fonda.

tine's Day Massacre, Bloody Mama), as well as science fiction and horror. At the time he produced his first film, *Monster from the Ocean Floor* (1954), Corman didn't have any lofty ideas about creating great art. "The whole idea," he says, "was to tell an interesting, visually entertaining story that would draw young people to the drive-ins and hardtop cinemas, and not take yourself too seriously along the way."[3] On the basis of his next film, *The Fast and the Furious* (1954), Corman secured a three-picture deal with a small distributor — the American Releasing Corporation, soon to be known as American International Pictures (AIP), and decided to direct. Although many of his earliest films have been forgotten, a few have become cult classics — in part for the way they tackle major cultural anxieties of the day.

It Conquered the World (1956) was one of Corman's earliest successful sci-fi pictures. This poor man's *Invasion of the Body Snatchers* features Lee Van Cleef as a scientist who makes contact with an alien from Venus. The alien, resembling a huge upended vegetable, coerces Van Cleef's Dr.

Anderson to aid its plans for world domination. As in *Invasion of the Body Snatchers*, the threat is vaguely Communist: bat-like scavengers turn authority figures into emotionless slaves of Earth's new "benefactor," who plans to imprison the masses and kill the dissidents. Anderson already convinced that the downfall of western civilization is immanent, hopes that the alien will reform the human race and create a better world for future generations. He explains to his colleague, Paul Nelson, that in the alien's world "only the waste is gone — the hate, the bitterness, the dreams, all the foolish nonsense." Nelson angrily responds, "This is your land, your world.... You're a traitor." Once he convinces Anderson of his patriotic duty, the doctor saves the world by jamming a road flare into the squatty alien's eye.

Corman's next film, *Not of This Earth* (1957), elaborates on the nature of its alien threat. In the opening scene, a man wearing a dark suit and sunglasses stalks a young girl in the middle of the night, searching for blood. We soon learn that the mysterious "Mr. Johnson" is a survivor of a dying planet of vampires, weakened by years of nuclear warfare. His arrival on earth is a reminder of the threat of atomic annihilation. *Attack of the Crab Monsters* (1957) expands on the subject. It begins when a group of scientists become stranded on an uncharted atoll that is slowly crumbling into the ocean, apparently due to the presence of giant ... talking ... land crabs. Since the film begins with a montage of A-bomb newsreel footage and an ominous pseudo–Biblical quotation, the viewer can safely assume that the cranky crustaceans are a product of the government's experiments in atomic warfare. The scientists in the film, however, seem oblivious to the significance of their discovery, and the monsters are more like schoolyard bullies or bitter gameshow hosts than horrifying omens of impending doom. When attacked, one of the crabs haughtily responds, "So, you have wounded me.... I must grow a new claw. Well, good. For I can do it in a day. But will you grow new lives when I have taken yours from you?"

Corman continued to direct and produce quirky films that exploited the prevailing anxieties of the day. Following the publication of Morey Bernstein's bestseller *The Search for Bridey Murphy,* he took advantage of a brief public interest in reincarnation with *The Undead* (1957); he also rushed *War of the Satellites* (1958) into production immediately after the launch of Sputnik. By 1958, foreign critics were beginning to pay attention to the director. With the release of *Machine-Gun Kelly,* some even recognized him as an artist. No one was more surprised than Corman himself, who writes in his autobiography, "To the French critics, the film expressed *themes,* I was making a *statement,* there was *significance* in certain moments, and the film had a *visual style* expressed through the camera."[4]

Kelly follows the criminal career of an American gangster — Charles Bronson in an early role — who commits acts of violence to maintain a macho public image, though he is a superstitious coward at heart. The film developed a theme that would become prevalent in Corman's career, and would be conveyed most effectively in *Death Race 2000* (1975). *Death Race* presents a satirical vision of future America — a world of minority privilege — in which politicians use a deadly sport to keep the masses subjugated. Corman expounds on the meaning of it all: "[In pre-historic times] for the human race to endure and not be wiped out, we had to be violent in the jungles and forest of predators who were bigger and tougher and swifter. Violence was absolutely necessary. The ironic, or perhaps tragic, twist is that violence is no longer necessary. But the violence that enabled us to survive is now the violence that may defeat and destroy us. The A-bomb is the earliest example. There's bacteriological warfare. There is gang violence, random street violence. We are, indeed, capable of wiping ourselves out one way or another."[5] After the release of *Machine-Gun Kelly*, with these concerns in mind, Corman consciously attempted to imbed socially-redeeming messages in many of his films.*

By late 1958, he had enough confidence to establish his own production company, Filmgroup, and immediately produced his first horror film. *The Wasp Woman* (1960) is a simple story, indebted to *The Fly* (1958). Janice Starling, CEO and poster girl for a major cosmetics company in New York, is afraid that she is beginning to look her age, and tries to restore her youthful glow with enzyme extracts from wasps. The youth serum turns Starling into a bug-eyed vampire, and the film ends abruptly when the wasp woman learns that she can't fly.

Trying to revitalize a genre that was struggling to define itself, Corman and his frequent collaborator, screenwriter Charles B. Griffith, cooked up a trio of darkly comic horror films—*A Bucket of Blood* (1959), *The Little Shop of Horrors* (1960) and *Creature from the Haunted Sea* (1961). In a sense, the films predicted the future of the genre, which would be largely defined in the 1970s by the cynicism of independent filmmakers. *A Bucket of Blood* is an outrageous send-up of beatnik culture. It begins at the Yellow Door Coffee Shop, where a timid busboy named Walter Paisley — played by Corman regular Dick Miller — seeks the respect of a hipster poet. The poet tells Walter that "life is an obscure hobo bumming a ride on the omnibus of art" and that "to be uncreative is death." His senseless

---

*In this regard, he was lampooned by Paul Bartel in Hollywood Boulevard.

aphorisms prompt Walter to take up sculpting, Completely lacking any natural talent, he begins to create his art through murder, like Vincent Price in *House of Wax* (1953). First, he covers his landlady's dead cat in clay and passes it off as his first masterpiece (aptly titled "Dead Cat"). Later, he kills an undercover cop with a frying pan and gives the corpse the same treatment, calling it "Murdered Man." Once Walter grows accustomed to the attention that an artist receives, he is only too willing to commit murder to safeguard his reputation.

Eager to top the madcap energy of *A Bucket of Blood*—and to boast the world's shortest feature film shooting schedule (two days)—Corman directed a similar Griffith script, *The Little Shop of Horrors*. This time, the unwitting murderer is Seymour Krelborn, a ne'er-do-well who breeds a blood-sucking plant named Audrey Jr. in a Skid Row flower shop. After committing a series of murders so that he can feed the corpses to Audrey Jr., Seymour feeds himself to the plant and—like Walter Paisley—becomes one with his creation. In effect, the monster wins. The same thing happens at the end of *Creature from the Haunted Sea*, in which American gangsters cook up a story about a sea monster in order to scare a group of Cubans away from the treasure they have been hired to guard. "What none of us knew," the hero explains, "was that the monster Renzo had invented had already been invented by somebody else ... by a couple of other monsters, I guess." The film ends with a shot of the bug-eyed monster (a 50–cent Creature from the Black Lagoon) sitting on his treasure at the bottom of the ocean. With this image, Corman brought the first phase of his career to a close, and started dreaming up new horrors.

In 1958, public interest in horror films was revived. Hammer's remakes of the classic Universal monster movies injected new blood into old genre traditions; though Hammer's films bore the names of the classics, they were much more bold, shamelessly indulging in graphic scenes of sex and violence. Corman, growing tired of exploitative quickies, followed the trend toward traditional Gothic horror, though his horrors were—at least initially—less gruesome than Hammer's.

House of Usher (1960) diverges sharply from Corman's earlier films; it is more firmly rooted in the horror genre than in the science fiction genre, reflecting a resurgence in popularity of the genre in America. The slow rot of the American Dream is echoed in the solemn declarations of Roderick Usher: "Once this land was fertile. The earth yielded its riches at harvest time. There were trees and plant life, flowers, fields of grain. There was great beauty here.... But this was long before my time. Then a suffering swept across the land and blasted it. The trees lost their foliage. The flowers languished and died. Shrubs grew brown and shriveled. The grain fields perished. The lakes and ponds became black and stagnant. And the land withered as before a plague."

Usher spurned a new wave of similar horror films at AIP, and kicked off a long-term collaboration between Corman and actor Vincent Price. The director clearly took inspiration from Price's earlier films, especially *House of Wax,* and the two creators seemed to work well together. Price's acting abilities allowed Corman to convey his outrageous ideas with increasing subtlety, and Corman's lofty interpretations of Poe's stories apparently amused the star. According to Corman, "Vincent commented to somebody, something about, 'I didn't necessarily believe everything Roger said, but it was really interesting to listen to!'"[6]

The director and actor joined forces again almost immediately to make *Pit and the Pendulum* (1961). Since the source material for that film was so thin — only the final scene in the film comes from in Poe's story — Corman and screenwriter Richard Matheson decided to fill it out with the kind of dark humor popularized by E.C. Comics in the 1950s. As a result, *Pit* was more irreverent than *Usher,* and would set the tongue-in-cheek tone for future Poe adaptations.

In 1961, after the overwhelming success of the Poe films, Corman embarked on an even more ambitious project. *The Intruder*, based on a novel by Charles Beaumont, tells the story of a rabble rouser named Adam Cramer, who arrives in a Southern town to stem the tide of racial integration. Like Machine Gun Kelly, Cramer is more interested in the way the masses perceive him than in the message he sends. Though he is the villain of the film, Cramer — played by a pre–*Star Trek* William Shatner — is also remarkably human, making the film more powerful than a political treatise. For Corman, it was "the first film I directed from a deep political and social conviction."[7] It was also his first commercial failure and, in hindsight, "the greatest disappointment of my career."[8] This time, Corman's attempt to create a socially relevant film had backfired. Although *The Intruder* is now widely recognized as the first serious film about the civil rights era, it hit too close to home for audiences of the day. At the time of the film's May 1962 release, Corman told an interviewer, "I didn't make *The Intruder* to make money or lose money. I believe in the subject. I'm just hoping for a good public response. If I can only get back what I put in, why, then I'll make more pictures like this. If not, there's always horror."[9] In 1962, he promptly went to work on *The Premature Burial.*

By this time, Corman had inspired a trend toward film adaptations of literary horrors, many of which were produced by AIP and featured Vincent Price. There were adaptations of works by Guy de Maupassant

(*Diary of a Madman,* 1963) H.P. Lovecraft (*The Haunted Palace,* 1963, *The Dunwich Horror,* 1970), Nathaniel Hawthorne (*Twice-Told Tales,* 1963), and of course Poe, whose macabre stories inspired no fewer than nine films during the decade (*House of Usher, Pit and the Pendulum, The Premature Burial, Tales of Terror* [1962], *The Raven* [1963], *The Masque of the Red Death* [1964], *The Tomb of Ligeia* [1965], *War-Gods of the Deep* [1965], and *The Oblong Box* [1969]).

In 1963, Corman made a brief departure from the Poe series and directed a film that was simultaneously indebted to his early sci-fi pictures and a hint of things to come. *X: The Man With the X-Ray Eyes* (1963) is the story of a brilliant scientist who creates a serum that allows him to see through things—first, clothes; then, flesh, bone, steel and finally the Earth itself. Unable to use his new gift for a good cause, Dr. James Xavier becomes reckless and finally ends up at a religious revival in the Nevada desert. Dr. X, looking a bit like the alien in *Not of This Earth,* tells the preacher that "there are great darknesses, farther than time itself, and beyond the darkness, a light that glows and changes, and in the center of the universe the eye that sees us all." The preacher coldly responds, "If thine eye offends thee, pluck it out," which prompts one of the all-time great shock endings.

Corman says, "I realized it was the concept that was important: a researcher moving through science toward a religious mystical experience. The theme of *X-Ray Eyes* was rather similar to *2001: A Space Odyssey,* made five or six years later, in that there is at the end of the odyssey an hallucinogenic, mystical vision of light and motion. Kubrick's trip was through space; *X*'s was interior."[10] For much of his remaining career as a director, Corman would oscillate between stark docudrama realism (*The St. Valentine's Day Massacre, Bloody Mama* and *Von Richtofen and Brown*) and mystical surrealism (*The Masque of the Red Death, The Trip,* and *Gas-s-s-s!*). It was as if Corman had split into two personalities—one increasingly rational and one endlessly imaginative. His final adaptation of Edgar Allan Poe illustrates the director's conflict. *The Tomb of Ligeia* is the only film in the Poe series to have a realistic setting and to make Vincent Price's character explicitly aware that the true danger to him lies in the power of his own mind.

Corman's apparent conflict might be interpreted as a reflection of his status in Hollywood. Though he was revered as an independent filmmaker, he was an outsider among the studio filmmakers. The only film he made for a major studio, *The St. Valentine's Day Massacre* (1967), led to disillusionment and bitterness. Afterwards, Corman went to work on a film about outcasts, *The Wild Angels* (1966). In his autobiography, he reflects,

"It was apparent that I was not about to emerge as a 'star' director in the Hollywood Establishment. Perhaps that is why the photograph of those outrageous and defiant bikers, living as outlaws on the fringe, openly flaunting society's conventions, so intrigued me. I wanted to make a realistic, possibly even sympathetic film about them."[11] The Hell's Angels were a subject of much curiosity in 1966, in part due to gonzo journalist Hunter S. Thompson, who wrote a book called *Hell's Angels*, based on his travels with the gang. Like Corman, Thompson wanted to present an honest, unapologetic picture of the outlaws, and summed up their mystique as follows: "Their real motivation is an instinctive certainty as to what the score really is. They are out of the ballgame and they know it. The outlaw motorcyclist views the future with the baleful eye of a man with no upward mobility at all. In a world increasingly geared to specialists, technicians and fantastically complicated machinery, the Hell's Angels are obvious losers and it bugs them. But instead of submitting quietly to their collective fate, they have made it the basis of a full-time social vendetta. They don't expect to win anything, but on the other hand, they have nothing to lose."[12] Corman's image of the bikers as the last American outlaws turned *The Wild Angels* into AIP's biggest hit.[13]

Peter Fond starred as gang leader Blues in *The Wild Angels*, and also became the counterculture hero of Corman's next film, *The Trip* (1967). "Like the Angels and their bikes," Corman says, "the drug subculture was in the headlines. LSD, grass, hash, speed, the drug and hippie movement, dropping out, tuning in, free love — it was all part of a pervasive 'outlaw' anti–Establishment consciousness in the country during the Vietnam era. More and more 'straight' people were dropping out and 'doing their own thing.' I wanted to tell that story as an odyssey on acid."[14] Once again, Corman had his finger on the pulse of the moviegoing public, and his idea attracted the talents of actors Fonda and Dennis Hopper and screenwriter Jack Nicholson.

The Trip was the final peak of Corman's career as a director. His next effort was a hodgepodge of ideas from his films throughout the 1960s. The director says *Gas-s-s-s!* (1970) was intended as "an apocalyptic, Strangelovian political satire."[15] It follows a group of hippies who try to create a peaceful, sex-and-drug-loving society in Mexico after a biological weapon kills everyone over the age of 25. The hippies are sure that the world will be a better place now that the old Republicans are dead, but their utopia is soon overrun by a militaristic high school football team. Only the intervention of a wisecracking deity prevents all-out war. In the final moments, Edgar Allan Poe (apparently reincarnated as a Hell's Angel) shows up to survey the resolution. His mama asks, "Aren't they going to rape, cheat, steal, loot, fight and kill?" The raven on Poe's shoulder responds, "Nevermore." The film is every bit as outrageous as it sounds, but not as funny. *Gas-s-s-s!* was one of Corman's few commercial failures. He has directed only two films since.

In 1970, Corman founded New World Pictures. Today, his legacy lives on thanks to A-list filmmakers who learned their craft at the unofficial Roger Corman Film School. Among the honorary graduates are Stephanie Rothman (director — *The Student Nurses*, 1970), Jonathan Demme (director — *Caged Heat*, 1974, *Crazy Mama*, 1975), Pam Grier (actress — *The Big Doll House* — 1971, *Women in Cages*, 1972, *Black Mama White Mama*, 1972, *The Big Bird Cage* — 1972), Martin Scorsese (director — *Boxcar Bertha*, 1972), Sylvester Stallone (actor — *Death Race 2000*, 1975), Joe Dante (director — *Hollywood Boulevard*, 1976), Ron Howard (actor — *Eat My Dust!*, 1976, and director — *Grand Theft Auto*, 1977), John Sayles (screenwriter — *Piranha*, 1978) and James Cameron (special effects — *Battle Beyond the Stars*, 1980). Other former employees include Academy Award winners Francis Ford Coppola, Robert Towne and Peter Bogdanovich.

Bogdanovich's first film, *Targets* (1968), provides a link between Corman's career as a director and the future of the horror genre in film. Boris Karloff, in one of his final roles, plays himself as Byron Orlock, an aging star of classic horror movies. After completing his most recent film, Orlock decides to retire, telling a screenwriter, "I'm an anachronism.... My kind of horror isn't horror any more." To prove his point, he holds up a newspaper that reads "Youth Kills Six in Supermarket." Soon after, he finds himself in the crosshairs of a deranged sniper, who begins picking off innocent moviegoers at the drive-in premiere of Orlock's new film. In its most haunting moments, *Targets* follows the sniper home, where he seems to lead a normal, functional life. There are no clues about what motivates him to kill, and his rampage is stopped only when he is confronted by Orlock — a familiar monster who turns out not to be such a bad guy after all. Ironically, Corman's own film *The Terror* is used as Orlock's movie-within-a-movie, implying that the director's horror films had already become anachronistic.

FEATURE FILMS PRODUCED AND DIRECTED BY CORMAN:

Five Guns West (1955)
Apache Women (1955)
Day the World Ended (1956)

The Oklahoma Woman (1956)
Gunslinger (1956)
It Conquered the World (1956)

13. Roger Corman

Not of This Earth (1957)
Attack of the Crab Monsters (1957)
The Undead (1957)
Rock All Night (1957)
Sorority Girl (1957)
Carnival Rock (1957)
Teenage Doll (1957)
Naked Paradise (a.k.a. *Thunder Over Hawaii*) (1957)
The Saga of the Viking Women and Their Voyage to the Waters of the Great Sea Serpent (1957)
War of the Satellites (1958)
Machine-Gun Kelly (1958)
I, Mobster (1958)
Teenage Caveman (1958)
A Bucket of Blood (1959)
Ski Troop Attack (1959)
The Little Shop of Horrors (1960)
The Wasp Woman (1960)
The Last Woman on Earth (1960)
Creature from the Haunted Sea (1961)
House of Usher (1960)
Atlas (1961)
Pit and the Pendulum (1961)
The Intruder (1962)
The Premature Burial (1962)
Tales of Terror (1962)
The Raven (1963)
The Haunted Palace (1963)
The Terror (1963)
The Young Racers (1963)
X: The Man With the X-Ray Eyes (1963)
The Masque of the Red Death (1964)
The Tomb of Ligeia (1965)
The Wild Angels (1966)
The St. Valentine's Day Massacre (1967)
The Trip (1967)
Bloody Mama (1970)
Gas-s-s-s! or How It Became Necessary to Destroy the World in Order to Save It (1970)

14

George A. Romero: The Fall of Camelot

In a February 2002 interview in the *Pittsburgh Post-Gazette*, director George A. Romero admitted that, prior to September 11, 2001, he was working on a long-awaited fourth entry in his *Night of the Living Dead* series. Immediately after the fall of the World Trade Center, he says, nobody was interested in making a horror movie.[1] Ironically, Romero made his breakthrough horror film *Night of the Living Dead* during one of America's darkest hours — at the height of the Civil Rights era, on the eve of the Tet offensive in Vietnam. In 1968, Americans had more than enough horror in their daily lives without adding fears of a zombie holocaust. The year, heralded a revolution in cinema — independent filmmakers were suddenly unwilling to reassure audiences of a "better tomorrow," as Hollywood studio films had for decades. Instead, they reflected the chaos of life in America, where wartime casualties at home and abroad were being routinely delivered, via television, into living rooms across the country for mass consumption. Romero, like many outspoken members of his generation, embraced this revolution, recognizing possibilities for both a bleak future and a better tomorrow. Unfortunately, his later films have been less than optimistic about the outcome of the revolution that began, for him, in a Pittsburgh farmhouse in 1967. In George Romero's America, the more things change, the more they stay the same.

In 1967, Romero and a group of friends in Pittsburgh, Pennsylvania, scraped together $6,000 to make a feature,[2] ultimately deciding to make a horror film because they believed it would give them the quickest return on their investment.[3] The result, *Night of the Living Dead*, begins when a

14. George A. Romero

George Romero and friends on the set of *Day of the Dead* (Laurel, 1985).

woman and her brother visit a secluded graveyard. Dusk seems to fall in the middle of the day, and a flash of lightning illuminates the tombstones. A stranger lumbers toward them, unthreatening. A moment later, before we know what has happened, the brother is dead and the woman is running for her life, pursued by a man who is not quite a man. He mumbles and groans and chases her like a desperate, frenzied drug addict. We briefly entertain the notion that he is some kind of sex-crazed half wit but, in the back of our minds, we sense that he wants to do something much worse than rape her (which begs the question: "What is worse than rape?").

The woman escapes to a nearby farmhouse, where she encounters other strangers who are on the run. At this point, the unnatural framing and jagged editing of a backyard horror movie disappear and the story begins to unfold in the style of a documentary newsreel. We learn that, whatever is happening, the entire nation is at risk and nobody—not the newsmen, not the scientists and certainly not the politicians—can provide an explanation or a solution. (There is no mention of other countries in any of the *Dead* films, with one significant exception in *Day of the Dead*. The zombie disease seems to be symptomatic of American life.)

On its most ambitious level—and this is a level that Romero wisely tried to avoid in the text of the film itself—*Night of the Living Dead* is an indictment of modern life in America. It conveys the anxieties of life in a time of theological and political uncertainty, suggesting that we as a nation are overwhelmed by faceless, irrational and blindly destructive forces, and are incapable of creating a united front to drive them back. T.S. Eliot conveyed the same mind-consuming anxieties for Europeans at the dawn of the Industrial Age. *The Waste Land* (published in 1919) was the poet's desperate attempt to suture centuries worth of religious and philosophical thoughts into a coherent view of a world worth living in. He was overwhelmed by too many disparate ideas, a "heap of broken images," a world ready to burst at the seams. For Romero, the only way to restore meaning to life was with the active threat of armageddon. The strangers in the farmhouse fend off the zombies for several hours, then begin to fight among themselves. It is their inability to work together that seals their fates. "The most frightening thing," Romero says, "is that nobody communicates. Everybody is isolated and alone with their own version of the world. They're all kinda insane. The trouble is that they can see that the afterlife is no better. Even if you're good there are no guarantees."[4] As Johnny announces, prophetically, in the opening moments of the film, "There's not much sense in my going to church." In the closing sequence, a redneck militia storms the house and kills the only survivor. The militia members are scarcely more empathetic than the zombies, and we are left without hope for the future.

As soon as the film was cut, Romero drove to New York City to seek a distributor. He arrived on April 4, 1968, the night of Martin Luther King's assassination. A month later, just after the assassination of Robert Kennedy, the film was screened for representatives of the Walter Reade Organization, who eventually released the film theatrically.[5] Most critics, including Roger Ebert, complained that the film was demoralizing, and should be banned. Audiences, however, flocked to the film, as they had flocked to *Dracula* in 1931. When asked if the film's success was due to its social relevance and cultural resonance, Romero responds, "It was 1968, man. Everybody had a 'message.' I was just making a horror film, and I think the anger and the attitude and all that's there is just there because it was 1968.... I won't abandon the allegory in the zombie films—I earnestly do think about it and try to make it work, but the biggest job is subduing all those thoughts, because those things can easily interfere with what you're doing, and what you're doing on the surface is making a comic book."[6]

After two unsuccessful films, a hippie melodrama called *There's Always Vanilla* (1970) and a 1973 feminist allegory called *Jack's Wife* (later released as *Season of the Witch*), Romero returned to the themes he had explored in *Night*. *The Crazies* (1973) is an all-too-obvious comment on the Vietnam War. In the film, the citizens of Evans City, Pennsylvania, are subjected to a government-enforced quarantine after the military accidentally discharges a dangerous biochemical agent into their water supply. When the citizens resist (as any American who holds dear the Articles of Confederation is apt to do), we learn that the cagey politicians in Washington are planning to wipe the town off the map. The battle lines are clear. Romero has shifted the focus of *Night of the Living Dead* so that the battle for survival is no longer between the dead and the undead, but between the corrupt American government and its citizen-subjects. The message-heavy film failed to find an audience.

After several years on hiatus, Romero delivered his most intelligent film. *Martin* (1978) is the story of a lonely teenager who is desperate to feel alive. He clings to the vampire mythology as a source of magic in life. When the world fails to inspire anything like awe or compassion, Martin kills innocent victims — always young, attractive women — to cure his boredom and loneliness. He subdues his victims with drugs, then cuts them open apologetically. With John Amplas in the lead role, it is difficult not to empathize with Martin. He is never especially threatening or contemptible, like so many movie monsters. Neither is he easy to dismiss, like Frankenstein or Romero's zombies, as inhuman. He is too familiar; he craves what we all crave — not blood, but life. Martin is a garden-variety sociopath, not the ordinary horror movie villain.

Accordingly, there is no charismatic screen hero to root for in the film. The only person who knows that Martin is dangerous is his elder cousin, Cuda, a religious fanatic. Cuda, however, does not believe that Martin is mentally unstable; he believes that Martin is Nosferatu. Cuda fuels the boy's fantasies, insisting that he is a vampire from a long line of vampires. After the local priest (Romero, in a telling cameo) and law enforcement fail to do anything about the boy's after-hours activities, Cuda sneaks up on Martin while he is sleeping and drives a wooden stake through his heart. The battle between Martin and Cuda is not between Good and Evil; it is fought in a kind of spiritual void, where ideas of Good and Evil are overwhelmed by a mundane reality. For Romero, the horror is not Evil, but violence.

In almost all of his films, Romero exposes a spiritual void in America that is reminiscent of the void that T.S. Eliot found in London after World War I. (Whether this is Romero's indictment of American culture or simply a byproduct of living in Pittsburgh is debatable.) The connection between people is lost. The ability to transcend habits of being through Imagination has been forgotten or ignored. Romero believes that this deep-rooted malaise has been present in the American temperament since the 1960's: "We've lost it in religion," he says, "We've lost it in sex. We've lost it even in our feelings about a city like New York. It's really gone and tarnished. We're trying to operate on a very realistic plane. I find that to be a very devastating thing as life goes on — you can't analyze it all. We're not meant to operate that way. You have to leave some room for emotion, and you have to leave some room for love and romance, or you're not really complete, and you find that you just want more." [7]

Romero took his criticism of American life even further in the first sequel to *Night of the Living Dead*. *Dawn of the Dead* (1978) picks up right where the original left off: Zombies are roaming the countryside, spreading like a plague at such a fast pace that there is little hope of containment. Four Pittsburgh residents realize that there is little hope in trying to hold onto their old lives. They fuel up a news helicopter and take off in search of a new home that remains unaffected by the curse. After only hours of searching, they stop at an abandoned mall to rest. It doesn't take the three men — Peter, Stephen and Roger — very long to realize that they are sitting on a consumer's dream. They start raiding stores for the best of everything that can be mass-produced. Only Fran, Stephen's pregnant wife, wants to keep searching. She warns them, "This is exactly what we're trying to get away from."

Romero's criticism of consumer culture is blissfully obvious. Zombies of all shapes and sizes (and religions) roam the mall, bargain hunting and listening to Muzak. After *Dawn of the Dead,* the zombie in film became something of a parody of modern man — a slow-moving, narrow-minded consumer, instinctively hungry for *more*. Lucio Fulci's unofficial sequel to *Dawn,* titled *Zombie* (1979), ends with a scene in which hordes of rotting corpses amble across the Brooklyn Bridge toward Manhattan's financial district, echoing Eliot's nightmare of dispirited workers making their way across London Bridge into the financial district; "I had not thought death had undone so many."

Dawn of the Dead, like *Night,* is a cinematic comic book, but it dares to consider the breakdown of society as we know it, and to show possibilities for a new beginning. Before the four friends flee the old world, a wandering priest offers sage advice: "We must stop the killing, or lose the war." Later in the film, a gang of motorcycle-riding outlaws raid the mall and destroy the group's happy home. They fight back, instinctively, before finally attempting — for the second time — to leave the old world behind. In the final moments, Peter and Fran take to the sky in the news chopper. They have little fuel and no plan, but they at least have some shred of hope that a new order is possible.

With his next film, *Knightriders* (1981), Romero again explores the challenge that consumerism poses to a meaningful life. Ed Harris stars as King Billy, the leader of a motorcycle gang that travels across the country, staging medieval jousting tournaments for "sucker-headed American driftwood." Billy has created a closed community in which to live out his dream of the way life should be — full of magic and honor — but he is constantly torn between his fantasy world and the real world that treats him like a novelty. He becomes increasingly withdrawn from reality until he finally creates a rift between himself and his subjects, who insist that he cannot survive without outsiders. "Money makes the world go round," they say, "Even *your* world." Billy fights back: "It's tough to live by the Code. It's real hard to live for something that you believe in. People try and they get tired of it like they get tired of diets, exercise or their marriage or their kids or their jobs or themselves or they get tired of their God. You can keep the money you make off this sick world! I don't want any part of it." Romero regards Billy as a hero but admits that he is doomed to live a life of isolation.

Knightriders may be best described as a film about a generation of dreamers who sold out. The mention of King Arthur and the Knights of the Round Table calls to mind the media's label of the Kennedy dynasty in the 1960s as "Camelot." *Knightriders* ends with the death of Billy and, presumably, the fall of Camelot. The others mourn his death, but there is no indication that the new king, Morgan, will follow in Billy's footsteps. *Knightriders* echoes the finale of *Easy Rider* (1969), in which Peter Fonda's Captain America is randomly gunned down on his motorcycle. Billy, by contrast, is the cause of his own death in *Knightriders*. He is daydreaming when an oncoming truck hits him. Billy dies with a smile on his face, but the manner of his death does nothing to confirm his convictions.

In the early 1980s, Romero retreated into a world of nostalgia. He teamed up with bestselling author Stephen King for 1982's *Creepshow,* an anthology based on the E.C. comics that influenced them both as children, and then went to work on a similar television series *Tales from the Darkside*. For a while, he considered filming an adaptation of King's most intimidating novel, *The Stand*.[8] Of all of King's works, this would have been the one most suited to Romero's vision of America.

The Stand, first published in 1982, is a sprawling, post-apocalyptic novel heavily influenced by T.S. Eliot, Richard Matheson and Romero himself. It begins with a deadly virus that wipes out 99 percent of the world's population. The survivors, led by mystical dreams, band together in two camps — one in the mountains of Colorado and one in the Arizona desert, to prepare for a final battle between Good and Evil that will determine what kind of new world is to be built on the ruins of the old. Unfortunately, budgetary concerns kept Romero's adaptation from being made, and he did not work with Stephen King again until *The Dark Half* (1993).

Romero's next film, *Day of the Dead* (1985), was set in a post-apocalyptic world with no such Manichean conflicts. *Day* picks up at least several months after the end of *Dawn of the Dead*. Following a helicopter sweep of the East Coast, one of the characters remarks that the "power's off on the mainland ... and all the shopping malls are closed." In Florida, a group of 12 scientists and soldiers have taken refuge in an underground compound. They have lost contact with the outside world and are forced to assume that there are no other survivors of the zombie holocaust. As one scientist, nicknamed Dr. Frankenstein, tries desperately to domesticate zombies and create a new order, tensions rise between the soldiers and the scientists.

Two survivors, hired to maintain a helicopter that is the only means of escape from the secured compound, sit idly by, avoiding the politics. John, a laid-back West Indian who may be the sanest member of the group, tries to convince his friends that they should abandon their attempts to restore order, saying, "Let's get in that old whirlybird there, find us an island someplace, get juiced and spend what time we got left soakin' up some sunshine." Sarah, a scientist, fires back, "You could do that, couldn't you? With all that's going on?" He shrugs. "Shit, I could do that even if all this wasn't going on." John is Romero's most outspoken character and is the heart of the film. He expresses what is, so far, the director's strongest message regarding Establishment America: Give up on society and save yourself. John finally makes Sarah see the impossibility of her efforts to save a civilization that deserved to collapse.

Romero originally had much more ambitious plans for *Day of the Dead*. He intended to present a world in which zombies were being trained as soldiers. The surviving humans would face the threat of a war in which zombies become the weapons of a power-hungry elite. When the smoke cleared, a few madmen would control the lives of the masses. Romero's punchline: in essence, nothing would have changed since 1968.[9] The filmed version of *Day of the Dead* ends on a tropical island. Two men and one woman are beached there, having finally given up on life as they knew it. We have no way of knowing whether or not they are the only three people left in the world or if, having escaped the continental United States, they have escaped the nightmare.

In 1985, Romero's indictment of modern American life (and implied condemnation of a generation of hippies-turned-yuppies) did not sit well with audiences, and *Day of the Dead,* unlike its predecessors, was a box office failure. Audiences in the carefree, consumer-friendly 1980s apparently did not feel the need for such a serious examination of personal and societal values. They flocked instead to Dan O'Bannon's *Return of the Living Dead,* an outrageous parody of the 1968 film. *Return* was pure postmodern escapism. It has since spawned two sequels, while Romero's nightmare vision has gone unanswered.

Since the disappointing reception to *Day,* Romero has seemed somewhat reluctant to tackle ambitious projects. He has continued to explore the dark side of human nature in minor films like *Monkey Shines: An Experiment in Fear* (1988) and *The Dark Half* (1993). His most recent feature film, *Bruiser* (2000), is a slight return to form for the director. *Bruiser* is firmly rooted in a time and place: the cutthroat business world of late 1990s America. Its antihero is Henry, a soft-spoken, put-upon rat-racer who goes postal when he realizes that everyone in his life is taking advantage of him. One morning, Henry looks in the mirror and sees that he has become faceless. In a desperate attempt reclaim his identity and his place in the world, has lashes out at those who have ignored or cheated him.

According to Romero, the inspiration was Henri-Georges Clouzot's *Eyes Without a Face* (1959), a film about a surgeon whose daughter is disfigured and must wear a mask: "I thought the image was startling, but I couldn't figure out what to do with it until Columbine. I just had this thought that this disenfranchisement and lack of identity is more than anything else what frustrates people and makes them want to shoot back."[10] Henry, who works for a sleazy magazine editor, is at odds with a world in which human decency is destroyed by the media and its commercial substitutes for love and respect. Like Martin, he just wants to make human contact, but finds that the only way to make lasting contact is through violence.

In an interview about *Night of the Living Dead,* Romero says that the message of his first film was that "you're not talking to each other, electronic media doesn't work, people don't communicate."[11] He might just as easily be talking about *Bruiser,* or any of the films in between. Romero has tried desperately, over the course of the last three and a half decades, to deliver a wake up call to audiences. "Horror is radical," he says, "It can take you into a completely new world, new place, and just rattle your cage and say, wait a minute — look at things differently. That shock of horror is what horror's all about. But in most cases, at the end of the story, people try to bring everything back — the girl gets the guy and everything's fine and things go on just the way they were. Which is really why we are doing this in the first place. We don't want things the way they are or we wouldn't be trying to shock you into an alternative place."[12]

Feature Films Written and Directed by Romero:

Night of the Living Dead (1967)
There's Always Vanilla (1970)
Jack's Wife (a.k.a. *Season of the Witch*) (1972)
The Crazies (a.k.a. *Code Name: Trixie*) (1973)
Martin (1978)
Dawn of the Dead (1978)
Knightriders (1981)
Creepshow (1982)
Day of the Dead (1985)
Monkey Shines: An Experiment in Fear (1988) — adapted screenplay
Two Evil Eyes (1990) — "The Facts in the Case of M. Valdemar" segment
The Dark Half (1993) — adapted screenplay
Bruiser (2000)

15

John Carpenter: Space-Age Cowboys

When asked what his favorite film genre is, John Carpenter says, "I got into this business wanting to make Westerns. And that just hasn't worked out. I made some Westerns, but they're not really Westerns. They're hidden Westerns."[1] In fact, though Carpenter has written several Western scripts, including one that was designated as a vehicle for John Wayne,[2] he has never directed one. Instead, he has tackled a wide variety of other genres, crossbreeding many of them with Western plots. The heroes in Carpenter's films are often modeled on the fearless gunslingers immortalized by John Wayne and Clint Eastwood, who take a stand against corrupt value systems, even when — perhaps *especially* when — forced to stand alone. His heroines are strong, independent women, like Angie Dickinson and Lauren Bacall in the films of Howard Hawks (*Rio Bravo, To Have and Have Not, Key Largo*). In many of Carpenter's films, these noble characters become trapped together and are forced to make a desperate last stand, whether they are facing ruthless gang members (*Assault on Precinct 13*), ghosts (*The Fog*), aliens (*The Thing, Ghosts of Mars*), vampires (*Vampires*) or Evil Incarnate (*Halloween, Prince of Darkness*). Carpenter has made a career for himself by creating archetypal myths in which Good and Evil, Past and Present square off on a frontier where one person can make a difference. His is a world of space-age cowboys, living the dream. The Western is "the only myth storytelling that we have in America," Carpenter says. "The West is where our ideas of individualism and freedom and some of our values come from and that's why those myths, when you retell them, they resonate."[3]

Around the time that Carpenter began making a student film at USC in 1970, the Western was a struggling genre. In 1962, John Ford — the genre's undisputed master — had made *The Man Who Shot Liberty Valance*, which sounded a kind of death knell for the classic Western. In it, John Wayne's gunslinger proves to be an anachronism compared to Jimmy Stewart's big city lawyer, who arrives in California to tame the savage lifestyle of America's closed frontier. In the end, it is Stewart's tenderfoot who wins the girl and the respect of the people. In 1964, Italian filmmaker Sergio Leone appropriated the American genre, casting Clint Eastwood as the laconic Man with No Name in *A Fistful of Dollars*. In Leone's "spaghetti western," Eastwood's gunslinger walks alone, unwilling to trust anyone. When asked if he has any respect for peace, he responds, "It's not easy to like something you know nothing about." Eastwood's character has no faith in institutions of law and order and little fath in human decency; he too is a hero out of time and place in a desolate "new west." In 1969, Sam Peckinpah conclusively de-mythologized the Western with *The Wild Bunch*, which graphically depicts the "last stand" of a group of decidedly un-heroic gunslingers. It was clear that the Western was on its way out, and a new generation of filmmakers was setting its sights on the next great American frontier: outer space.

Carpenter's first film, *Dark Star* (1974), explored this new frontier rather than the Old West, and it was hardly an archetypal myth. Instead, *Dark Star* was a parody of *2001: A Space Odyssey* (1968), about a trio of dimwitted astronauts who are not the least bit concerned with Manifest Destiny. His second feature film, *Assault on Precinct 13* (1976), was a more ambitious neo–Western. *Assault* is a loose remake of Howard Hawks's *Rio Bravo* (1959), cross-bred with elements of George Romero's *Night of the Living Dead* (1968) and set in L.A. gangland. In the film, a group of strangers are trapped in an abandoned police station, surrounded by an army of unseen snipers. As in both *Rio Bravo* and *Night of the Living Dead*, the central character is a self-reliant man who is able to keep his cool in the face of adversity. Lt. Bishop forms an alliance with Napoleon Wilson, a convict with a devil-may-care attitude, and Leigh, a beautiful woman with an iron will. Each of these characters is an independent thinker, but their survival depends on their ability to trust each other. This is a dynamic that was frequently emphasized by Howard Hawks (*Red River, Rio Bravo, El Dorado, Rio Lobo*) and John Ford (*Stagecoach, My Darling Clementine, Fort Apache, The Searchers*), whose films were reminders that America was founded on a spirit of community as well as independence.

Carpenter's deepest loyalty seems to be to Napoleon Wilson, the outlaw. Wilson calls to mind Howard Hawks' most rugged gunfighters as well as the incorrigible characters portrayed by Humphrey Bogart. At the end of *Assault on Precinct 13*, when the trio realize that they have survived their ordeal, a police officer attempts to take Napoleon Wilson back into protective custody. Lt. Bishop pushes him away, then turns to Wilson and says, "It would be an honor if you would walk outside with me." Without missing a beat, Wilson replies, "Of course it would."

Carpenter followed up *Assault on Precinct 13* with *Halloween* (1978), one of the highest grossing independent films of all time. *Halloween* — influenced more by the films of Val Lewton and Alfred Hitchcock than Howard Hawks and John Ford — reminded audiences that, even in the most civilized and domesticated parts of America, there are eruptions of disorder. The town of Haddonfield looks safe enough, with its cookie-cutter houses and its neatly manicured lawns, but the slow-moving camera reminds us that there is something lurking in the shadows during the characters' most vulnerable moments. With this film, Carpenter shattered the illusion of safety in suburbia for middle-class Americans just as *Jaws* (1975) had turned vacationers away from the beach. "Suburbia is supposed to be safe," Carpenter says, "Your house is supposed to be a sanctuary. Nowadays, maybe because of conditions beyond our control, there is no sanctuary. And I think that is in the audience's mind."[4] (Looking back on the *Halloween* phenomenon today, Carpenter remarks that violence has become so widespread and so random that audiences no longer go to the movies for the kind of scare that the original film delivered.[5] Accordingly, in a recent sequel to *Halloween*, Laurie Strode returns and takes a very proactive role in disposing of her supposedly indestructible brother.)

Unlike Carpenter's neo–Westerns, *Halloween* offers no heroes to restore order in Haddonfield. Laurie Strode is a survivor-type, but she is characterized by her *reactions* rather than her actions, and she stands alone in all efforts. The ineffectiveness of the would-be hero, Dr. Sam Loomis, becomes obvious in the final moments of the film, when six bullets fail to keep Michael Myers on the ground. "Was it the Boogeyman?" Strode asks. Loomis, looking stunned despite his repeated warnings to the townfolk that Michael Myers is more than a man, responds, "As a matter of fact, it was."

In 1981, after *The Fog* and a sequel to *Halloween*, John Carpenter could have made just about any film he wanted, and he chose another "hidden Western." This time, the hero bore a stronger resemblance to Clint Eastwood's Man With No Name (or, for that matter, Dirty Harry) than to John Wayne's traditional gunslinger. Kurt Russell, who had already worked with the director on the TV movie *Elvis* (1979), starred as Snake Plissken, a war hero turned outlaw who, like Eastwood, speaks softly and carries a big gun. The director says that Plissken "represents my ultimate hatred of authority."⁶

Carpenter wrote the original story for *Escape from New York* in 1974, as a response to that year's *Death Wish*, which starred Charles Bronson — a veteran of Leone's Westerns — as Paul Kersey.⁷ After his wife is killed and his daughter raped by thugs in New York City, Kersey escapes to Tucson, Arizona, where he becomes enchanted with the Western mythos. When an acquaintance tells him that "around here, muggers will just plain get their asses blown off," Kersey returns to New York to carry out "the old American social custom of self-defense." He later finds himself staring down a punk with a gun, and says, with a twisted smile, "Draw." As his crusade continues, crime statistics drop and the media hails the unknown vigilante as a hero.

In *Escape*, New York is even more desperately in need of a hero. The island of Manhattan has become so crime-infested that it is converted into a maximum security prison, surrounded by 50-foot containment walls and maintained by the Liberty Island Patrol. The United States of the future (1997, to be exact) is a military regime, on the brink of war with the Soviet Union and China. Twenty-four hours before the President is

Kurt Russell as Snake Plissken in *Escape from New York* (AVCO Embassy, 1982).

scheduled to appear at a peace conference to prevent a nuclear holocaust, Air Force One is shot down over the Big Apple by soldiers of the "National Liberation Front ... acting in the name of all the oppressed of this imperialist country." The U.S. government turns to Snake, an unlikely ally, to single-handedly carry out a search-and-rescue operation.

When he is brought in, Snake meets with Police Commissioner Bob Hauk (played by Leone regular Lee Van Cleef). When Hauk explains that the President is in danger, he sarcastically asks, "President of what?" Like Eastwood in *A Fistful of Dollars,* he pretends to be a completely self-absorbed loner. We eventually learn that Snake is willing to fight for the survival of the human race — but not for the survival of the United States government. Carpenter's Man With No Name emerges as a Man With No Country. This futuristic "tech noir" is arguably more bleak than any of the film noirs of the 1940s. It spells out certain doom for a future-perfect America in which technological and political advancements have destroyed the founding principles of the past.

Equipped with various futuristic weapons, Snake lands a jet glider on the top of the darkened Twin Towers of the World Trade Center, then descends and begins to wander a nightmarish parody of Manhattan, where bored criminals role-play rape scenarios and drag queens overrun Broadway. Eventually, Snake locates the President, who is held captive by the self-appointed Duke of New York. Donald Pleasence is featured as an unlikely U.S. President — perhaps because Carpenter wanted to attribute some of Dr. Loomis' madness to the most powerful politician in the world. Later in the film, after he has escaped from Manhattan with Snake, the President picks up an automatic weapon and guns down the Duke of New York, while screaming hysterically. It is an image of a power-hungry America that acts only out of fear and revenge — an American that Snake does not wish to save. By destroying a tape that will (somehow) help the United States to establish peace with its enemies, he plunges the United States into a world war. The message is extreme: Snake calls for a new American Revolution.

The defeatist tone of *Halloween* and *Escape from New York* carried over into Carpenter's next film, a 1982 remake of Howard Hawks' *The Thing from Another World.* Kurt Russell stars as Macready, a pilot who is stationed with seven other men at a remote government outpost in the Arctic. In the film's opening moments, they are visited by a Norwegian, who is angrily pursuing a sled dog. They kill the Norwegian and lock up the sled dog inside the outpost. At this point, only Ennio Morricone's ominous music hints that there is anything wrong at U.S. National Science Institute Station 4. Then, without warning, the Norwegian's sled dog undergoes a grotesque transformation, morphing into human shape before the eyes of the Americans. Despite their efforts to contain it, the alien creature gets loose in the complex and the relationship among the men quickly deteriorates as they realize that the monster is capable of taking any form — any one of them could become the Thing. "I don't know who to trust," one of the men barks at Macready. "I know what you mean," Mac responds, "Trust is a tough thing to come by these days." In a 1982 interview, Carpenter said, "People today are experiencing ... paranoia in their everyday lives. You read a headline about a murder and, the next day, you begin looking at the person walking next to you a bit more carefully. This movie takes that underlying feeling and lets it grow."[8] At the end of the film, only two men — Macready and Childs — remain alive. From the viewer's perspective, either one of them could be inhuman. The outcome of mankind's "last stand" is uncertain.

After the commercial failure of *The Thing*, Carpenter took on a few "safe" projects — a second sequel to *Halloween*, a 1983 adaptation of Stephen King's bestseller *Christine*, and the surprisingly light-hearted alien romance *Starman* (1984). His next film, *Big Trouble in Little China* (1986), took his love for the Western in a different direction. Kurt Russell stars as Jack Burton, an American truck driver who moves and talks like John Wayne, but has an arrogance all his own. Somehow, Jack finds himself in the middle of a "Chinese standoff," fighting side by side with a soft-spoken kung fu expert named Wang. It's East meets West and, though the American hero finds himself completely out of his league, it is ultimately his partnership with Wang that allows Good to triumph over Evil.

In 1987, after the big-budget *Big Trouble* failed to generate substantial box office receipts, Carpenter decided to return to his roots and make two independent features. *Prince of Darkness* expanded on themes from *Assault on Precinct 13*, *The Fog* and *The Thing*, in which a group of strangers are trapped together and forced to fight for their lives (and, in fact, the future of mankind). *They Live* (1988) is a much more comic film, though not necessarily less ambitious. In fact, it is a sharp (if overindulgent) examination of Carpenter's views on American values in the 1980s.

At the time of the film's release, Carpenter said, "I'm disgusted by what we've become in America. I truly believe there is brain death in this country. Everything we see is designed to sell us something. My awareness became so acute ... that I couldn't even watch MTV. It's all about wanting us to buy something. The only thing they want to do is take our money." [9] Every reactionary has a Them. Carpenter's Them is yuppie decision-makers and the Establishment that protects them. Carpenter's "proof" of the alien invasion is the widening gap between the rich and the poor in post–Reagan America. He shows that the homeless and the disenfranchised — who are, in this film, all of the people that still blindly believe in the founding principles of America — are being enslaved by alien body snatchers. In *They Live,* America is no longer a place where a hard worker can make his dreams come true, no matter what Rowdy Roddy Piper says. Carpenter places blame on the politicians, the police, the rich and the media.

The film begins in a Depression-style shantytown on the outskirts of Los Angeles. A drifter named John Nada (Piper) wanders into the district around the time that a rebel group begins to take action. By chance, Nada stumbles into the headquarters of the resistance and is given a pair of sunglasses that allow him to see the truth: Aliens are among us, disguised as humans, and subliminal advertising is being used to keep the masses obedient and oblivious. On TV, a politician quells all thoughts of civil unrest, saying, "It's a new morning in America. Fresh. Vital. The old cynicism is gone. We have faith in our leaders. We're optimistic.... We don't need pessimism." Carpenter does not agree. "I wanted to make some political statements," he says, "One of the biggest being that everybody is proud to be an American as long as they can make money at it."[10] For Nada, who claims to still believe in America, it is time to send the world a wake-up message; he destroys the satellite that allows the aliens to remain hidden, so that humans can finally see politicians and yuppies for what they really are.

In the final moments of the film, Carpenter pokes fun at a specific element of "the Establishment" that frequently targets horror directors like him. The destruction of the satellite reveals a pair of Siskel-and-Ebert-type critics to be aliens, exposing the bogus motives of conservative film critics who argue that horror films are potentially dangerous. Seven years later, Carpenter expands on this idea with *In the Mouth of Madness* (1995), his first truly ambitious film of the 1990s.

Madness presupposes that the warning of the conservative critics — that fictional violence will beget violence in reality — is prophetic. "I wanted to direct the movie," Carpenter says, "because of the relevance it has to what's happening both in America and Britain. This ludicrous argument that television / radio violence is the cause of society's ills. When I was growing up it was horror comics that said 'Religion seeks discipline through fear.' That's what the current moral crusade is all about. It's called Dominion Theology. Government under God, and you only have to look at Iran to see where this avenue of thought ends up."[11] Audiences stayed away from the film, perhaps because the warning seemed too pretentious. Carpenter, however, did not abandon the idea.

Escape from L.A. (1996) is a far more biting, and even more outrageous, satire of right-wing demands for a return to "traditional values." Though it is practically a remake of *Escape from New York,* the subtext of *Escape from L.A.* is different. In this dystopian future, the island of Los Angeles—cut off from the continental United States by a massive millennium earthquake—is a prison for those deemed "undesirable or unfit to live in the new moral America." A fascist President amends the Constitution, granting himself a lifetime term in office, and proceeds to outlaw smoking, drinking, drugs, sex ("unless, of course, you're married"), guns, foul language, atheism and red meat. Only the President's daughter, Utopia, is able to get close enough to undermine his power. Stealing a weapon capable of shutting down all of the world's electronics, she escapes to the island of L.A., where a revolutionary named Cuervo Jones has promised to protect her.

Once again, Snake Plissken is blackmailed into saving the United States. By the time he gets to L.A., Utopia has realized that Cuervo Jones is just another meglomaniacal politician, trying to deny his followers their basic freedoms. She escapes with Snake, who knows that the only hope for the future of the country ("America, "he says, "died a long time ago") is the destruction of existing politics, authorities and institutions—a *real* return to traditional values. With the push of a button, he sends the U.S. "right back to the dark ages."

The film, and its hero, failed to draw audiences to theaters in 1996, probably because Carpenter's reactionary, anti-technology message is as out of place in this day and age as the Western. To some, Plissken may be reminiscent of Ted Kaczynski, who also wanted to shut down the motor of America and start from scratch. In his Manifesto, the Unabomber suggests that Americans must look to the past, rather than the future, for a more meaningful life. "The conservatives are fools," he says. "They whine about the decay of traditional values, yet they enthusiastically support technological progress and economic growth. Apparently it never occurs to them that you can't make rapid, drastic changes in the technology of the economy of a society without causing rapid changes in all other aspects of the society as well, and that such rapid changes inevitably break down traditional values."[12] Kaczynski blames the industrial and technological advances of the 20th century (as well as the political systems that support these advances) for the social ills that are consistently pointed out in sci-fi and horror films: the decline of religion, the destruction of nature and the disintegration of family / community values. His solution: "It would be better to dump the whole stinking system and take the consequences."[13] That's precisely what Snake Plissken does, returning America to its 19th century state of "innocence," without the violence of terrorism.

15. John Carpenter

Since *Escape from L.A.*, Carpenter's films have been less political. *Vampires* (1998) and *Ghosts of Mars* (2001) are genre films that borrow Western themes, without becoming too ponderous. *Vampires* is essentially a supernatural remake of John Ford's *The Searchers* (1956), in which John Wayne stars as Ethan Edwards, a no-nonsense gunman living in post–Civil War Texas. Ethan is consumed by bitterness toward "savage" Native Americans and over-civilized Union soldiers. After his niece is kidnapped by a tribe of Comanches, he heads north with a small group of hunters to find her and exact his revenge. As time passes, the hunters become the hunted and the group disbands, leaving only Ethan and his nephew to carry on the crusade. Over time, the nephew realizes that Ethan means kill his niece when he finds her. After spending years with savages, he says, white women "ain't white any more." Only in the final moments of the film does Ethan change his mind. He returns her to her family, then heads north again, still desperate to conquer his demons.

In *Vampires,* James Woods stars as Jack Crowe, a no-nonsense slayer who unknowingly leads his team of vampire hunters into a deadly trap in New Mexico. Aided by the only surviving member of his team, Jack seeks vengeance on an immortal named Valek. Along the way, his partner is bitten by a vampire and Jack, realizing that his friend will soon be less than human, prepares to kill him. Only in the final moments of the film does he show mercy, promising his friend two days to escape before he continues his crusade against the race of savage monsters.

Ghosts of Mars is a pretty straightforward game of "cowboys and Indians," set in a Martian terraform colony in the year 2176. When a disturbance is reported among the colonists, military personnel are sent to investigate. They quickly learn that the colonists have become irrational, masochistic savages. A survivor explains that they are possessed by the original inhabitants of Mars, who are trying to protect their planet from the invading humans. The characters and the plot structure are culled straight out of *Rio Bravo* and *Assault on Precinct 13,* reinforcing Carpenter's belief that, even in the distant future when we're faced with new frontiers, the Western mythology will always be a part of the American story.

Feature Films Written and Directed by Carpenter:

Assault on Precinct 13 (1976)*
Halloween (1978) written with Debra Hill*
The Fog (1980) written with Debra Hill*
Escape from New York (1981)

written with Nick
   Castle*
Prince of Darkness (1987) written
   as "Martin Quatermass"*
They Live (1988) adapted by
   "Frank Armitage"*

Escape from LA (1996) written
   with Debra Hill & Kurt
   Russell*
Ghosts of Mars (2001) written
   with Larry Sulkis*

Feature Films Directed by Carpenter

Dark Star (1974)
Elvis (1979)
The Thing (1982)
Christine (1983)*
Starman (1984)*
Big Trouble in Little China (1986)*

Memoirs of an Invisible Man
   (1992)
In the Mouth of Madness
   (1995)*
Village of the Damned (1995)*
Vampires (1998)*

Feature Films Written and Produced by Carpenter

The Eyes of Laura Mars (1978)
Halloween 2 (1981)
*Halloween 3: Season of the
   Witch* (1982)

The Philadelphia Experiment
   (1984)
Black Moon Rising (1985)

*Carpenter also composed the score.

16

Larry Cohen: Outside in America

It is no surprise when the screen fantasies of an independent filmmaker exhibit a strong outsider mentality, especially among directors working in the horror genre, which has traditionally focused on disenfranchised (if not disembodied) outsiders. In the modern era of the American horror film, Larry Cohen was at the forefront of a new wave of filmmakers working outside of Hollywood. Few noteworthy directors are as fiercely independent as Cohen, who admits that he has "always been interested in anyone who lives on the edge of what is, supposedly, accepted normality."[1] His films have consistently questioned forms of "otherness" that threaten the status quo. Robin Wood notes that this was a common theme in horror films of the 1970s, many of which explored lifestyles that "bourgeois ideology cannot recognize or accept." The otherness in these films, he says, functions "not simply as something external to the culture or to the self, but also as what is repressed (though never destroyed) in the self and projected outward in order to be hated and disowned."[2] This type of inner-struggle, stemming from conflicts of personal identity, is particularly prevalent in Cohen's work, prompting some critics to theorize that the American-born Jewish director is expressing anxieties about his own ancestry and religious background. Cohen casually admits, "Living up at the end of World War II, being just a little kid at the end of that period and hearing about concentration camps and attempts to murder Jews might have had some effect on me."[3]

Cohen describes the first "Larco" production, *Bone* (1972), as "a satire of American racial conflicts."[4] Bone, an imposing black man, is a character out of step with the times, trying to find his place in American society. The film is set in 1970, when "the most powerful nation on earth wages war against one of the poorest countries—which it finds impossible to defeat." In the opening scene, Bone appears in the yard of a wealthy white Beverly Hills couple. He offers no explanation for his presence, so the couple nervously employ him to pull a dead rat out of their pool. When the deed is done, Bone orders the husband to go to the bank and make a withdrawal, and threatens to rape the wife if he doesn't return within the hour. "Unfortunately," Cohen says, "many black people choose to play the stereotypical roles whites have chosen for them. As Bone says, 'I'm just a big black buck doing what's expected of him.'"[5] When the husband fails to return, Bone seems conflicted over his real motivation, and the wife becomes consoling. "Well," she says, "I guess like everybody today you're under great social pressure." Bone complains, "I had the nigger mystique. And then they changed it."

On the basis of *Bone,* AIP producer Sam Arkoff hired Cohen to direct *Black Caesar* (1973), conceived as a "blaxploitation" film like *Shaft* (1971) and *Superfly* (1972), which depicted strong, street-wise African-Americans thumbing their noses at white authority. Cohen's film, however, is not as stereotypical; the director himself points out that, in *Black Caesar,* "all the genre rules are violated."[6] *Black Caesar* is based more on the classic gangster film *Little Caesar* (1931) than on *Shaft* or *Superfly*. Like Edward G. Robinson in *Little Caesar,* Fred Williamson's Tommy Gibbs hides an intense inferiority complex beneath his devil-may-care attitude. Tommy would like everyone to believe that he is dismantling the hierarchy of authority in Harlem in the name of racial justice, but as the film progresses, we realize that he is doing it because he hates the color of his own skin.

At the beginning of the film, teenage Tommy takes a message to an Irish police chief named McKinney, who berates him, calling him a nigger. McKinney goes to great lengths to make sure that the delivery boy knows his place, and it quickly becomes clear to young Tommy that, in New York City, there are two masters—Irish cops and Sicilian gangsters. These two authorities have a mutual respect for each other, and an equal disrespect for the black hoods in Harlem. Tommy aims to change that. He learns Italian, then approaches the Sicilians with a plan to organize the Harlem streets. He, gradually moves into a position of power and wealth, but never quite gains the respect he so desperately craves. He lives in a white man's house and wears a white man's clothes, but those who know him best assure him that he is nothing but a "white nigger." The film's most telling moment comes when Tommy is finally able to exert his power over

McKinney. In what should be his ultimate moment of triumph, Tommy smears black shoe polish on the white man's face and begins to sob, helplessly, "You the nigger, McKinney."

The commercial success of *Black Caesar* prompted an immediate sequel, *Hell Up in Harlem* (1973), but Cohen was already at work on a very different type of film. *It's Alive* (1974) begins when a California woman goes into labor in the middle of the night. Her husband, anxious but never overly concerned, takes her to the hospital. While he stands by in the waiting room, his wife gives birth to a violent mutant baby that chews its way out of the womb and promptly kills the doctor and the nurses in attendance.

For the majority of the picture, the baby's father, Frank Davis, helps authorities hunt the mutant baby, which leaves a trail of mutilated victims in its wake. Davis repeatedly insists that the baby is not his, and loudly encourages its destruction, desperate to clear his good name. When he finally comes face to face with his son in the Los Angeles sewers, he realizes that the infant has been acting purely on an instinct for self-preservation. In his father's arms, the child appears docile and even a bit scared. The peaceful reunion is shattered when intolerant authorities arrive. Davis, realizing that they will never accept the truth, throws the razor-toothed infant at them.

In the sequel, Frank Davis has become a crusader for mutant baby rights. At the beginning of *It Lives Again* (1976), he approaches a couple at a baby shower and warns them that they are being watched by government agents. Somehow, authorities have learned to predict when a pregnant woman will give birth to one of Them. Davis tells the newlyweds not to be afraid. "Monster," he says, "They use that word too easily, don't they? Because it's different. I wounded my own child, but he forgave me. Is that an animal? Is it? Is that a monster that can forgive?" The focus of the sequel, like the first film, is on the parents rather than the children. Davis and the expectant parents go into hiding, trying to protect the newborns from a society that destroys what it doesn't understand.

Cohen explains that "the best parts of the *It's Alive* films do not involve monsters, but so called normal people acting in an aberrant manner because of the unreal situation they find themselves in."[7] According to him, the films address real problems in everyday America: "At the time that we made the picture, it was the drug era and parents were looking at their kids who were suddenly coming home with long hair, smoking grass, talking LSD and talking strangely, listening to music that the parents didn't understand. The parents didn't understand who was in their house, how this person came about. This wasn't the child they raised. And in a number of cases fathers actually killed their children, shot their teenage sons who came home stoned and the parents were terrified."[8]

The *It's Alive* films also address ecological concerns of 1970s America. At the beginning of *It's Alive*, Davis listens to another anxious father-to-be talk about his job as an exterminator. The father says that a new breed of cockroaches, resistant to old pesticides, has evolved. In *It Lives Again*, Cohen expands on the implication of the first film that the Davis baby may be a progressive step in human evolution. Davis and his group of radical pro-lifers name the first two mutant babies in their protective custody Adam and Eve, speculating that the children—with their more developed instincts and heightened immune system—are "a way humans can survive the pollution of this planet." The masses, of course, continue to regard the mutant babies as a threat and, eventually, even the crusaders doubt the possibility of a better world in which the mutant babies constitute normalcy. One hopeful father argues, "If you believe in God, they must be here for some reason." Another father, having witnessed the carnage that his son is capable of, responds, "I don't believe in God. Not any more."

During this period, Larry Cohen seems to have had religious doubts of his own that affected the way his characters viewed the changing world and their roles in it. In 1977, Cohen wrote and directed *God Told Me To* (a.k.a. *Demon*), a science-fiction thriller that remains his most ambitious work. *God Told Me To*, like so many of Cohen's films (*Black Caesar, Hell Up in Harlem, Q: The Winged Serpent, Special Effects, Perfect Strangers, Maniac Cop* and *The Ambulance*) is set in New York City. It opens on a busy street in midtown Manhattan on a summer day. Against the already-hectic city landscape, chaos erupts. A man is thrown from his bike by an invisible force. Nearby, another victim collapses rather ungracefully on the sidewalk. It does not take the bystanders long to realize that there is a sniper above them, picking off random targets with incredible accuracy. The sniper claims 12 more victims before an NYPD detective named Peter Nicholas climbs the tower and attempts to talk him down.

Nicholas makes conversation with the shooter, a nervous, wiry young man who introduces himself as Harold Gorman. When Nicholas asks why he is killing people, Gorman responds, "God told me to," and then leaps to his death. On the street below, the shooter's mother argues that her son was perfectly sane. "He was a good student," she says, convinced that her son is the victim of some kind of conspiracy. Before he has a chance to decipher Gorman's cryptic final words, Nicholas is called to another crime scene, where a man invokes the Biblical story of Abraham and Isaac to justify the cold-blooded murder of his wife and children. "God told me to," he explains.

Detective Peter Nicholas (Tony LoBianco) prepares to talk down a sniper in *God Told Me To* (New World, 1978).

While others in the police department dismiss the similarities in the two cases, arguing that there have always been crazies who blame their crimes on God, Nicholas is profoundly affected. He seems to believe in the possibility of a God who speaks to His followers, but he does not understand why God would order people to kill. We learn that, for all of his life, Nicholas has gone to church and confessed his sins every morning; only his estranged wife seems to understand his need for guilt and forgiveness. In one scene, she asks him, "You truly believe, but where is the happiness that it's supposed to bring you?" Unable to answer the question, Peter continues to search for the common link between the murderers. Eventually, he learns that the killers were each seen in the presence of the same man — a hippie with no distinguishing features who goes by the name Bernard Phillips.

The detective tracks down Phillips' mother, who attacks him with a kitchen knife before he can get any answers out of her. After she is killed in a fall, the coroner explains that Bernard Phillips' mother was a virgin. While investigating the apparently supernatural origins of the mystery man, Peter Nicholas begins to investigate his own history, seeking out his mother for the first time in his life. Eventually, he learns that she was abducted by aliens in the 1950s and realizes that, like Bernard Phillips, his father was not human. "All my life I felt so close to God," he says, "and it wasn't Him after all." Soon after he learns the truth, a stranger shows up to take Peter to meet his "brother," who has convinced a group of affluent businessmen that he is the risen Jesus. Cohen explains, "Imagine a creature from another planet born and brought up here, not knowing his origins, realizing that he has supernatural powers enabling him to control people. This alien might soon begin to believe that he is God, particularly in a Christian society like ours where it is preached that God came to Earth in human form with unique powers. When he makes other people accept him as God, he believes this to be the truth. My screenplay isn't so far from being the dark side of the Superman legend."[9] The lasting impact of the film, however, is not in its speculation about aliens, but in its assumption that there are so many individuals willing to commit mass murder in the name of any God that will present itself.

Cohen's 1982 film *Q: The Winged Serpent* speaks to the same concerns, though with a more dismissive cynicism. *Q* begins almost the same way as *God Told Me To*; this time, the everyday hustle and bustle of the New York City streets is disrupted by a shower of red rain. Pedestrians stop and look up to see a winged dinosaur-creature — like something out of a Ray Harryhausen movie — soaring between the skyscrapers. In its jaws is the body of an unfortunate man who was washing windows on of one of the city's tallest buildings. A New York City detective named Shepard opens an investigation and learns, from a group of religious eccentrics, that the monster is Quetzalcoatl, an ancient Aztec god that demands human sacrifices. Shepard casually comments that this isn't "the first time in history that a monster has been mistaken for a god."

The unlikely hero of *Q* is not Shepard, but Jimmy Quinn (played by Cohen's onscreen alter ego, Michael Moriarty), a small time crook who is constantly being muscled by everyone. After a foiled bank robbery in midtown Manhattan, Quinn escapes to the top floor of the Chrysler Building, where he discovers a gigantic egg belonging to the city's new Kong. Quinn decides to exploit his discovery, promising local authorities that he will disclose the location of the monster for a large sum of money. Unfortunately, the city bureaucrats stiff Jimmy and, adding insult to injury, he is taken hostage by members of the religious order that worships Quetzalcoatl, strapped to a table and prepared as a human sacrifice for the flesh-eating prehistoric bird. Under the circumstances, he remains surprisingly calm. When the cult members ask Quinn to pray, he flatly refuses and, since Quetzalcoatl cannot receive sacrifices that have not been "blessed" by prayer, Quinn buys himself enough time to make an escape. In effect, the self-absorbed hero saves his ass (the only thing he has any faith in) by renouncing God. "When I was young," Cohen says, "some kids on the street used to say 'You Jews! You killed Christ.' I'd go home and ask, 'Is that true?' Stupid things like that can affect a child. You begin to think you are a part of a group that killed God. In many of my movies, you have people who are basically Judas characters like those in *God Told Me To* and *Q*."[10] In this film, Judas is the only true survivor.

Cohen's films throughout the 1980s continued to be allegorical, but most were less ambitious than *God Told Me To* or even the *It's Alive* films. *Full Moon High* (1981) is a hilarious send-up of *I Was a Teenage Werewolf* (1957) that transplants the 1950s monster onto the similarly conservative 1980s. At the beginning of the film, a wholesome teen named Tony Walker travels to Romania with his father, a CIA agent (Ed McMahon) who describes the breeding ground of Gothic nightmares as "a country warped by ignorance and fear." While the old man is getting it on with a couple of Romanian hookers ("Let's find out what Communist infiltration is all about"), Tony goes for a walk and is attacked by a werewolf. As he lies bleeding, he contemplates mortality: "Killed by a wolf.... It could happen to anybody over here. It's like getting run over [back in the States]."

Upon his return to the U.S., Tony begins sprouting hair in strange places. After he tries to attack his father, the old man locks himself in a fortified bomb shelter and rants to a framed photograph of Senator Joseph McCarthy: "The Commies turned my son into a werewolf.... I don't know how they did it.... Maybe something in the water. Fluoride! They say fluoride is good for your teeth. Did you get a load of his teeth?!" Tony disappears for several decades before returning home in the 1980s. Not having aged a day in 30-odd years, he passes himself off as his own son and resolves to help his old high school football team win the big game.

After writing and directing two very effective Hitchcockian thrillers, one highlighting the dangers of divorce culture (*Perfect Strangers,* 1984) and one on the power of film to distort reality and personal identity (*Special Effects,* 1984), Cohen made another satirical horror film. *The Stuff* (1985) is Cohen's least subtle statement about the horrors of conformity, and is heavily indebted to *Invasion of the Body Snatchers* (1956) as well as *The Blob* (1958). In the film, America is obsessed with a yogurt-like product called The Stuff. Addicts turn into commercial-savvy zombies, arguing that the manufacturers are "giving us the food that will nourish all and guide us to a new order in life." The only problem: Nobody seems to know where The Stuff is manufactured or what's in it. Michael Moriarty plays a sleazy industrial spy named Moe Rutherford ("Every time people give me something, I always want some mo") who discovers that consumers are not eating The Stuff; it is eating them.

Rutherford calls in Col. Spears, a conservative militant who quickly rounds up his soldiers to kick some Commie ass and keep the world "safe for ice cream." "They're no match for the American boys," Spears says sternly, "We have never lost a war!" (When reproached about Vietnam, he answers, "We lost that war at home.") Spears and company save the mindless consumers from the alien goo by sabotaging the distribution company. At the end of the film, however, The Stuff is being sold on the black market, and is more popular than ever.

Perhaps Cohen's most insightful film of the past two decades was his next, and (to date) last, collaboration with Michael Moriarty. *A Return to Salem's Lot* (1987) is a loose sequel to Stephen King's *Salem's Lot*, but Cohen made the material his own. In King's novel, the citizens of the sleepy New England town of Salem's Lot begin disappearing shortly after an elusive European aristocrat arrives. By the end of the novel, so many of the locals have been turned into vampires that the only thing for the surviving humans to do is run. In Cohen's film, the vampires inhabiting Salem's Lot arrived with the earliest American colonists and the only remaining humans are slaves who protect the town's secret during the daylight hours. The vampire children go to school at night, where they learn a peculiar version of U.S. history. (One wonders why they must continue to go to school, since the vampires have presumably been alive for several centuries.) Asked to name the ship that brought "us" to the New World, one child begins, innocently enough, by talking about the Mayflower. Another student interrupts, "Not the Mayflower. The *other* ship, which everybody thought had sunk." Their teacher shares the history of the *Speedwell* and its passengers: "We thought it best that others should believe we perished at sea.... Far from persecution, far from witch trials, far from crazy mobs trying to drive stakes through our hearts." The vampires of Salem's Lot are proud Americans, but they are also proud of their heritage as "the oldest race in humanity." The see themselves as both a master race and a persecuted race.

Axel, the town Judge, summons an anthropologist named Joe Webber (Moriarty), who spent summers in Salem's Lot as a child, to write about their days in exile. Webber arrives in Salem's Lot with his son, Jeremy, who has spent most of his childhood living with his mother and being forced to constantly act older than he is. Feeling robbed of his own youth, he immediately falls in love with the town, where the children live forever in the magic of the night, oblivious to the "horrors" of the outside world. Webber is not so easily converted. For all of the jokes made about his inhumanity, Joe regards humans—not the vampires—as the real victims. And he is not alone. A feisty Jewish wanderer named Van Meer (played by independent filmmaker Samuel Fuller) arrives in Salem's Lot, and claims to be hunting an escaped Nazi. After his confrontation with Axel, Van Meer flees the town with Joe and Jeremy. On their way to warn the State Police about the danger in Salem's Lot, Jeremy asks, "Who'll believe in vampires?" Van Meer responds, "In 500 years, who'll believe in Nazis?" This is perhaps Cohen's ultimate statement on the horror genre: We must recognize the real monsters in our world, which can appear perfectly normal on the surface, and be careful not to persecute anyone too hastily, though they may appear monstrous on the surface.

Cohen followed up *A Return to Salem's Lot* with *Wicked Stepmother* (1989), a forgettable variation on the television show *Bewitched* that boasted Bette Davis' final performance. He has continued to write stories about crises of identity (including the TV movie *As Good as Dead*) and to criticize American institutions—focusing on the public services sector in the *Maniac Cop* series (1988–92) and *The Ambulance* (1990)—but he has been increasingly less involved in production.

In 1997, Cohen wrote a sarcastic ode to the American military when he turned a Gulf War vet into an undead psycho-killer in *Uncle Sam*. After Sam Harper is killed by friendly fire and fails to return home, his young nephew starts to idolize him. "When I grow up," Jody tells his teacher (a Vietnam draft dodger), "I'm going in the Army, just like Sam did, and I'll do whatever the President says to do, because he knows better." When Sam returns from the dead soon after, the teacher and Jody's mother's beau (a lawyer who cheats the IRS) become the first targets because, as Sam says, "People who don't respect the American way of life deserve to have their butts kicked."

Only a WWII vet named Crowley is able to save Jody from Sam's corrupting influence; he explains that Sam simply liked killing. "Isn't that what makes a hero?" Jody asks. "There are no heroes," Crowley tells him, and goes on to say that the soldiers who fought in the Gulf War died only to keep some Arabs rich. At a 4th of July carnival where the local kids burn flags and mangle "The Star-Spangled Banner" ("Hell, it's a lousy song—nobody can ever remember the words!"), Sam shows up in the guise of Honest Abe. After a few more murders, Jody realizes that the American military and his uncle are both power-hungry monsters, and helps to put his uncle to rest.

Throughout his career, Cohen has continually made films about the duality of the monster; his "horrors" stem from a struggle between individual and society. The problems in his films—homicidal infants, aliens, werewolves, zombies and killer yogurt—may be ridiculous on the surface, but for Cohen they represent dangerous forces at work in America.

Chris Neville, the deranged director in *Special Effects,* speaks for Cohen: "People assume special effects means taking models, miniatures, tricking them up, making them look real. I'm taking reality and making it look like make-believe."

FEATURE FILMS WRITTEN, PRODUCED AND DIRECTED BY COHEN

Bone: A Bad Day in Beverly Hills (1972)
Black Caesar (1973)
Hell Up in Harlem (1973)
It's Alive (1974)
The Private Files of J. Edgar Hoover (1977)
God Told Me To (1977)
It Lives Again (1978)
Full Moon High (1981)
Q: The Winged Serpent (1982)
The Stuff (1985)
It's Alive 3: Island of the Alive (1987)
A Return to Salem's Lot (1987)
Wicked Stepmother (1989)
As Good as Dead (1995)

FEATURE FILMS WRITTEN AND DIRECTED BY COHEN

Original Gangstas (1996)

FEATURE FILMS DIRECTED BY COHEN

Special Effects (1984)
Perfect Strangers (1984)
Deadly Illusion (1987)
The Ambulance (1993)

FEATURE FILMS WRITTEN BY COHEN, DIRECTED BY WILLIAM LUSTIG

Maniac Cop (1988)
Maniac Cop 2 (1990)
Maniac Cop 3: Badge of Silence (1992)
Uncle Sam (1997)

17

David Lynch: American Beauty?

The films of David Lynch offer a vision of American life that is arguably more personal and more challenging than that of any other mainstream filmmaker working today. The director has explored small town life and the open road, Hollywood and the "nowhere part" of America that characterizes film noir, though he has seldom grounded his films in a real time or place. To do so, it seems, would betray the honesty of his creations. "I want to make films that occur in America," he says, "but that take people into worlds where they may never go."[1] Since 1978, he has been doing just that, traveling over the rainbow and into the depths of his own private hell.

Eraserhead, Lynch's first feature film, explores many of the obsessions that have defined his career. The narrative revolves around Henry, a bushy-haired young urbanite with the constant, wide-eyed fear of someone who has been struck by lightning at least twice. (Power surges are not uncommon when Henry is in the room.) He lives in a squalid hotel in a run-down, washed-out neighborhood where the only sign of life is the hypnotic hum of machinery at a local steel mill. Lynch says that this sterile environment reflects his post-college years in Philadelphia.[2] Having grown up in the rural Northwest, he was unsettled by the atmosphere of the city: "In a large city, I realized there was a large amount of fear, because so many people were living close together. You could feel it in the air. I think people in the city obviously get used to it, but to come into it from the Northwest it kind of hits you like a train."[3] The contrast between urban and rural environments would appear in films through the director's career — most notably, in *Dune* (1984), *Blue Velvet* (1986) and *Twin Peaks* (1990) — and it hinted at yet another obsession explored in *Eraserhead*.

Lynch, like fellow director David Cronenberg, is intrigued with the comparison of the mechanical and the organic. His camera gazes lovingly at factories and smokestacks (just as Cronenberg gazes lovingly at flesh); the industrial sounds throughout his first film are almost ethereal; and Henry finds his greatest solace in the hiss of an old radiator. By contrast, biological functions — a litter of pups feeding, or Henry's attempt to have sex with a neighbor — are the subjects of crude, revolting scenes that rival the worst moments in Roman Polanski's *Repulsion* (1965), a disturbing exploration of "a virgin's worst nightmares." Lynch explains his fascination: "Human beings are like little factories, and all these fluids, and timings and changes, and all these chemicals somehow capturing life, and coming out and splitting off and turning into another thing ... it's unbelievable."[4] Henry is equally awe struck, but more than a little terrified. He desires the purity of mass production, not the messiness of human reproduction.

The opening sequence of *Eraserhead* revolves around a celestial birth. Henry watches with horror as a man with some kind of skin disease pulls a lever and jettisons an umbilical cord into a cesspool. The undefined organic matter travels down what appears to be a birth canal, toward a white light, and the horror begins. Henry is called to his girlfriend's house for dinner and he goes, reluctantly, to meet her parents. Mary's father, with a sloppy grin, serves miniature chickens for dinner. "Man-made," he tells Henry, gleefully. As Henry attempts to cut into one, the drumsticks begin to thrust obscenely and, as the food oozes blood onto his plate, Mary's father suffers an epileptic seizure — performing demonic cunnilingus like Linda Blair in *The Exorcist* (1973). By now, we instinctively understand that Mary is pregnant, and are not surprised when her mother angrily barks at Henry, "There's a baby." The shock comes when Mary adds, "They're still not sure it *is* a baby."

Henry and Mary try, for one night, to live together like a normal couple, but the crying mutant "baby" drives her away, leaving Henry alone with his hideous offspring. (To this day, Lynch refuses to say exactly what the baby was made from, though some fans have speculated that the director turned the undeveloped fetus of a farm animal into a hand puppet.) Desperate to escape, Henry pays a conjugal visit to a female neighbor and appears to drown in a bed filled with a milky white substance. Later, he derives some kind of momentary peace from a daydream of a musical lady in his radiator, who gleefully squishes sperm-like creatures that rain down on her miniature stage. "In Heaven, everything is fine," she reassures him, but soon even his dreams of her become nightmarish. The Lady in the Radiator turns into the Man in the Planet, the God-figure from the beginning of the film, who appears to have the same skin disease that Henry's baby has. Henry finally decides to end the baby's — and, by extension, his own — suffering. The final images in the film are the Man in the Planet hopelessly trying to re-set a huge piece of machinery, as it throws off sparks, and Henry embracing the Lady in Heaven. The music swells in a finale that might be compared to the end of *2001: A Space Odyssey* (1968), wherein a celestial newborn manifests hope for the future of mankind.

Henry's hope for the future is a very different kind. The "birth" at the beginning of the film is the opposite of an apotheosis; the baby's murder

The Man in the Planet (Jack Fisk), from the opening sequence of *Eraserhead* (AFI, 1977).

at the end of the film appears to be liberating. The God-figure's actions are, for lack of a better word, mechanical — it is Henry who takes control, acting out of desperation and madness. His actions, as contemptible as they might be, provide him with an escape from a life that is tedious, lonely, nonsensical and nauseating — a Kafkaesque nightmare. Lynch does not directly address questions of morality and metaphysics, but conveys a sense that Henry is in a better place after committing the murder. To the existentialist, this may be viewed as an optimistic ending; Henry has simply asserted control over the chaos of his life. Lynch himself seems somewhat hopeful when he muses on the possibility of eventual escape from that cold, insane reality, resigning his hope to the idea that "this world is maybe not the brightest place one could be."[5]

Though some were quietly baffled, many filmmakers proclaimed *Eraserhead* a work of genius. Lynch was offered a wide variety of projects, including such unlikely material as *Fast Times at Ridgemont High* (1982), *Return of the Jedi* (1983) and *Beverly Hills Cop* (1984). It was comedian Mel Brooks who led Lynch to his next project, *The Elephant Man* (1980), which tells the true story of John Merrick. Born around the turn of the century with a severe facial deformity, Merrick was treated like a carnival sideshow freak until he met a doctor who vowed to improve his quality of life. The film, set in London during the Industrial Revolution, allowed Lynch to indulge his obsession with a world where bodies and machines collide haphazardly. Merrick intrigued Lynch as an illustration of this: "Pictures of explosions — big explosions — they always reminded me of those papillomatous growths on John Merrick's body. They were like slow explosions. And they started erupting from the bone."[6] The real-life story also provided him with a character, unlike Henry, whose search for understanding amid cruelty and chaos leads not to violence, but to love. At the end of the film, Merrick explains that "people are frightened by what they don't understand." Realizing this, he is able to accept the way that he has been treated, and to die happily. Most of Lynch's subsequent films have embraced a similar philosophy — that it is possible to find peace in a world that can be cruel and chaotic. In fact, this may be an apt expression of the director's perception of life in America.

The Elephant Man was a major critical success and Lynch was nominated for the Best Director Academy Award in 1981, which put him in a position of authority to choose his next project. He decided to direct a big-budget adaptation of Frank Herbert's sci-fi novel *Dune* for producer Dino DeLaurentiis. Despite lofty ambitions, the film was a failure in many respects, and Lynch learned that such large-scale, studio projects would not allow him the intimacy he needed with his material. It did, however, introduce Lynch to Kyle McLachlan, the actor who would quickly become the director's onscreen alter ego.

In *Dune*, McLachlan stars as a messianic prince who is destined to save his people in a time of war. Believing that McLachlan effectively conveyed both the naiveté of a child and the promise of a great leader, Lynch later cast McLachlan as Jeffrey Beaumont — an all–American teenager on the cusp of manhood — in *Blue Velvet*. At the beginning of the film, Jeffrey is innocent and curious. When he finds a severed human ear in a field near his home, he becomes curious and begins unraveling a perverse murder mystery that opens his eyes to a dark, twisted reality.

Blue Velvet begins on "a sunny, woodsy day" in Lumberton, USA, a sleepy town in which the spirit of the 1950s has been magically preserved. For Lynch, the decade of his childhood epitomizes the American Dream. Waxing nostalgic, he says, "There were a lot of advertisements in magazines where you see a well-dressed woman bringing a pie out of an oven, and a certain smile on her face, or a couple smiling, walking together up to their house, with a picket fence. Those smiles were pretty much all I saw." At the same time, he acknowledges that those perfect smiles were "strange smiles. They're the smiles of the way the world should be or could be."[7] *Blue Velvet* is a neo-noir for the Reagan era, peeling back the façade of normalcy that hides the cynicism of the 1970s just as Eisenhower's golden era stifled a climate of postwar malaise; it effectively shatters the picture-perfect vision of small-town Americana within the first few minutes of screen time.

After finding the severed ear, Jeffrey follows clues to an apartment on the wrong side of the tracks in Lumberton. With the help of his neighbor Sandy, he breaks into the apartment of a troubled lounge performer named Dorothy, whose husband has been kidnapped by an obsessive fan. When Dorothy finds Jeffrey hiding in her closet, she forces him to strip, at knifepoint, then seduces him and begs him to hurt her. Immediately, Jeffrey is drawn into Dorothy's tantalizing world of sex and violence. Lynch associates the character's awakening with his own coming of age, and describes both with awe: "I could see a world opening — this sexual dream. It was another great indication that life was really great and worth living. And it kept on going, because I see that the vast realm of sex has all these different levels, from lust and fearful, violent sex to the real spiritual thing at the other end. It's the key to some fantastic mystery of life."[8] Jeffrey is not repelled by the threat of violence that follows; rather, he embraces it, lamenting his loss of innocence with wide-eyed wonder: "It's a strange world." Lynch says, "This is the way America is to me. There's a very innocent, naïve quality to life, and there's a horror and a sickness as well. It's everything. *Blue Velvet* is a very American movie."[9]

The film was another critical hit for David Lynch, and he used the momentum to orchestrate a very unlikely new project — a pilot for a television series co-created with *Hills Street Blues* producer Mark Frost. *Twin Peaks* takes place in a woebegone lumber mill town in the Northwest. The images in the opening credits are of smokestacks and a circular saw throwing sparks. Instead of the sounds of industry, however, we hear a sad, ominous composition by Angelo Badalamenti. An equally brooding piece plays over the first scene, which provides the catalyst for the series: A man goes fishing and finds a the body of a young woman, wrapped in plastic. The local sheriff recognizes her as Laura Palmer, a local high school student. Through the course of the pilot, we're introduced to a number of eccentric characters, including Dale Cooper, an FBI agent who is assigned to investigate the murder. Kyle McLachlan brings the boyish curiosity of

Jeffrey Beaumont to the role of Cooper, adding an element of other-worldly wisdom. Cooper believes that Laura's death is the work of a highly unusual serial killer.

As the first season of the television series progressed, the investigators got closer to identifying the killer, but the episodes focused just as much on building the mystique of the dead girl. They learn that the picture-perfect prom queen of Twin Peaks was a habitual drug user and a prostitute, exploited by at least one of the community's leaders. Cooper's job becomes more than a simple murder investigation — he has to look beneath the surface and learn the secrets of the entire town, in order to find the killer. Along the way, he encounters a full bag of Lynchian absurdities — a one-armed schizophrenic, a one-eyed amnesiac, a uniformed giant who speaks in riddles, a uniformed dwarf who speaks backwards and a "Log Lady." Through it all, Cooper remains fascinated by the mystery (and the simple pleasures of the local diner), even after being shot. "It's not so bad," he says, "if you can keep the fear from your mind. I guess you can say that about anything in life."

After initiating the series, Lynch began work on another feature, *Wild at Heart* (1990), based on a novel by Barry Gifford. The film is, in the director's words, "a picture about finding love in Hell."[10] As with *Blue Velvet*, Lynch is searching for some kind of spiritual stronghold in a country that seems to be dangerously out of control. At the heart of the film are Sailor and Lula, two young lovers separated by violence. Sailor is a rebel, born under a bad sign without much "parental guidance"; he wears a snake-skin jacket as a "symbol of individuality" and "belief in personal freedom." Lula is equally tormented by her upbringing — by the murder of her father, the domineering presence of her mother and a childhood rape.

When Sailor is convicted on murder charges and sent away to prison, Lula retreats into a fantasy world inspired by *The Wizard of Oz* (1939). At times when reality becomes too much to bear, she clicks her heels together hopefully and dreams of a place better than home. After Sailor's release, the lovers set out for California, which is — in Lula's mind — the closest thing to the Emerald City. For these characters, the only way to survive is to escape from reality. Lynch's film proposes that this may be the only way to remain sane in an increasingly insane world. "We're kind of getting used to the world being crazy," Lynch said in a 1999 interview, "but I swear to you, in 1988 or '89 or whenever it was I first read the book [Barry Gifford's *Wild At Heart*], it wasn't so much like that."[11] Dazed by reports of violence in her own life and across the nation, Lula sums up: "It's just shocking sometimes," she says, "when things aren't the way you thought they were." She begins to question whether or not it is worth living in a world that is so "wild at heart and weird on top, it's just shit." Sailor blindly promises, "I ain't gonna let things get no worse."

Soon after, the lovers break down on the yellow brick road and Sailor is tricked into participating in a bloody bank robbery, which lands him back in jail. After he is released for the second time, he convinces himself that he does not belong in a sane world, a functional family or a loving relationship. He turns his back on Lula and their son, only to be rescued in a daydream by the Good Witch of the North, who explains, "If you're truly wild at heart, you'll fight for your dreams. Don't turn away from love." Sailor runs back to Lula, his faith restored. With this scene, Lynch suggests that our saving grace may be our denial of reality, our faith in something that makes more sense than logic. Dorothy's remarks to her family at the end of *The Wizard of Oz* sum up Lynch's America: "Some of it wasn't very nice, but most of it was beautiful."

If *Wild at Heart* is "a picture about finding love in Hell," his next film might be labeled "a picture about not finding love in Hell." Audiences reacted angrily to *Twin Peaks: Fire Walk with Me* (1992) because it had none of the levity of the television show. The film, a prequel to the series, details the last days of Laura Palmer, a slightly schizophrenic teenager victimized by her family, her friends and herself. In the ongoing series, Lynch presented Laura to audiences through the fond memories of her friends, family and an entire community. *Fire Walk with Me* revolves instead around a self-destructive and self-loathing young woman who is doomed from the beginning. To audiences, this may have seemed unmerciful; there is no reassurance in Laura's nightmarish descent into a private hell.

Lynch's next film, *Lost Highway* (1997), is more complex. It is the director's dark night of the soul, the Limbo of his Divine Comedy. It begins, simply enough, with a murder mystery. A jazz composer named Fred Madison receives a visitor at his Los Angeles home. The unseen visitor leaves a voice message that Dick Lurant is dead. This prompts us, like Fred Madison, to wonder, "Who is Dick Lurant, and why and how did he die?" The following day, Fred receives another cryptic message — a videotape left on his front doorstep. He suspiciously asks his wife Renee if she knows anything about it, but she claims ignorance. When Fred plays the tape, he sees only a few seconds of footage, shot during the night in front of their house. Renee nervously dismisses it as the work of a real estate agent. The following day, a second videotape is left on the doorstep. This time, the footage was filmed inside their bedroom while they slept. Fred contacts the police, explaining that the strange occurrences are particularly unnerving to him because he does not like recordings. "I like to remember things my own way," he explains, "Not necessarily the way they happened."

That night, Fred and Renee go to a party thrown by Renee's friend Andy, and Fred meets a bald, pasty-faced Mystery Man who says, "We've met before." Fred tells him that he is mistaken, then asks, "Where was it you think we met?" The stranger responds, "At your house. Don't you remember?" Wide-eyed, he adds, "As a matter of fact, I'm there right now." Fred tries to escape the nonsensical conversation, but the stranger thrusts a cell phone at him and insists, "Call me." When Fred calls home, he hears the Mystery Man's voice on the other end of the line. Fred and Renee promptly leave the party.

Back at home, Fred finds yet another videotape. On this one, he sees himself standing over the bloody corpse of his wife. Moments later, he is being interrogated by homicide detectives. For the duration of the film, the audience must try desperately to play catch-up. The initial questions are the simplest: Is Renee really dead? Or has she set him up somehow? Is someone trying to make him look crazy? Or has Fred Madison really gone crazy? So far, it is a fairly typical example of film noir. It is clear that Fred does not trust his beautiful wife, perhaps simply because she is beautiful and not very affectionate. He has in fact confessed that, in his dreams (and, in this film, who's to say where they end and reality begins?), she only *looks* like the woman he married. Renee is the type of femme fatale that an obsessive man would kill for. Questions remain: Who are the murderers and who are the victims?

In classic films noir, trust always proved unwise and hope unrealistic. At best, the characters were set adrift in a world without providence. At worst, they were the helpless targets of cruel Fates. In David Lynch's variation on *Night and the City* (1950), the death of the main character is just the beginning of an exploration of greater mysteries of the universe. When Fred Madison wakes up in a jail cell, he is a completely different person — a teenager, bruised and battered, suffering from amnesia. The cops identify him as Peter Raymond Dayton, a mechanic with a history of auto theft convictions. Lynch does not explain the mystery of Fred Madison's transformation into Peter Raymond Dayton. (Blame it on reincarnation, UFO abduction, expensive plastic surgery...) What intrigues Lynch are the inexplicable parallels between the two men's lives. Pete works for a porn producer named Mr. Eddie, who the local cops identify as Lurant. Mr. Eddie introduces Pete to a tantalizing blonde named Alice, who looks exactly like Renee Madison. Pete, Mr. Eddie and Alice end up at a party thrown by Renee's friend Andy, and cross paths with the same bald, pasty-faced Mystery Man who spoke to Fred Madison. The Mystery Man tells Pete that "in the Far East, when a person is sentenced to death, they're sent to a place where they can't escape, never knowing when an executioner may step up behind them and fire a bullet in the back of their head."

After that, Pete learns what it means to live in fear. Alice manipulates him into helping her steal Andy's money so that they can run away together. After the murder, he follows Alice to a house in the desert, unsure of whether he can trust her. Moments before their arrival, we see the house implode — a reversal of the final apocalyptic scene in Robert Aldrich's seminal film noir *Kiss Me Deadly* (1955). Outside the house, Renee begins to seduce him and, at the moment when his desire reaches fever-pitch, she says, "You'll never have me," and disappears inside. In that moment, Pete becomes Fred again.

Inside the house, he finds the Mystery Man, who explains, "Her name is Renee. If she told you her name is Alice, she's lying." In a fit of rage, Fred leaves the house and tracks Mr. Eddie ("Lurant") and Renee to the Lost Highway Motel, where he kills them both. Afterwards, he visits his own home and leaves a voice message ("Dick Lurant is dead.") before driving into the desert, pursued by dozens of cop cars. Like the murderer in *Detour* (1945), who blames fate for his misfortunes, Fred Madison can apparently blame his "other self," just as Laura Palmer's murderer could. Both men are unable to accept responsibility or to take control of their lives, and so are left to wander the open highway, followed by personal demons. In Lynch's strange Limbo where time and identity have no relevance, Fred Madison's actions at the end of the film reset the stage for everything that has happened, bringing him full circle, and dooming him to repeat his nightmare.

Mulholland Drive (2001), which finds Lynch back in the realm of neo-noir, is a more than worthy successor to *Lost Highway*. It begins with a stretch limo cruising the Hollywood hills. On Sunset Boulevard, the limo driver pulls a gun on the dark-haired woman in the back and orders her to get out. As she is doing so, a car comes over the ridge from the opposite direction and collides with the limo, killing everyone except the dark-haired woman, who staggers toward the lights of Los Angeles, unable to remember who she is or how she got there.

The following morning, Betty, a naïve young woman from Ontario who dreams of becoming a star, arrives in L.A. and finds the dark-haired woman — who adopts the name Rita — in her new apartment. Betty is intrigued by Rita's mystery, and the contents of her purse: several thousand dollars in cash, and a blue key. When Rita suddenly remembers a name from her past, the two women set out to learn her identity. Instead, they discover the weeks-old corpse of someone named Diane Selwyn. As the mystery becomes more complex, they begin to fall in love.

In what seems to be a digression, the film follows a troubling week in the life of a precocious Hollywood director named Adam, who finds his wife cheating on him and is kicked off of his latest film for refusing to hire an actress named Camilla Rhodes.

As the mystery unravels, in cryptic David Lynch style, Betty and Rita find a box that fits the blue key. Inside the box, they find an alternate reality, where Rita is a bitchy actress named Camilla Rhodes and Betty is Diane Selwyn, Camilla's jilted lover. When Camilla announces her engagement to a precocious Hollywood director named Adam, Betty / Diane makes arrangements to have her killed. After the hit fails, Betty / Diane kills herself. Lynch has created another imperfect circle, where the end is the beginning and the path between them is inexplicable. His is a world of dream logic, but what resonates above the chaos in *Mulholland Drive* is the love of the two women for each other. The final image in the film is of Betty and Rita, enveloped in a shower of light, similar to the final image in *Eraserhead*. If we follow Lynch's dream logic, Camilla has escaped the murder attempt on Sunset Boulevard only to become Rita. Diane Selwyn has died only to be reborn as Betty, with renewed opportunities for success as an actress, and for love.

In Lynch's film-reality, the vicious circle of *Lost Highway*'s Limbo is broken in *Mulholland Drive* when Betty and Rita visit a Hollywood club called Silencio. In the club, they observe a minimalist performance in which a Spanish vocalist begins a soulful song, only to collapse halfway through. Her voice continues on a pre-recorded tape even as her body is carried off the stage. The moment has a profound effect on Betty and Rita, who seem to realize that the same thing has happened to them. Their lives, and the film up to this point, have been a dream — incorporating random fragments (some good and some bad) of a previous life, and perfecting the love that ended it. In *Mulholland Drive,* Lynch makes the City of Angels seem a little bit like Heaven.

The progression from *Eraserhead* to *Mulholland Drive* illustrates one man's evolution of ideas, reflecting a highly personal view of American culture as well as the world at large. The films mirror the dark side of the American Dream, just as surely as they reflect the wild-at-heart energy of the dreamers who make it beautiful. For Lynch, the two aspects are co-dependent, at least in this life. "Being in darkness and confusion is interesting to me," he says, "but behind it you can rise out of that and see things the way they really are. That there is some sort of truth to the whole thing, if you could just get to that point where you could see it, and live it, and feel it ... I think it's a long, long way off. In the meantime, there's suffering and darkness and confusion and absurdities, and it's people kind of going in circles. It's fantastic. It's like a strange carnival: it's a lot of fun, but it's a lot of pain."[12]

FEATURE FILMS WRITTEN & DIRECTED BY LYNCH

Eraserhead (1977)
The Elephant Man (1980) written with Christopher de Vore and Eric Bergren
Dune (1984) based on a novel by Frank Herbert
Blue Velvet (1986)
Twin Peaks: The Pilot (1990) written with Mark Frost
Wild at Heart (1990) based on a novel by Barry Gifford
Twin Peaks: Fire Walk With Me (1992) written with Robert Engels
Lost Highway (1997) written with Barry Gifford
Mulholland Drive (2001)

18

Wes Craven: The New Myths

For over three decades, Wes Craven has been a trend setter among horror filmmakers. In the 1970s, he broke the Hollywood taboos on sex and violence with *The Last House on the Left* (1972) and *The Hills Have Eyes* (1977), and helped to usher in the modern era. In the 1980s, he created one of the silver screen's most recognizable icons, Freddy Krueger — a character so charismatic that neither the director, the actor in the role (Robert Englund) nor the genre itself have been able to escape his shadow. In the 1990s, Craven revitalized the genre with *Scream* (1996), a postmodern homage to many of the films that have defined the past two decades of horror. Through his approach to the genre has changed over the years, the director has continually focused his films on conflicts within the family — in particular, on children whose worlds are full of grim fairy tales. "To me," Craven says, "the most poignant and powerful area of our memory is childhood, and that almost exclusively takes place in regular, residential houses. In fact, for the first five years of our lives, we don't get away very much from the house and the yard at all. That's where you encounter most of the really primal events of your experience, and that's why you're afraid of the attic, the basement, the dark, and everything else."[1]

Craven's filmmaking career began with a rape-revenge screenplay entitled *Night of Vengeance*, an exploitative version of Ingmar Bergman's *The Virgin Spring* (1960), which was itself based on a Norwegian folk tale about a father who avenges the rape and murder of his daughter. He teamed up with producer Sean S. Cunningham, who re-titled the script *Sex Crime of the Century* and later *The Last House on the Left*, to make a film that would shock horror film audiences with its unflinching depiction of realistic violence. The film begins with a disclaimer that "the events you are about to witness are true," but left most audiences clinging to the promotional tag line — "Keep telling yourself: It's only a movie!" Though the plot was modeled on a centuries-old folk tale, *Last House on the Left* was more like a true crime documentary.

Five years earlier, Richard Brooks had brought the true crime genre to the silver screen with his adaptation of Truman Capote's novel *In Cold Blood*. The film drew praise for the same reason that *Last House on the Left* drew harsh criticism; there was no moral center. *In Cold Blood* did not pass judgment on the criminals; it simply recounted the facts in the real-life case of Dick Hickox and Perry Smith, two aimless criminals who murdered a family in the Midwest. The crime, it seems, was committed mostly on a whim, and the film resonated a warning that — in a world where this type of criminal exists — "if this can happen to a decent God-fearing family, nobody's safe anymore."

Craven's film might easily be interpreted as a warning, but most critics interpreted it as exploitation. The director insists that, for him, it was something like a personal protest document: "I found that I was writing about things that I had very strong feelings about. I was drawing on things from very early in my own childhood, things that I was feeling about the war, and they were pouring into this very simple B-movie plot."[2] *The Virgin Spring*, *In Cold Blood* and *Last House on the Left* are all, on some level, tales of revenge. After the father takes his revenge in *The Virgin Spring*, he asks God for forgiveness; after the state executes the two murderers in *In Cold Blood*, the narrator assures us that justice has been served. In comparison, no words follow the bloody chainsaw murder in *Last House*. We are left with the confused, dissatisfied and disoriented faces of the avenging parents. We are left with only a sense of loss.

Last House marked the end of innocence for a generation, and for the director himself, whose experiences at college were eye-opening. He was raised in a sternly religious family where "a great amount of time, energy and study was spent on things other than the physical or material reality of this world."[3] Craven admits that "in many ways a religious upbringing ... can weigh heavily on your wild years. Because it tells you no, you can't do anything. So when you break free, you really break free."[4] Making *Last House*, he says, was "almost like doing a pornographic film if you'd been a fundamentalist."[5]

It was followed by *The Hills Have Eyes*, another independent film that merged legend and exploitative violence. The story, Craven says, "resulted from a week I spent at the Forensics Department of the New York Public

Library, where I discovered an account of a savage family that lived in England in the seventeenth century.... There was a district between London and Scotland that was considered haunted because travelers kept disappearing, over several generations. Nobody could figure out exactly what was happening until a husband and wife on horseback were attacked by what the husband later described as a half-naked group of savages. His wife was dragged off her horse and killed, and the man barely managed to escape with his life."[6] In *Hills,* the younger generation of a vacationing family survives this type of attack by becoming equally savage.

Last House on the Left and *The Hills Have Eyes* laid the groundwork for Craven's future films, which would also focus on threats to the nuclear family. His next project was a television movie called *Summer of Fear* (1978), which starred Linda Blair as a teenager whose world is turned upside down by the arrival of Julia, her orphaned cousin. Julia steals Rachel's "solid fellar," kills her horse, curses her with boils on prom night, and turns her parents against her before Rachel finally proves that her cousin is a witch. The film brought Craven to the attention of Hollywood executives and, in 1981, he was hired to direct his first studio film, *Deadly Blessing*.

The film, about a series of gruesome murders in a Pennsylvania Hittite community, allowed Craven to address anxieties about his own religious upbringing. It begins with black-and-white stills of "a simple farm community, untouched by time," where the Hittites have "been protected for generations" from evil. Their lifestyle is jeopardized when one of the Hittite men marries a woman from the outside world (they call her the Incubus), and mysteriously dies soon after. The widow, Martha, believes that he was killed by members of his former "family," who disapproved of the marriage, and she fears that she might be next. Martha invites two attractive female friends to stay with her, but their presence only stirs up the Hittites even more — encouraging several of the men to stray from the simpler pleasures of farming life. In the film's most genuinely unsettling scene, the community Elder canes a young boy for spying on the women. After more murders, Martha learns that the killer is not a member of the Hittite community, but a hermaphroditic local who wants to destroy them. Her death seems to resolve the mystery.

"It was an interesting notion," Craven says, "to first of all look at the hypocrisy of the religion and then at the very end to say that it wasn't them [that were evil] either."[7] Despite his personal interest in the subject, the director correctly guessed that the film "would live or die on its images rather than rely on great storytelling coherence"[8] and decided to add an unexpected twist to the end of the film. In the final scene, a surly demon rips through the floorboards of Martha's living room and pulls her down into Hell, proving that the Hittites were right about the Incubus. This surreal finale and two dream sequences in the film were stylistic precursors to Craven's future projects, which would be more imaginative and more focused on the supernatural.

Over the next few years, the director remained busy. He wrote and directed a feature-length adaptation of DC Comics' *Swamp Thing*, crafted a sequel to *The Hills Have Eyes* and returned to the small screen to direct *Invitation to Hell* (1984). *Invitation* begins when Matt Winslow, a die-hard nonconformist, accepts a job working for Corporate America. His wife Patricia, awed by their upward mobility, comments that "the days of out-of-tune pianos and beat-up furniture are over." She and their two kids are even more impressed by an invitation to join the exclusive Steaming Springs country club — little suspecting that the price of membership is eternal damnation. Luckily, Matt maintains his independence, and refuses to "sell out"— despite the protests of his increasingly hostile wife and two children who would give The Exorcist a run for his money. Eventually, Matt must use his latest invention — a flame retardant space suit — to rescue his family from the depths of Hell.

In 1984, Craven also wrote a screen adaptation of V.C. Andrews's bestseller *Flowers in the Attic*. The novel revolves around four children whose idyllic lives are shattered when their father dies, and their mother abandons them to the care of a hateful grandmother who promises to give food and shelter, but never kindness. For months, the children are locked away in an attic and slowly poisoned. For Craven, the story was particularly unsettling: "There's something about innocent children being held captive and abused by people they are supposed to look up to and trust that touches a very large and unpleasant nerve. The idea of parents as monsters represents an almost quintessential evil in people."[9] Like Craven's earlier films, *Flowers in the Attic* exhibited a fairy tale quality —"Hansel and Gretel on a big scale."[10] Despite his passion for adapting the project, however, Craven's screenplay was not used for the film version, released two years later. As he continued to wander into the realm of myth and fantasy, Craven was primed for his watershed project.

The inspiration for *A Nightmare on Elm Street* (1984) came from a series of articles in *The L.A. Times*. "Over a period of about a year and a half," the director says, "there were incidents of people having severe nightmares, telling their families about them, about how these dreams were worse than anything they'd ever had before. All of them had a similar reaction — they didn't want to sleep again. They were afraid of going back to the dreams. They tried, one way or another, to stay awake. The next time these people fell asleep, they died."[11] Based on the idea of potentially fatal nightmares, Craven began to build his most indelible modern myth.

A Nightmare on Elm Street begins with a dream in which a teenage girl wanders through a labyrinthine boiler room, knowing instinctively that she is being stalked, but seeing and hearing only a frightened lamb. The imagery is powerfully evocative; the dreamer and the audience anticipate a slaughter. Tina escapes the dream, but finds a series of unexplainable slashes in her nightgown. At school the next day, she tells her friend Nancy about the nightmare, suggesting that "maybe we're about to have a big earthquake. They say things get really weird just before."

That night, Tina invites her friend Nancy and Rod, her boyfriend, to stay at her house. Her parents, like Nancy's, are divorced, so she relies on friends for support. Once Tina falls asleep, however, she faces the boogeyman alone. He confronts Tina in a dream, extending long, inhuman arms, as if to embrace her. When she tries to escape, she finds that the boogeyman is everywhere at once, and the damage he inflicts with a razor-tipped glove is fatal in the waking world. Tina's boyfriend, Rod, watches her thrashing in the bed, as deep lacerations appear on her body, but he is unable to see the killer.

The next day, none of the adults are willing to believe Rod's story, and he is charged with Tina's murder. Soon after, Nancy falls asleep in her high school English class and begins to dream of her dead friend, who leads her down into the school's boiler room. There, she is confronted by Tina's nightmare man. Terrified, Nancy screams, "It's only a dream," but she soon realizes that she is wrong, and saves herself by thrusting her arm against a scalding pipe. The pain brings her back to reality, where she notices a very real burn scar on her arm and realizes that Rod was telling the truth. After Rod is found hanged in his prison cell, Nancy tries to warn her parents that she will be next, but they dismiss her fears as stress-induced hallucinations.

Finally, she accepts the fact that the battle is one she must fight alone; only she believes in the boogeyman, so only she can fight him. In her next dream, Nancy tests the boundaries of the dream reality and escapes with the killer's hat, which helps to identify him as Fred Krueger. Confronted with the name, Nancy's mother confesses that Krueger was a child murderer who was killed years earlier by a local lynch mob, but she continues to deny the real danger of Nancy's dreams. Nancy then prepares for an all-out war, setting up booby traps inside her house with the intention of bringing

Freddy into the real world where, she hopes, he can die like anyone else. Her plan works, up to a point. Craven says that his original script ended when Nancy turns her back on Freddy, effectively stripping him of his power: "He leaps for her and he goes screaming off into nothingness. The kids drive off into the fog and you never know if the whole thing is a dream or not."[12] The filmed version sets the stage for an imminent sequel.

Freddy would continue to dominate impressionable teens—acting the part of a maniacal father figure—over the course of 7 (to date) sequels. According to Craven, much of this "father figure" subtext was part of his original concept of the monster: "I just felt that Freddy was the paradigm of the threatening adult. Freddy stood for the savage side of male adulthood. He was the ultimate bad father. It's a sickness where youth is hated. Childhood and innocence are hated. From the very beginning that's how I saw him."[13] This idea carried over to Craven's next theatrical feature. *Deadly Friend* drew some of its inspiration from a failed attempt to update Mary Shelley's *Frankenstein* for producer Roger Corman. "It was a futuristic horror story," Craven says, "a new version of the myth updated to the twenty-first century. It was a very bizarre examination of the barriers between organic life and machine life, about the frontiers of human evolutionary barriers."[14] Corman eventually used another writer and directed the film himself, while Craven transplanted the Frankenstein myth onto suburbia.

Deadly Friend (1986) involves a teenage whiz kid named Paul, who moves to California with his mother and Beebee, a super-intelligent robot that he designed himself. Soon after moving in, Paul becomes infatuated with Samantha, the girl next door, and is devastated when she is accidentally killed by her alcoholic father. Paul sneaks into the morgue and implants Beebee's computer chip brain into Samantha's body. The result: Samantha returns from the dead with superhuman strength and a very icy disposition. Her first order of business is to burn her father alive. Unfortunately, as Craven points out, this eliminates "the one person you're afraid of in the movie," leaving it nowhere to go.[15] From that point on, the film and its heroine lose momentum.

After *Deadly Friend*, Craven returned to familiar territory for Freddy Krueger's third outing. *A Nightmare on Elm Street 3: Dream Warriors* (1987) re-introduces Nancy Thompson, Freddy's arch-nemesis. Five years after her first battle with the boogeyman, Nancy is working with troubled teens at a Springwood psychiatric hospital. Though they have been labeled as anti-social suicide cases by parents and other authority figures, she understands what the kids are up against. "That was one of the points of the film," Craven says. "We were aware of teenage suicide and the notion was to show that it's not just some drug or something that's making them do it, it's a real perception of evil. A real teenager committing suicide doesn't want to do it, he wants somebody to know what's going on inside of him, so he can be understood and not just seen as sick."[16]

After Nancy gains their trust, she begins to teach the kids how to battle the nightmare man. According to the film's mythology, in the dream world, each person has a gift that they can use to combat Freddy — Taryn is an adept street fighter, Will is a powerful wizard, Kincaid has superhuman strength. Eventually, the dream warriors learn as much about Freddy as he knows about them, and they are able to turn the tables on him. Subsequent films in the *Nightmare* series used the ideas in *Nightmare 3* as a jumping-off point. Alice, the heroine of the fourth and fifth outings, is able to channel the dream powers of each of her victimized friends in order to wage war on Freddy, who harnesses his power from the souls of the same kids.

Craven's next film expanded on some of the ideas about dreams and reality that were explored in *A Nightmare on Elm Street*. In *The Serpent and the Rainbow* (1988), Dr. Dennis Alan travels to Haiti to study the botanical secrets of voodoo. While there, he encounters Captain Peytrard, a spiritual medium who — like Freddy — is able to control people through their dreams. "I can be there every time you close your eyes," he promises. Dr. Alan soon learns the truth of this threat, and his life becomes a waking nightmare. Horace Pinker, the mass murderer in *Shocker* (1989), has a similar ability to control his victims. Pinker possesses people's bodies through touch, his essence traveling from place to place via electrical impulses. Pinker is, to quote David Cronenberg, "the new flesh." After these films failed to re-capture the magic of *A Nightmare on Elm Street*, Craven re-focused on the family.

The inspiration for his next feature came from a news article about "a house that was burglarized in a very nice neighborhood. When the police went to investigate, they discovered that the parents were away at work. Still, they heard sounds and went in with guns drawn, and discovered at the back of the house two or three rooms that had been sealed off and were inhabited by teenage children who had never been outside!"[17] *The People Under the Stairs* (1991) follows Fool, a poor black kid from the L.A. ghetto. When a rich white landlord threatens to evict his family, Fool goes with a couple of thieves to the landlord's house, intent on robbing it. Getting in proves relatively easy, but they soon learn that even the flies can't get out.

The inhabitants of the house are a somewhat unusual family. Mother likes to bake. Father likes to dress up in a full-body leather suit and march around the house with a shotgun. They have a brow-beaten daughter named Alice, who has been well-trained not to see, hear or speak any evil. There are also, Fool learns, *other* children. When it appears that she's cleaned her dinner plate a little too well, Mother reprimands Alice for "feeding that thing between the walls again." As Father prepares to beat her ("Just remember not to bruise her face"), Fool pulls her into an elaborate maze behind the walls. He calmly assesses the situation: "You're father's one sick mother. Actually, your mother's one sick mother too." Pursued by the angry parents, Fool and Alice hide in the bowels of the house, with the other adopted children — those who didn't live up to the parents' expectations. Alice explains that, when they were bad, "Daddy cut out the bad parts and put them in the cellar." They live in cages — pale, emaciated creatures.

The parents in *The People Under the Stairs* are perhaps Craven's most outrageous example of demonic authority figures, and some critics interpreted the film as a broad criticism of America's authority figures. "It was meant as a political allegory," the director explains. "Siskel and Ebert claimed the two antagonists were meant to be Nancy and Ronald Reagan. That was not true, it was not meant to be that specific. They're just conservatives, or actually people who would elect Nancy and Ronald.... [There] was a political cartoon which ran when Bush was seeking election which had Bush creeping up these rickety stairs and it had our *The People Under the Stairs* logo and was captioned 'Terror on the way to the Polls.' Underneath were all the poor and disenfranchised."[18] The political allegory ends with a symbolic redistribution of wealth: Fool finds a vault filled with riches and dynamite; when he lights a match, the ghetto is showered with money.

By 1994, Craven admits, he was having trouble taking the genre seriously.* When he resurrected Freddy for *Wes Craven's New Nightmare*, he concocted a plot that acknowledged the other films in the series as works of fiction, and attempted to make his creation scary again. *New Nightmare* takes place in "real world" Hollywood, where actress Heather Langenkamp — Nancy Thompson in *Nightmares 1* and *3* — is struggling to connect with her own son, Dylan, after the mysterious death of her husband. One night, while trying to assuage Dylan's fears of the boogeyman, Heather begins to read him a bedtime story. She stops when "Hansel and Gretel" becomes too violent, worried that it will give him nightmares. Dylan begs her to continue until the witch has been burned alive in the furnace. "It's *important*," he says.

---

*See Vampire in Brooklyn *(1995) for proof.*

Heather soon learns that Dylan is being haunted by a boogeyman she knows all too well — Freddy has somehow escaped the world of fiction and is now terrorizing the people who created him. For Craven (who is among the targets in the film), this belief illustrates a personal belief that Freddy is "an entity that has been around for a very long time. He stands for something ancient and probably goes back to the very roots of mankind. In each age, storytellers try to grab on to those elements that are mysterious and hidden and ineffable and give them shapes and give them names. In my case, I called it Freddy."[19]

Mother and son confront the boogeyman in a dream, sparring with him in a Gothic inferno until Freddy finally corners Dylan in an oversized furnace like the one in "Hansel and Gretel." With his mother's help, the boy traps Freddy in the furnace and sets him on fire while they escape into the waking world. Leaving the real horror behind, Heather lulls Dylan to sleep with the fictional horrors of a modern fairy tale — the script of *Wes Craven's New Nightmare*. The implication is none-too-subtle: Horror films are the "allowable insanity" that help us cope with real-life horror. "I think horror films serve the same functions as nightmares serve in the human condition," Craven explains. "They are a vent for disturbing but very powerful and important thoughts. I think films process very powerful primal fears and trepidations. It's life and death, blood and guts. But people come out of it at the end. There's a sense of exhilaration. They survive."[20]

Scream (1996) takes the idea one step further, demonstrating that today's youth have absorbed these myths, studied them line by line, frame by frame. Many are bored with the formulas: It's always about "some stupid killer chasing some big-breasted girl who can't act who's always running up the stairs when she should be running out the front door." As a result, they have decided to *create* real horror, killing their classmates in the style of their favorite movies. Craven justifies the satire by saying, "Kids today have fears and they need to process their terror in a positive and funny manner. *Scream* accomplished this with scenarios of intense anxiety as well as playfulness."[21]

Perhaps because he genuinely believes in the cathartic power of horror films, Wes Craven continues to be a driving force in the genre. He has directed two sequels to *Scream* and produced a number of low-budget horror films in recent years (e.g. "Wes Craven Presents" *Mind Ripper, Wishmaster, Carnival of Souls, Dracula 2000* and *They*). "I do have a capacity to generate horror films, horror images," he says, "Somehow those images from our own culture affect me profoundly and I'm able to put them onto film…. I'm trying now to be more mature about it and admit that there is a part of me that is this wild maniac, that loves these crazy images, that loves to scare people and enjoys going into these very dark labyrinths of human consciousness."[22] It seems a safe bet that, as long as Craven and his peers willing to wander down the dark corridors, audiences will follow.

Feature Films Directed by Craven:

The Last House on the Left (1972)*
The Hills Have Eyes (1977)*
Summer of Fear (a.k.a. *Stranger in Our House*) (1978)
Deadly Blessing (1981)*
Swamp Thing (1982)*
Invitation to Hell (1984)
The Hills Have Eyes Part 2 (1985)*
A Nightmare on Elm Street (1984)*
Chiller (1985)
Deadly Friend (1986)
The Serpent and the Rainbow (1988)*
Shocker (1989)*
Night Visions (1990)
The People Under the Stairs (1991)*
Wes Craven's New Nightmare (1994)*
A Vampire in Brooklyn (1995)
Scream (1996)
Scream 2 (1997)
Music of the Heart (1999)
Scream 3 (2000)

*Wes Craven received a screenwriting credit.

Filmography

The Student of Prague (Germany, 1913); Hans Heinz Ewers, Stellan Rye
The Golem (Germany, 1915); Henrik Galeen, Paul Wegener
Homunculus (Germany, 1916); Otto Rippert
The Wicked Darling (USA, 1919); Tod Browning
The Cabinet of Dr. Caligari (Germany, 1920); Robert Wiene
The Golem: How He Came into the World (Germany, 1920); Carl Boese, Paul Wegener
Outside the Law (USA, 1920); Tod Browning
Nosferatu: A Symphony of Horror (Germany, 1922); F.W. Murnau
The Hunchback of Notre Dame (USA, 1923); Wallace Worsley
Waxworks (Germany, 1924); Paul Leni
The Hands of Orlac (Austria, 1925); Robert Wiene
The Unholy Three (USA, 1925); Tod Browning
The Bat (USA, 1926); Roland West
The Black Bird (USA, 1926); Tod Browning
The Student of Prague (USA, 1926); Henrik Galeen
The Cat and the Canary (USA, 1927); Paul Leni
London After Midnight (USA, 1927); Tod Browning
The Unknown (USA, 1927); Tod Browning
The Haunted House (USA, 1928); Benjamin Christensen
The Cat Creeps (USA, 1930); Rupert Julian, John Willard
Dracula (USA, 1931); Tod Browning
Dracula (USA, 1931); George Melford, Enrique Tovar Avalos
Dr. Jekyll and Mr. Hyde (USA, 1931); Rouben Mamoulian
Frankenstein (USA, 1931); James Whale
Little Caesar (USA, 1931); Mervyn LeRoy
Doctor X (USA, 1932); Michael Curtiz
Freaks (USA, 1932); Tod Browning
The Most Dangerous Game (USA, 1932); Irving Pichel, Ernest B. Schoedsack
The Mummy (USA, 1932); Karl Freund

Murders in the Rue Morgue (USA, 1932); Robert Florey
The Old Dark House (USA, 1932); James Whale
Vampyr (Germany, 1932); Carl Theodor Dreyer
The Invisible Man (USA, 1933); James Whale
Island of Lost Souls (USA, 1933); Erle C. Kenton
King Kong (USA, 1933); Merian C. Cooper, Ernest B. Schoedsack
Mystery of the Wax Museum (USA, 1933); Michael Curtiz
The Black Cat (USA, 1934); Edgar G. Ulmer
It Happened One Night (USA, 1934); Frank Capra
Bride of Frankenstein (USA, 1935); James Whale
Mad Love (USA, 1935); Karl Freund
Mark of the Vampire (USA, 1935); Tod Browning
The Raven (USA, 1935); Lew Landers
The Thirty-Nine Steps (UK, 1935); Alfred Hitchcock
The Devil-Doll (USA, 1936); Tod Browning
Dracula's Daughter (USA, 1936); Lambert Hillyer
Mr. Smith Goes to Washington (USA, 1939); Frank Capra
Son of Frankenstein (USA, 1939); Rowland V. Lee
Stagecoach (USA, 1939); John Ford
The Wizard of Oz (USA, 1939); Victor Fleming
The Devil Bat (USA, 1940); Jean Yarbrough
Rebecca (USA, 1940); Alfred Hitchcock
Mr. and Mrs. Smith (USA, 1941); Alfred Hitchcock
Suspicion (USA, 1941); Alfred Hitchcock
The Wolf Man (USA, 1941); George Waggner
Black Dragons (USA, 1942); William Nigh
Cat People (USA, 1942); Jacques Tourneur
The Ghost of Frankenstein (USA, 1942); Erle C. Kenton
The Gorilla Man (USA, 1942); D. Ross Lederman
Invisible Agent (USA, 1942); Edwin L. Marin
Saboteur (USA, 1942); Alfred Hitchcock
Frankenstein Meets the Wolf Man (USA, 1943); Roy William Neill
Ghosts on the Loose (USA, 1943); William Beaudine
A Guy Named Joe (USA, 1943); Victor Fleming
I Walked with a Zombie (USA, 1943); Jacques Tourneur
The Leopard Man (USA, 1943); Jacques Tourneur
The Mysterious Doctor (USA, 1943); Benjamin Stoloff
Shadow of a Doubt (USA, 1943); Alfred Hitchcock
The Seventh Victim (USA, 1943); Mark Robson
Revenge of the Zombies (USA, 1943); Steve Sekely
The Curse of the Cat People (USA, 1944); Robert Wise, Gunther von Fritsch
Gaslight (USA, 1944); George Cukor
House of Frankenstein (USA, 1944); Erle C. Kenton
Laura (USA, 1944); Otto Preminger, Rouben Mamoulian
Lifeboat (USA, 1944); Alfred Hitchcock
The Return of the Vampire (USA, 1944); Lew Landers, Kurt Neumann
Son of Dracula (USA, 1944); Robert Siodmak

To Have and Have Not (USA, 1944); Howard Hawks
The Uninvited (USA, 1944); Lewis Allen
Weird Woman (USA, 1944); Reginald LeBorg
Detour (USA, 1945); Edgar G. Ulmer
House of Dracula (USA, 1945); Erle C. Kenton
Isle of the Dead (USA, 1945); Mark Robson
It's a Wonderful Life (USA, 1946); Frank Capra
My Darling Clementine (USA, 1946); John Ford
The Spiral Staircase (USA, 1946); Robert Siodmak
Abbott & Costello Meet Frankenstein (USA, 1948); Charles Barton
Fort Apache (USA, 1948); John Ford
Key Largo (USA, 1948); Howard Hawks
Red River (USA, 1948); Howard Hawks
Rope (USA, 1948); Alfred Hitchcock
Night and the City (USA, 1950); Jules Dassin
The Day the Earth Stood Still (USA, 1951); Robert Wise
Strangers on a Train (USA, 1951); Alfred Hitchcock
The Thing from Another World (USA, 1951); Christian Nyby, Howard Hawks
The Beast from 20,000 Fathoms (USA, 1953); Eugene Lourie
House of Wax (USA, 1953); Andre de Toth
Invaders from Mars (USA, 1953); William Cameron Menzies
War of the Worlds (USA, 1953); Byron Haskin
The Fast and the Furious (USA, 1954); Roger Corman
Gojira (Godzilla, King of the Monsters) (Japan, 1954); Ishiro Honda
Monster from the Ocean Floor (USA, 1954); Wyott Ordung
Rear Window (USA, 1954); Alfred Hitchcock
Them! (USA, 1954); Gordon Douglas
Apache Women (USA, 1955); Roger Corman
Diabolique (France, 1955); Henri Georges-Clouzot
Five Guns West (USA, 1955); Roger Corman
It Came from Beneath the Sea (USA, 1955); Robert Gordon
Kiss Me Deadly (USA, 1955); Robert Aldrich
The Quatermass Xperiment (aka The Creeping Unknown); (UK, 1955); Val Guest
Rebel Without a Cause (USA, 1955); Nicholas Ray
Tarantula (USA, 1955); Jack Arnold
The Bad Seed (USA, 1956); Mervyn LeRoy
The Day the World Ended (USA, 1956); Roger Corman
Gunslinger (USA, 1956); Roger Corman
Invasion of the Body Snatchers (USA, 1956); Don Siegel
It Conquered the World (USA, 1956); Roger Corman
The Oklahoma Woman (USA, 1956); Roger Corman
The Searchers (USA, 1956); John Ford
The Wrong Man (USA, 1956); Alfred Hitchcock
Attack of the Crab Monsters (USA, 1957); Roger Corman
Beginning of the End (USA, 1957); Bert I. Gordon
Blood of Dracula (USA, 1957); Herbert L. Strock

Carnival Rock (USA, 1957); Roger Corman
The Curse of Frankenstein (UK, 1957); Terence Fisher
The Deadly Mantis (USA, 1957); Nathan Juran
I Was a Teenage Frankenstein (USA, 1957); Herbert L. Strock
I Was a Teenage Werewolf (USA, 1957); Gene Fowler Jr.
The Incredible Shrinking Man (USA, 1957); Jack Arnold
Not of This Earth (USA, 1957); Roger Corman
Quatermass 2 (aka Enemy From Space); (UK, 1957); Val Guest
Rock All Night (USA, 1957); Roger Corman
The Seventh Seal (Sweden, 1957); Ingmar Bergman
Sorority Girl (USA, 1957); Roger Corman
Teenage Doll (USA, 1957); Roger Corman
The Undead (USA, 1957); Roger Corman
Attack of the 50-Foot Woman (USA, 1958); Nathan Juran
The Blob (USA, 1958); Irvin S. Yeaworth Jr.
Earth vs. the Spider (USA, 1958); Bert I. Gordon
The Fly (USA, 1958); Kurt Neumann
Horror of Dracula (UK, 1958); Terence Fisher
I Mobster (USA, 1958); Roger Corman
Macabre (USA, 1958); William Castle
Machine-Gun Kelly (USA, 1958); Roger Corman
The Return of Dracula (USA, 1958); Paul Landres
Vertigo (USA, 1958); Alfred Hitchcock
War of the Satellites (USA, 1958); Roger Corman
A Bucket of Blood (USA, 1959); Roger Corman
Eyes Without a Face (France, 1959); Georges Franju
House on Haunted Hill (USA, 1959); William Castle
North By Northwest (USA, 1959); Alfred Hitchcock
Rio Bravo (USA, 1959); Howard Hawks
House of Usher (USA, 1960); Roger Corman
The Little Shop of Horrors (USA, 1960); Roger Corman
Psycho (USA, 1960); Alfred Hitchcock
The Wasp Woman (USA, 1960); Roger Corman
The Virgin Spring (Sweden, 1960); Ingmar Bergman
Creature from the Haunted Sea (USA, 1961); Roger Corman
Gorgo (UK, 1961); Eugene Lourie
Homicidal (USA, 1961); William Castle
The Intruder (USA, 1961); Roger Corman
Pit and the Pendulum (USA, 1961); Roger Corman
The Man Who Shot Liberty Valance (USA, 1962); John Ford
The Premature Burial (USA, 1962); Roger Corman
Tales of Terror (USA, 1962); Roger Corman
What Ever Happened to Baby Jane? (USA, 1962); Robert Aldrich
The Birds (USA, 1963); Alfred Hitchcock
Blood Feast (USA, 1963); Herschell Gordon Lewis
Charade (USA, 1963); Stanley Donen
The Day of the Triffids (USA, 1963); Steve Sekely

Dementia 13 (USA, 1963); Francis Ford Coppola
Diary of a Madman (USA, 1963); Reginald LeBorg
The Haunted Palace (USA, 1963); Roger Corman
The Raven (USA, 1963); Roger Corman
The Terror (USA, 1963); Roger Corman
Twice-Told Tales (USA, 1963); Sidney Salkow
X: The Man with the X-Ray Eyes (USA, 1963); Roger Corman
A Fistful of Dollars (USA, 1964); Sergio Leone
Hush... Hush, Sweet Charlotte (USA, 1964); Robert Aldrich
The Last Man on Earth (USA, 1964); Sidney Salkow, Ubaldo Ragona
Marnie (USA, 1964); Alfred Hitchcock
The Masque of the Red Death (USA, 1964); Roger Corman
Strait-Jacket (USA, 1964); William Castle
Repulsion (West Germany, 1965); Roman Polanski
The Tomb of Ligeia (USA, 1965); Roger Corman
2001: A Space Odyssey (USA, 1968); Stanley Kubrick
War-Gods of the Deep (USA, 1965); Jacques Tourneur
The Wild Angels (USA, 1966); Roger Corman
El Dorado (USA, 1967); Howard Hawks
In Cold Blood (USA, 1967); Richard Brooks
The St. Valentine's Day Massacre (USA, 1967); Roger Corman
The Trip (USA, 1967); Roger Corman
2001: A Space Odyssey (USA, 1968); Stanley Kubrick
Night of the Living Dead (USA, 1968); George A. Romero
Rosemary's Baby (USA, 1968); Roman Polanski
Targets (USA, 1968); Peter Bogdanovich
Easy Rider (USA, 1969); Dennis Hopper
The Oblong Box (USA, 1969); Gordon Hessler
The Wild Bunch (USA, 1969); Sam Peckinpah
Bloody Mama (USA, 1970); Roger Corman
Count Yorga: Vampire (USA, 1970); Bob Kelljan
The Dunwich Horror (USA, 1970); Daniel Haller
Gas-s-s-s! (USA, 1970); Roger Corman
Rio Lobo (USA, 1970); Howard Hawks
The Student Nurses (USA, 1970); Roger Corman
There's Always Vanilla (USA, 1970); George A. Romero
The Vampire Lovers (UK, 1970); Roy Ward Baker
Vampyros Lesbos (Spain, 1970); Jess Franco
The Big Doll House (USA, 1971); Jack Hill
Jack's Wife (USA, 1971); George A. Romero
Let's Scare Jessica to Death (USA, 1971); John Hancock
Lust for a Vampire (UK, 1971); Jimmy Sangster
Shaft (USA, 1971); Gordon Parks
There's Always Vanilla (USA, 1971); George A. Romero
Twins of Evil (UK, 1971); John Hough
Twitch of the Death Nerve (Italy, 1971); Mario Bava
Von Richtofen and Brown (USA, 1971); Roger Corman

Women in Cages (USA, 1971); Gerardo de Leon
The Big Bird Cage (USA, 1972); Jack Hill
Black Mama White Mama (USA, 1972); Eddie Romero
Blacula (USA, 1972); William Crain
Bone: A Bad Day in Beverly Hills (USA, 1972); Larry Cohen
Boxcar Bertha (USA, 1972); Martin Scorsese
Deliverance (USA, 1972); John Boorman
Frenzy (USA, 1972); Alfred Hitchcock
Frogs (USA, 1972); George McCowan
The Last House on the Left (USA, 1972); Wes Craven
Night of the Lepus (USA, 1972); William F. Claxton
Superfly (USA, 1972); Gordon Parks
Black Caesar (USA, 1973); Larry Cohen
The Crazies (USA, 1973); George A. Romero
The Exorcist (USA, 1973); William Friedkin
Hell Up in Harlem (USA, 1973); Larry Cohen
Jack's Wife (a.k.a. Season of the Witch) (USA, 1973); George A. Romero
Scream Blacula Scream (USA, 1973); Bob Kelljan
Sisters (USA, 1973); Brian DePalma
Andy Warhol's Dracula (a.k.a. Blood of Dracula); (USA, 1974); Paul Morrissey
Black Christmas (USA, 1974); Bob Clark
Caged Heat (USA, 1974); Jonathan Demme
Dark Star (USA, 1974); John Carpenter
Death Wish (USA, 1974); Michael Winner
It's Alive (USA, 1974); Larry Cohen
Phantom of the Paradise (USA, 1974); Brian DePalma
Phase IV (USA, 1974); Saul Bass
Seizure (USA, 1974); Oliver Stone
The Texas Chain Saw Massacre (USA, 1974); Tobe Hooper
Bug (USA, 1975); Jeannot Szwarc
Crazy Mama (USA, 1975); Jonathan Demme
Death Race 2000 (USA, 1975); Paul Bartel
Deep Red (Italy, 1975); Dario Argento
Eat My Dust! (USA, 1975); Charles B. Griffith
Jaws (USA, 1975); Steven Spielberg
The Stepford Wives (USA, 1975); Bryan Forbes
Assault on Precinct 13 (USA, 1976); John Carpenter
Carrie (USA, 1976); Brian DePalma
God Told Me To (a.k.a. Demon); (USA, 1976); Larry Cohen
Grizzly (USA, 1976); William Girdler
Hollywood Boulevard (USA, 1976); Joe Dante, Allan Arkush
Obsession (USA, 1976); Brian DePalma
The Omen (USA, 1976); Richard Donner
Squirm (USA, 1976); Jeff Lieberman
Ants! (USA, 1977); Robert Scheerer
Day of the Animals (USA, 1977); William Girdler

Eraserhead (USA, 1977); David Lynch
Grand Theft Auto (USA, 1977); Ron Howard
The Hills Have Eyes (USA, 1977); Wes Craven
Kingdom of the Spiders (USA, 1977); John "Bud" Cardos
The Bees (USA, 1978); Alfredo Zacarias
Dawn of the Dead (USA, 1978); George Romero
Halloween (USA, 1978); John Carpenter
I Spit on Your Grave (USA, 1978); Meir Zarchi
Invasion of the Body Snatchers (USA, 1978); Philip Kaufman
It Lives Again (USA, 1978); Larry Cohen
Martin (USA, 1978); George Romero
Piranha (USA, 1978); Joe Dante
Summer of Fear (a.k.a. Stranger in Our House); (USA, 1978); Wes Craven
The Swarm (USA, 1978); Irwin Allen
Alien (USA, 1979); Ridley Scott
The Amityville Horror (USA, 1979); Stuart Rosenberg
Dracula (USA, 1979); John Badham
Elvis (USA, 1979); John Carpenter
Love at First Bite (USA, 1979); Stan Dragoti
Prophecy (USA, 1979); John Frankenheimer
Salem's Lot (USA, 1979); Tobe Hooper
Zombie (Italy, 1979); Lucio Fulci
Battle Beyond the Stars (USA, 1980); Jimmy T. Murakami
Dressed to Kill (USA, 1980); Brian DePalma
The Elephant Man (USA, 1980); David Lynch
The Fog (USA, 1980); John Carpenter
Friday the 13th (USA, 1980); Sean S. Cunningham
He Knows You're Alone (USA, 1980); Armand Mastroianni
Motel Hell (USA, 1980); Kevin Connor
Prom Night (USA, 1980); Paul Lynch
The Shining (USA, 1980); Stanley Kubrick
Terror Train (USA, 1980); Roger Spottiswoode
An American Werewolf in London (USA, 1981); John Landis
Deadly Blessing (USA, 1981); Wes Craven
Escape from New York (USA, 1981); John Carpenter
The Evil Dead (USA, 1981); Sam Raimi
Full Moon High (USA, 1981); Larry Cohen
The Funhouse (USA, 1981); Tobe Hooper
Graduation Day (USA, 1981); Herb Freed
Happy Birthday to Me (USA, 1981); J. Lee Thompson
Hell Night (USA, 1981); Tom DeSimone
The Howling (USA, 1981); Joe Dante
Knightriders (USA, 1981); George A. Romero
Ms. 45: Angel of Vengeance (USA, 1981); Abel Ferrara
My Bloody Valentine (USA, 1981); George Mihalka
Night School (USA, 1981); Ken Hughes
The Prowler (USA, 1981); Joseph Zito

Alone in the Dark (USA, 1982); Jack Sholder
Amityville II: The Possession (USA, 1982); Damiano Damiani
Basket Case (USA, 1982); Frank Henenlotter
Cat People (USA, 1982); Paul Schrader
Creepshow (USA, 1982); George A. Romero
Fast Times at Ridgemont High (USA, 1982); Amy Heckerling
Halloween 3: Season of the Witch (USA, 1982); John Carpenter
Poltergeist (USA, 1982); Tobe Hooper
Q: The Winged Serpent (USA, 1982); Larry Cohen
Swamp Thing (USA, 1982); Wes Craven
The Thing (USA, 1982); John Carpenter
Christine (USA, 1983); John Carpenter
Cujo (USA, 1983); Lewis Teague
The Dead Zone (USA, 1983); David Cronenberg
The Hunger (USA, 1983); Tony Scott
Return of the Jedi (USA, 1983); Richard Marquand
Twilight Zone: The Movie (USA, 1983); Joe Dante, John Landis, Steven Spielberg, George Miller
Videodrome (USA, 1983); David Cronenberg
Beverly Hills Cop (USA, 1984); Martin Brest
Body Double (USA, 1984); Brian DePalma
Dune (USA, 1984); David Lynch
Ghostbusters (USA, 1984); Ivan Reitman
Gremlins (USA, 1984); Joe Dante
Invitation to Hell (USA, 1984); Wes Craven
A Nightmare on Elm Street (USA, 1984); Wes Craven
Perfect Strangers (USA, 1984); Larry Cohen
Special Effects (USA, 1984); Larry Cohen
Starman (USA, 1984); John Carpenter
Cat's Eye (USA, 1985); Lewis Teague
Day of the Dead (USA, 1985); George Romero
Fright Night (USA, 1985); Tom Holland
The Hills Have Eyes Part 2 (USA, 1985); Wes Craven
A Nightmare on Elm Street Part 2: Freddy's Revenge (USA, 1985); Jack Sholder
Re-Animator (USA, 1985); Stuart Gordon
The Return of the Living Dead (USA, 1985); Dan O'Bannon
The Stuff (USA, 1985); Larry Cohen
Teen Wolf (USA, 1985); Rod Daniel
Aliens (USA, 1986); James Cameron
Big Trouble in Little China (USA, 1986); John Carpenter
Blue Velvet (USA, 1986); David Lynch
Deadly Friend (USA, 1986); Wes Craven
Poltergeist II: The Other Side (USA, 1986); Brian Gibson
The Texas Chain Saw Massacre Part 2 (USA, 1986); Tobe Hooper
Flowers in the Attic (USA, 1987); Jeffrey Bloom
The Lost Boys (USA, 1987); Joel Schumacher
Near Dark (USA, 1987); Kathryn Bigelow

A Nightmare on Elm Street 3: Dream Warriors (USA, 1987); Chuck Russell
Prince of Darkness (USA, 1987); John Carpenter
A Return to Salem's Lot (USA, 1987); Larry Cohen
The Stepfather (USA, 1987); Joseph Ruben
Maniac Cop (USA, 1988); William Lustig
Monkey Shines: An Experiment in Fear (USA, 1988); George A. Romero
The Serpent and the Rainbow (USA, 1988); Wes Craven
They Live (USA, 1988); John Carpenter
The Understudy: Graveyard Shift 2 (USA, 1988); Gerard Ciccoritti
Shocker (USA, 1989); Wes Craven
Wicked Stepmother (USA, 1989); Larry Cohen
The Ambulance (USA, 1990); Larry Cohen
Night of the Living Dead (USA, 1990); Tom Savini
Roger Corman's Frankenstein Unbound (USA, 1990); Roger Corman
Twin Peaks (USA, 1990); David Lynch
Wild at Heart (USA, 1990); David Lynch
The People Under the Stairs (USA, 1991); Wes Craven
The Silence of the Lambs (USA, 1991); Jonathan Demme
Subspecies (USA, 1991); Ted Nicolaou
Alien 3 (USA, 1992); David Fincher
Bram Stoker's Dracula (USA, 1992); Francis Ford Coppola
Candyman (USA, 1992); Bernard Rose
Dracula Rising (USA, 1992); Fred Gallo
Twin Peaks: Fire Walk with Me (USA, 1992); David Lynch
The Dark Half (USA, 1993); George A. Romero
To Sleep with a Vampire (USA, 1993); Adam Friedman
Interview with the Vampire (USA, 1994); Neil Jordan
Wes Craven's New Nightmare (USA, 1994); Wes Craven
The Addiction (USA, 1995); Abel Ferrara
As Good as Dead (USA, 1995); Larry Cohen
In the Mouth of Madness (USA, 1995); John Carpenter
Mind Ripper (a.k.a. The Outpost); (USA, 1995); Joe Gayton
Nadja (USA, 1995); Michael Almereyda
Vampire in Brooklyn (USA, 1995); Wes Craven
Escape From L.A. (USA, 1996); John Carpenter
Scream (USA, 1996); Wes Craven
Alien Resurrection (USA, 1997); Jean-Pierre Jeunct
Lost Highway (USA, 1997); David Lynch
Scream 2 (USA, 1997); Wes Craven
Uncle Sam (USA, 1997); Larry Cohen
Wes Craven Presents Wishmaster (USA, 1997); Robert Kurtzman
Blade (USA, 1998); Stephen Norrington
Vampires (USA, 1998); John Carpenter
Wes Craven Presents Carnival of Souls (USA, 1998); Adam Grossman
Bruiser (USA, 2000); George A. Romero
Scream 3 (USA, 2000); Wes Craven
Shadow of the Vampire (USA, 2000); E. Elias Merhige

Wes Craven Presents Dracula 2000 (USA, 2000); Patrick Lussier
Ghosts of Mars, 2001 (USA); John Carpenter
Hannibal (USA, 2001); Ridley Scott
Mulholland Drive (USA, 2001); David Lynch
Queen of the Damned (USA, 2002); Michael Rymer
Wes Craven Presents They (USA, 2002); Robert Harmon

Notes

Part I

1. Baldick xiii.
2. Bayer-Berenbaum.
3. Halberstam 2.
4. Walpole 7.
5. Clarens 37.
6. Skal: *Carnival* 155.

Chapter 1

1. Freud 220.
2. *Ibid*. 249.
3. Kracauer 29.
4. *Ibid*. 29–30.
5. *Ibid*. 32–33.
6. Wells 3.
7. Kracauer 65.
8. *Ibid*. 67.

Chapter 2

1. Kawin, "Mummy's" 550.
2. Skal: *Carnival* 156.
3. *Ibid*. 157.
4. Jensen 10.
5. *Ibid*. 38.
6. Gabler 207.
7. Kinnard 19.
8. Skal: *Monster* 180.
9. Wells 53.
10. Skal: *Monster* 181.
11. Mast 244.

Chapter 3

1. Gotlieb 200.
2. *Ibid*. 109.
3. Skal: *Monster* 217.
4. *Ibid*. 216–217.
5. Bansak 123.
6. *Ibid*. 128.
7. *Ibid*. 140.
8. Freud 214.
9. Day 10.
10. Evans 53.
11. Schickel 280.
12. Schrader 54.
13. Bansak 178.
14. *Ibid*. 205.
15. Schrader 59–61.

Chapter 4

1. Wells 62.
2. *Ibid*. 62.
3. Kawin: "Mummy's" 551.
4. *Ibid*. 552–53.
5. Skal: Monster 248.

Notes

Chapter 5

1. Castle 134.
2. McCarty 79.
3. Castle 136.
4. *Ibid.* 146.
5. McCarty 13.
6. Pirie 28.
7. *Ibid.* 40.
8. Corman 78.
9. *Ibid.* 78–79.
10. Spoto 416.
11. Barker 31.

Chapter 6

1. Wells 75.
2. Polanski 265.
3. Wexman 37.
4. Spoto 461.
5. Wells 82.
6. Gagne 37–38.
7. *Ibid.* 6.
8. Robb 24–26.
9. Wood *Hollywood* 128.
10. Graham 133.
11. Barker 41.
12. Tony Williams *Hearths* 175.
13. *Ibid.* 175.
14. Wood *Hollywood* 71.
15. *Ibid.* 92–93.
16. Sharrett 261.
17. Rodowick 325.
18. Fischer 251.
19. *Ibid.* 251.
20. Rodowick 330.

Chapter 7

1. Wood *Hollywood* 196.
2. Waller *Horrors* 5.
3. Biskind 223.
4. Wood *Hollywood* 151.
5. Kael 698.
6. King 171.
7. *Ibid.* 174.
8. Fischer 126.
9. Dika 98.
10. Linda Williams 577.
11. Derry 164.
12. Wood *Hollywood* 91.
13. Glover 31.
14. Halberstam 143.

Chapter 8

1. Lemkin 277.
2. Bradley 109.
3. Knight 120, 122.
4. Gagne 89.
5. King 142–143.
6. Lowe.
7. Baxter 313.
8. Edmundson 44–45.
9. Ewing 111.
10. Lofficier 61.
11. Rodley *Lynch* 5–6.
12. Kael 1114.
13. Wells 108.

Chapter 9

1. Gagne 71.
2. Wood *Hollywood* 109.
3. Waller, *Living* 10.
4. Conrich 80.
5. Robb 83.
6. Conrich 83–84.
7. Briefel 288.
8. Edmundson 63.
9. Muir 167.
10. Wells 35.

Chapter 10

1. Silver 209.
2. Pirie 87.
3. Freeland 149.
4. Ramsland 232.
5. Ressler 272.
6. Silver 155.

7. Ramsland 245.
8. *Ibid.* 257.
9. Ressler 275.
10. Edmundson 67–68.
11. Wood *Hollywood* 109.

Part II

1. Sarris "Notes" 586.
2. *Ibid.*

Chapter 11

1. Sarris *American* 228.
2. Skal: *Carnival* 155.
3. Skal: Monster Show 127.
4. Skal: *Carnival* 71.
5. *Ibid.* 82.
6. Blake 168.
7. Skal: *Carnival* 86–87.
8. Blake 331.
9. *Ibid.* 192.
10. Skal: *Carnival* 116–117.
11. *Ibid.* 137.
12. *Ibid.* 96.
13. Kracauer 73.

Chapter 12

1. Wood: *Hollywood* 96.
2. Truffaut 124–125.
3. Gotlieb 170.
4. *Ibid.*
5. Truffaut 131–32.
6. *Ibid.* 150.
7. Schickel 281–82.
8. Wood "Ideology" 479.
9. Spoto 257.
10. Truffaut 155.
11. Gotlieb 115.
12. Truffaut 216.
13. Gotlieb 134.
14. Spoto 333.
15. Mulvey 756.
16. Rebello 183.
17. Rebello 184.
18. Wood: *Hitchcock's* 154.
19. Bogdanovich 535.

Chapter 13

1. Sarris *American* 211.
2. Corman 236.
3. *Ibid.* 33.
4. *Ibid.* 55.
5. *Ibid.* 162.
6. Lucy Williams 170.
7. Corman 97.
8. *Ibid.* 103.
9. Gray 76.
10. Corman 118.
11. *Ibid.* 132.
12. Thompson 53.
13. Corman 143.
14. *Ibid.* 145.
15. *Ibid.* 163.

Chapter 14

1. Weiskind.
2. Barker 242.
3. Gagne 23.
4. Wells 82.
5. Gagne 34.
6. *Ibid.* 38.
7. *Ibid.* 147–48.
8. *Ibid.* 124.
9. *Ibid.* 147–48.
10. Weiskind.
11. Barker 243.
12. *Ibid.* 245–46.

Chapter 15

1. Abbott.
2. Muir 10.
3. Abbott.
4. Barker 64.
5. *Ibid.* 68.
6. Muir 49.

7. *Ibid.* 21.
8. *Ibid.* 28.
9. *Ibid.* 39.
10. *Ibid.* 40.
11. *Ibid.* 45.
12. Douglas 207.
13. *Ibid.* 257.

Chapter 16

1. Tony Williams *Larry* 352.
2. Wood *Hollywood* 73.
3. Tony Williams *Larry* 359.
4. *Ibid.* 303.
5. *Ibid.* 349.
6. *Ibid.* 311.
7. *Ibid.* 330.
8. Barker 196.
9. Tony Williams *Larry* 314.
10. *Ibid.* 350.

Chapter 17

1. Rodley *Lynch* 114.
2. *Ibid.* 37.
3. Breskin 55.
4. Rodley *Lynch* 103.
5. Breskin 73.
6. Rodley *Lynch* 103.
7. Breskin 55.

8. *Ibid.* 60.
9. Rodley 139.
10. *Ibid.* 193.
11. *Ibid.* 197.
12. Breskin 71–72.

Chapter 18

1. Goldberg 239–40.
2. Wood *Hollywood* 125.
3. Robb 11.
4. *Ibid.* 150.
5. Wood: *Hollywood* 125.
6. Russo 179.
7. Robb 46.
8. *Ibid.* 45.
9. *Ibid.* 150.
10. *Ibid.* 119.
11. *Ibid.* 61.
12. Barker 135.
13. *Ibid.* 138.
14. Robb 119.
15. *Ibid.* 122.
16. *Ibid.* 100.
17. Russo 180.
18. Robb 152.
19. Barker 137.
20. *Ibid.* 140.
21. Robb 178.
22. *Ibid.* 135.

Bibliography

Abbott, John. "Flashback: John Carpenter Interview" : July 21, 1999.
Baldick, Chris. *The Oxford Book of Gothic Tales.* New York: Oxford University Press, 1993.
Bansak, Edmund G. *Fearing the Dark: The Val Lewton Career.* Jefferson NC: McFarland, 1995.
Barker, Clive, and Stephen Jones. *Clive Barker's A to Z of Horror.* London: BBC Books, 1997.
Baxter, John. *Stanley Kubrick: A Biography.* New York: Carroll & Graf, 1997.
Bayer-Berenbaum, Linda. *The Gothic Imagination: Expansion in Gothic Literature and Art.* Rutherford NJ: Fairleigh Dickinson University Press, 1982.
Biskind, Peter. *Easy Riders, Raging Bulls: How the Sex Drugs and Rock and Roll Generation Saved Hollywood.* New York: Simon & Schuster, 1998.
Blake, Michael F. *A Thousand Faces: Lon Chaney's Unique Artistry in Motion Pictures.* New York: Vestal, 1995.
Bogdanovich, Peter. *Who the Devil Made It? Conversations with Robert Aldrich, George Cukor, Allan Dwan, Howard Hawks, Alfred Hitchcock, Chuck Jones, Fritz Lang, Joseph H. Lewis, Sidney Lumet.* New York: Ballantine, 1998.
Bradley, Matthew R. "An Interview with W.D. Richter." *They're Here ... Invasion of the Body Snatchers: A Tribute.* New York: Berkley Boulevard, 1999.
Breskin, David. *Inner Views: Filmmakers in Conversation.* New York: DaCapo Press, 1997.
Briefel, Aviva, and Sianne Ngai. "*Candyman*: Urban Space, Fear and Entitlement." *Horror Film Reader.* Ed Alain Silver & James Ursini. New York: Limelight, 2000.
Brunas, Michael, John Brunas and Tom Weaver. *Universal Horror: The Studio's Classic Films 1931–1946.* Jefferson, NC: McFarland 1990.
Castle, William. *Step Right Up! I'm Going to Scare the Pants Off America: Memoirs of a B-Movie Mogul.* New York: Pharos, 1992.
Clarens, Carlos. *An Illustrated History of the Horror Films.* New York: G.P. Putnam's Sons, 1967.

Conrich, Ian. "Seducing the Subject: Freddy Krueger, Popular Culture and the *Nightmare on Elm Street* Films." *Trash Aesthetics: Popular Culture and Its Audience.* Ed. Deborah Cartmell, I.Q. Hunter, Heidi Kaye, Imelda Whelehan. Chicago: Pluto Press, 1997.

Cook, David A. *A History of Narrative Film.* New York: Norton, 1996.

Corman, Roger, and Jim Jerome. *How I Made a Hundred Movies in Hollywood and Never Lost a Dime.* New York: DaCapo Press, 1998.

Cullen, Jim. *The American Dream: A Short History of an Idea That Shaped a Nation.* New York: Oxford University Press, 2003.

Day, William Patrick. *In the Circles of Fear and Desire: A Study of Gothic Fantasy.* Chicago: University of Chicago Press, 1985.

Derry, Charles. "More Dark Dreams: Some Notes on the Recent Horror Film." *American Horrors: Essays on the Modern American Horror Film.* Chicago: University of Illinois Press, 1987.

Dika, Vera. "The Stalker Film, 1978 – 81." *American Horrors: Essays on the Modern American Horror Film.* Chicago: University of Illinois Press, 1987.

Douglas, John, and Mark Olshaker. *Unabomber: On the Trail of America's Most Wanted Serial Killer.* New York: Pocket Books, 1996.

Edmundson, Mark. *Nightmare on Main Street: Angels, Sadomasochism, and the Culture of the Gothic.* Cambridge: Harvard University Press, 1997.

Eliot, T.S. *The Complete Poems and Plays, 1909–1950.* New York: Harcourt, Brace & Company, 1930.

Evans, Walter. "Monster Movies: A Sexual Theory." *Planks of Reason: Essays on the Horror Film.* Metuchen NJ: Scarecrow, 1984.

Ewing, Darrell, and Dennis Myers. "King of the Road." *Feast of Fear: Conversations With Stephen King.* Ed. Tim Underwood, Chuck Miller. New York: Carroll & Graf, 1989.

Fischer, Dennis. *Horror Film Directors 1931–1990.* Jefferson NC: McFarland, 1991.

Freeland, Cynthia A. *The Naked and the Undead: Evil and the Appeal of Horror.* Boulder CO: Westview Press, 2000.

Freud, Sigmund. "The Uncanny." *The Complete Psychological Works of Sigmund Freud Volume XVII: An Infantile Neurosis and Other Works.* London: Hogarth Press, 1955.

Gabler, Neal. *An Empire of Their Own: How the Jews Invented Hollywood.* New York: Anchor Books, 1989.

Gagne, Paul. *The Zombies That Ate Pittsburgh: The Films of George A. Romero.* New York: Dodd, Mead & Co., 1987.

Glover, Carol J. *Men, Women and Chainsaws: Gender in the Modern Horror Film.* Princeton NJ: Princeton University Press, 1992.

Goldberg, Lee, and Randy Lofficier and Jean-Marc Lofficier and William Rabkin. *The Dreamweavers: Interviews with Fantasy Filmmakers of the 1980s.* Jefferson NC: McFarland, 1995.

Gotlieb, Sidney. *Hitchcock on Hitchcock: Selected Writings and Interviews.* Los Angeles: University of California Press, 1995.

Graham, Allison. "The Fallen Wonder of the World: Brian DePalma's Horror Films." *American Horrors: Essays on the Modern American Horror Film.* Ed. Gregory A. Waller. Chicago: University of Illinois Press, 1987.

Gray, Beverly. *Roger Corman: An Unauthorized Biography of the Godfather of Indie Filmmaking*. Renaissance Books: Los Angeles, 2000.

Halberstam, Judith. *Skin Shows: Gothic Horror and the Technology of Monsters*. Durham NC: Duke University Press, 1995.

Hendershot, Cyndy. *The Animal Within: Masculinity and the Gothic*. Ann Arbor: University of Michigan Press, 1998.

Jensen, Paul M. *The Men Who Made the Monsters*. New York: Twayne Publishers, 1996.

Kawin, Bruce F. "*The Funhouse* and *The Howling*." American Horrors: Essays on the Modern American Horror Film. Ed. Gregory A. Waller. Chicago: University of Illinois Press, 1987.

_____. "*The Mummy's Pool*." Film Theory and Criticism: Introductory Readings. Ed. Gerald Mast, Marshall Cohen, Leo Braudy. New York: Oxford University Press, 1992.

Kael, Pauline. *For Keeps*. New York: Penguin, 1984.

King, Stephen. *Danse Macabre*. New York: Berkley Books, 1981.

Kinnard, Roy, and R.J. Vitone. *The American Films of Michael Curtiz*. Metuchen NJ: Scarecrow, 1986.

Knight, Tracey. "The Rorschach Plot of *Invasion II*: The Life and Death of Counterculture." They're Here ... Invasion of the Body Snatchers: A Tribute. New York: Berkley Boulevard, 1999.

Kracauer, Siegfried. *From Caligari to Hitler: A Psychological History of the German Film*. New York: Princeton University Press, 1947.

Lemkin, Jonathan. "Archetypal Landscape in *Jaws*." Planks of Reason: Essays on the Horror Film. Metuchen NJ: Scarecrow, 1984.

Lofficier, Randy. "Stephen King Talks About *Christine*." Feast of Fear: Conversations with Stephen King. Ed. Tim Underwood, Chuck Miller. New York: Carroll & Graf, 1989.

Lowe, Ed. "Long Island: Our Story / Chapter 9 / Transformation / 1974 The Horrors in Amityville / Six Murders on Ocean Avenue Become a Media Circus Rippling Around the World." *Newsday*: June 21, 1998.

Mast, Gerald, and Bruce Kawin. *A Short History of the Movies*. Needham Heights NJ: Allyn & Bacon, 1996.

McCarty, John. *The Fearmakers: The Screen's Directorial Masters of Suspense and Terror*. New York: St. Martin's Press, 1994.

Muir, John Kenneth. *The Films of John Carpenter*. Jefferson NC: McFarland, 2000.

Mulvey, Loura. "Visual Pleasure and Narrative Cinema." *Film Theory and Criticism: Introductory Readings*. Ed. Gerald Mast, Marshall Cohen, and Leo Braudy. New York: Oxford University Press 1992.

Pirie, David. *A Heritage of Horror: The English Gothic Cinema 1946–1972*. London: Gordon Fraser, 1973.

Polanski, Roman. *Roman*. New York: William Morrow & Co., 1984.

Ramsland, Katherine. *Piercing the Darkness: Undercover with Vampires in America Today*. New York: HarperPrism, 1998.

Rebello, Stephen. *Alfred Hitchcock and the Making of Psycho*. New York: Dembner, 1990.

Ressler, Robert K., and Tom Shachtman. *Whoever Fights Monsters*. New York: St. Martin's, 1992.
Robb, Brian J. *Screams and Nightmares: The Films of Wes Craven*. Woodstock NY: Overlook, 1998.
Rodley, Chris. *Cronenberg on Cronenberg*. New York: Faber & Faber, 1992.
_____. *Lynch on Lynch*. New York: Faber & Faber, 1999.
Rodowick, D.N. "The Enemy Within: The Economy of Violence in *The Hills Have Eyes*." *Planks of Reason: Essays on the Horror Film*. Metuchen NJ: Scarecrow, 1984.
Russo, John. *Scare Tactics*. New York: Dell, 1992.
Sarris, Andrew. *The American Cinema: Directors and Directions 1929 – 1968*. Da Capo Press: New York, 1996.
_____. "Notes on the Auteur Theory in 1962." *Film Theory and Criticism: Introductory Readings*. Ed Gerald Mast, Marshall Cohen, Leo Braudy. New York: Oxford University Press, 1992.
Schickel, Richard. *The Men Who Made the Movies*. Chicago: Ivan R. Dee, 2001.
Schrader, Paul. "Notes on Film Noir." *Film Noir Reader*. Ed. Alain Silver and James Ursini. New York: Limelight, 1996.
Sharrett, Christopher. "The Idea of Apocalypse in *The Texas Chainsaw Massacre*." *Planks of Reason: Essays on the Horror Film*. Metuchen NJ: Scarecrow, 1984.
Silver, Alain and James Ursini. *The Vampire Film: From Nosferatu to Interview with the Vampire*. New York: Proscenium, 1997.
Skal, David J. *The Monster Show: A Cultural History of Horror*. New York: Faber & Faber, 1993.
_____, and Elias Savada. *Dark Carnival: The Secret World of Tod Browning, Hollywood's Master of the Macabre*. New York: Anchor, 1995.
Spoto, Donald. *The Dark Side of Genius: The Life of Alfred Hitchcock*. New York: DaCapo, 1999.
Telotte, J.P. "Faith and Idolatry in the Horror Film." *Planks of Reason: Essays on the Horror Film*. Metuchen NJ: Scarecrow, 1984.
Thompson, Hunter S. *Hell's Angels: A Strange and Terrible Saga*. Ballantine Books: New York, 1966.
Truffaut, Francois. *Hitchcock*. New York: Simon & Schuster, 1983.
Waller, Gregory. *American Horrors: Essays on the Modern American Horror Film*. Chicago: University of Illinois Press, 1987.
_____. *The Living and the Undead: From Stoker's Dracula to Romero's Dawn of the Dead*. Chicago: University of Illinois Press, 1986.
Walpole, Horace. *The Castle of Otranto*. New York: Oxford University Press, 1996.
Weaver, Tom. *Poverty Row Horrors!* Jefferson NC: McFarland, 1993.
Weiskind, Rob. "Director Romero wants to break out of horror." *The Pittsburgh Post-Gazette*: February 14, 2002.
Wells, Paul. *The Horror Genre: From Beelzebub to Blair Witch*. London: Wallflower, 2000.
Wexman, Virginia Wright. "The Trauma of Infancy in Roman Polanski's *Rosemary's Baby*." *American Horrors: Essays on the Modern American Horror Film*. Ed. Gregory A. Waller. Chicago: University of Illinois Press, 1987.
Williams, Linda. "When the Woman Looks." *The Dread of Difference: Gender and the Horror Film*. Ed. Barry Keith Grant. Austin: University of Texas Press, 1996.

Williams, Lucy Chase. *The Complete Films of Vincent Price*. Carol Publishing Group: New York, 1995.

Williams, Tony. *Hearths of Darkness: The Family in the American Horror Film*. Cranbury NJ: Associated University Press 1996.

_____. *Larry Cohen: The Radical Allegories of an Independent Filmmaker*. Jefferson NC: McFarland.

Wood, Robin. *Hitchcock's Films Revisited*. New York: Columbia University Press, 1989.

_____. *Hollywood From Vietnam to Reagan*. New York: Columbia University Press, 1986.

_____. "Ideology, Genre, Auteur." *Film Theory and Criticism: Introductory Readings*. Ed. Gerald Mast, Marshall Cohen, Leo Braudy. New York: Oxford University Press, 1992

Index

Abbott and Costello Meet Frankenstein (1948) 20
The Addiction (1995) 92
Aldrich, Robert 5, 47, 159
Alfred Hitchcock Presents 43, 44
Alien (1979) 66
Alien Resurrection (1997) 67
Alien 3 (1992) 66, 67
Aliens (1986) 66, 67
Alone in the Dark (1982) 81
The Ambulance (1990) 144
The American Dream: A Short History of an Idea That Shaped a Nation 5
American Psycho (novel) 87
An American Werewolf in London (1981) 81
The Amityville Horror (1979) 71, 72
Amityville II: The Possession (1980) 72
Amplas, John 125
Andrews, V.C. 165
Andy Warhol's Dracula (1974) 88
Anson, Jay 71
Ants! (1977) 34
Apache Woman (1955) 112
Argento, Dario 62, 111
Arkoff, Sam 42, 142
As Good as Dead (1995) 149
Assault on Precinct 13 (1976) 131, 132, 133, 137, 139
Attack of the Crab Monsters (1957) 34
Attack of the 50 Foot Woman (1958) 57

Bacall, Lauren 131
The Bad Seed (1956) 36, 53
Badalamenti, Angelo 155
Badham, John 88
Balestrero, Christopher 108
Bansak, Edmund G. 27
Barker, Clive 83
Barrymore, Lionel 102
Bartel, Paul 115
Basket Case (1982) 81
The Bat (1926) 12
Battle Beyond the Stars (1980) 120
Bauhaus 89
Bava, Mario 62
The Beast from 20,000 Fathoms (1953) 33
Beaumont, Charles 117
Beckett, Samuel 92
The Bees (1978) 34
Beginning of the End (1957) 33
Bergman, Ingmar 51, 162
Bernstein, Morey 114
Beverly Hills Cop (1984) 154
The Big Bird Cage (1972) 120
The Big Doll House (1971) 120
Big Trouble in Little China (1986) 136
The Birds (1963) 6, 33, 48, 49, 50, 104, 105, 110
Bissell, Whit 36, 38
The Black Bird (1926) 99
Black Caesar (1973) 142, 143, 144
The Black Cat (1934) 16, 17, 18
Black Christmas (1974) 62

Index

Black Dragons (1942) 23
Black Mama White Mama (1972) 120
Blacula (1972) 78, 88
Blade (1998) 93
Blair, Linda 152, 164
Blake, Michael F. 100
Blatty, William Peter 52
The Blob (1958) 38, 147
Bloch, Robert 43
Blood Feast (1963) 48
Blood of Dracula (1957) 78
Bloody Mama (1970) 113, 118
Blue Velvet (1986) 76, 77, 152, 154, 155, 156
Bodeen, Dewitt 20
Body Double (1984) 111
Bogart, Humphrey 133
Bogdanovich, Peter 120
Bone: A Bad Day in Beverly Hills (1972) 141, 142
Bowie, David 89
Boxcar Bertha (1972) 120
Bram Stoker's Dracula (1992) 91
Bride of Frankenstein (1935) 18, 19
Briefel, Aviva 84
Brolin, James 72
Bronson, Charles 115, 134
Brooke, Hillary 32
Brooks, Richard 163
Brown, Charles Brockden 4
Browning, Tod 5, 15, 97–103, 106
Bruiser (2000) 129
A Bucket of Blood (1959) 40, 115, 116
Bug (1975) 33
Burroughs, William 92

The Cabinet of Dr. Caligari (1921) 9, 10, 101
Caged Heat (1974) 120
Cahiers du Cinema 95
Cameron, James 120
Candyman (1992) 83, 84
Capote, Truman 163
Capra, Frank 105, 106, 107
Carpenter, John 62, 75, 85, 111, 131–140
Carradine, John 81
Carrie (1976) 60, 61, 62, 63
Carrie (novel) 75
Castle, Nick 63
Castle, William 39, 40, 41, 44, 45, 47, 49, 111

The Cat and the Canary (1927) 12, 40
The Cat Creeps (1930) 12
Cat People (1942) 20, 23, 24, 25, 27, 57
Cat People (1982) 81
Cat's Eye (1985) 75
Cavett, Dick 83
Chandler, Helen 13
Chaney, Lon 12, 15, 40, 97, 98, 99, 100, 103
Chaney, Lon, Jr. 22
Charade (1963) 111
Chase, Richard Trenton 90
Christensen, Benjamin 40
Christine (1983) 75, 136
Christine (novel) 74, 75
Clarens, Carlos 4
Clark, Bob 62
Clouzot, Henri-Georges 39, 129
Cohen, Larry 53, 111, 141–150
Conrad, Joseph 15
Conrich, Ian 82, 83
Coppola, Francis Ford 91
Corman, Roger 4, 34, 39, 40, 41, 42, 45, 47, 80, 81, 91, 112–121, 167
Cotten, Joseph 26
Count Yorga: Vampire (1970) 78, 88
Craven, Wes 51, 52, 55, 56, 82, 83, 84, 86, 162–171
Crawford, Joan 46, 47
The Crazies (1973) 125
Crazy Mama (1975) 120
Creature from the Haunted Sea (1961) 115, 116
The Creeping Unknown (1954) (a.k.a. *The Quatermass Xperiment*) 41
Creepshow (1982) 75, 127
Cronenberg, David 75, 81, 152, 168
Cruise, Tom 91
Cujo (1983) 75
Cujo (novel) 74
Cukor, George 111
Cullen, Jim 5
Cunningham, Sean S. 51, 162
The Curse of Frankenstein (1956) 42
The Curse of the Cat People (1944) 28
Curtis, Jamie Lee 62
Curtiz, Michael 15

Danse Macabre (book) 30
Dante, Joe 80, 81, 120
The Dark Half (1993) 128, 129

Dark Star (1974) 132
Davis, Bette 45, 47, 149
Dawn of the Dead (1978) 6, 70, 71, 126, 128
Day, William Patrick 24
Day of the Animals (1977) 34
Day of the Dead (1985) 71, 81, 123, 128, 129
The Day of the Triffids (1963) 70
Day of the Woman (1978) (a.k.a. *I Spit on Your Grave*) 65
The Day the Earth Stood Still (1951) 31
Day the World Ended (1956) 34
The Dead Zone (1983) 75
The Dead Zone (novel) 74
Deadly Blessing (1981) 163
Deadly Friend (1986) 167
The Deadly Mantis (1957) 33
Dean, James 36, 90
Death Race 2000 (1975) 115, 120
Death Wish (1974) 134
Deep Red (1975) 111
DeLaurentiis, Dino 154
Deliverance (1972) 65
De Maupassant, Guy 117
Dementia 13 (1963) 48
Demme, Jonathan 120
Demon (1977) (a.k.a. *God Told Me To*) 144
Deneuve, Catherine 89
DePalma, Brian 58, 59, 60, 62, 63, 75, 81, 111
Depeche Mode 68
De Quincey, Thomas 41
Derry, Charles 64
Detour (1945) 159
The Devil–Doll (1936) 102, 103
Diabolique (1955) 39
Diary of a Madman (1963) 118
Dickinson, Angie 131
Dika, Vera 63
Dr. Jekyll and Mr. Hyde (1931) 14
Doctor X (1932) 15, 16
Donen, Stanley 111
Dracula (1931) 5, 11, 12, 13, 19, 57, 97, 100, 101, 124
Dracula (1931, Spanish) 11
Dracula (1979) 81, 88
Dracula (novel) 10, 87
Dracula (play) 100
Dracula Rising (1993) 91

Dracula's Daughter (1936) 24, 57
Dressed to Kill (1980) 63, 64, 65, 111
Dreyer, Carl Theodor 11
Dreyfuss, Richard 69
Du Maurier, Daphne 20, 105
Dune (1984) 152, 154
The Dunwich Horror (1970) 118

Earth vs. the Spider (1958) 33
Eastwood, Clint 131, 132, 133, 135
Easy Rider (1969) 127
Eat My Dust! (1976) 120
Ebert, Roger 124
Edmundson, Mark 85
El Dorado (1967) 132
The Elephant Man (1980) 154
Eliot, T.S. 124, 125, 126, 127
Ellis, Bret Easton 87
Elvis (1979) 133
An Empire of Their Own: How the Jews Invented Hollywood 14
Enemy from Space (1956) (a.k.a. *Quatermass II*) 41
Englund, Robert 83, 84, 162
Eraserhead (1978) 151, 152, 153, 160
Erickson, Leif 32
Escape from L.A. (1996) 137, 138, 139
Escape from New York (1981) 133, 134, 135, 138
The Evil Dead (1981) 81
The Exorcist (1973) 52, 58, 152
Eyes Without a Face (1959) 129

"The Fall of the House of Usher" 4, 41
The Fast and the Furious (1954) 113
Fast Times at Ridgemont High (1982) 154
Father Knows Best (television series) 75
Faulkner, William 4
Ferrara, Abel 92
Firestarter (novel) 74
A Fistful of Dollars (1964) 132, 135
Five Guns West (1955) 112
Florey, Robert 12
Flowers in the Attic (novel) 165
The Fly (1958) 40, 115
The Fog (1981) 131
Fonda, Peter 119, 127
Ford, John 132, 133
Fort Apache (1948) 132
Franco, Jess 88

Index

Frankenstein (1931) 5, 12, 13, 19, 53
Frankenstein: An Adventure in the Macabre 12
Frankenstein: A Modern Prometheus 8, 167
Frankenstein Meets the Wolf Man (1943) 20, 22, 28
Freaks (1932) 15, 101, 102
Freeland, Cynthia 89
Frenzy (1972) 110
Freud, Sigmund 6, 7, 42
Freund, Karl 5, 11, 13, 18, 97
Friday the 13th (1980) 62
Fright Night (1985) 81, 85
Frogs (1972) 33
From Caligari to Hitler: A Psychological History of the German Horror Film 1, 8
Frost, Mark 155
Fulci, Lucio 126
Full Moon High (1981) 147
Fuller, Samuel 149
The Funhouse (1981) 79

Gabler, Neal 14
Gabor, Zsa Zsa 83
Galeen, Henrik 7
Gaslight (1944) 111
Gas-s-s-s! or How It Became Necessary to Destroy the World in Order to Save It 118, 119, 120
Gein, Ed 44, 54
The Ghost of Frankenstein (1942) 20, 22
Ghostbusters (1984) 81
Ghosts of Mars (2001) 131, 139
Ghosts on the Loose (1943) 23
Gifford, Barry 156
Glover, Carol J. 2, 66
God Told Me To (1977) 144, 145, 146, 147
Godzilla, King of the Monsters (1956) 33
Gojira (1954) 33
The Golem (1920) 8
The Golem, or How It Came into the World (1913) 8
Gorgo (1961) 33
The Gorilla Man (1943) 23
Graduation Day (1981) 62
Graham, Allison 52
Graham, Winston 109
Grand Theft Auto (1976) 120

Grant, Cary 106
Gremlins (1984) 81
Grier, Pam 120
Griffith, Charles B. 115
Griffith, D.W. 97
Grizzly (1976) 33
Gunslinger (1956) 112
A Guy Named Joe (1943) 29
Gwenn, Edmund 34

Halberstam, Judith 66
Hall, Charles 11
Halloween (1978) 62, 63, 71, 79, 81, 131, 133, 135
Halloween 2 (1981) 136
Hamilton, George 88
Hamilton, Murray 69
The Hands of Orlac (1925) 18
Hannibal (2001) 93
"Hansel and Gretel" 165, 169, 170
Happy Birthday to Me (1981) 62
Harris, Ed 127
Harris, Thomas 90
Harryhausen, Ray 33, 146
The Haunted House (1928) 40
The Haunted Palace (1962) 45, 118
Hawks, Howard 31, 131, 132, 133, 135
Hawthorne, Nathaniel 4 , 118
He Knows You're Alone (1980) 62
Heart of Darkness (novel) 15
Hedren, "Tippi" 49, 110
Hell Night (1981) 62
Hell Up in Harlem (1973) 143, 144
Hell's Angels: A Strange and Terrible Saga 119
Henn, Carrie 66
Herbert, Frank 154
Hess, David 48
Heston, Charlton 85
Hickox, Dick 163
Hill, Debra 62
Hill Street Blues (television series) 155
The Hills Have Eyes (1977) 55, 162–164
The Hills Have Eyes Part 2 (1985) 165
Hitchcock, Alfred 20, 26, 27, 43–45, 48, 49, 58, 62, 81, 104, 105–111, 133
Hoffman, E.T.A. 7
Hollywood Boulevard (1976) 115, 120
Homicidal (1961) 45
Homunculus (1916) 8
Hooper, Tobe 54, 55, 65, 68, 75, 79, 111

Index

Hopkins, Anthony 91
Hopper, Dennis 119
The Horror Genre: From Beelzebub to Blair Witch 3, 9
Horror of Dracula (1958) 42, 88
House of Dracula (1945) 20, 22
House of Frankenstein (1944) 20, 22, 28
House of Usher (1960) 42, 43, 45, 116, 117, 118
House of Wax (1953) 40, 116, 117
House on Haunted Hill (1959) 40, 41
How I Made a Hundred Movies in Hollywood and Never Lost a Dime 112
Howard, Ron 120
The Howling (1981) 80
Hugo, Victor 98
The Hunchback of Notre Dame (1923) 98
The Hunger (1983) 88, 89, 90
Hunt, Jimmy 32
Hush, Hush ... Sweet Charlotte (1964) 47

I Mobster (1958) 112
I Spit on Your Grave (1978) 65
I Walked with a Zombie (1943) 23
I Was a Teenage Frankenstein (1957) 38
I Was a Teenage Werewolf (1957) 36, 37, 147
An Illustrated History of the Horror Films 4
In Cold Blood 163
In the Mouth of Madness (1995) 85, 86, 137
The Incredible Shrinking Man (1957) 33
Interview with the Vampire (1994) 91, 92
Interview with the Vampire (novel) 90
The Intruder (1962) 117
Invaders from Mars (1953) 31, 32, 33
Invasion of the Body Snatchers (1956) 6, 33, 35, 36, 41, 59, 113, 114, 147
Invasion of the Body Snatchers (1978) 6, 69, 81
Invisible Agent (1942) 22, 23
The Invisible Man (1933) 13
Invitation to Hell (1984) 165
Island of Lost Souls (1933) 15
Isle of the Dead (1945) 23
It Came from Beneath the Sea (1955) 33
It Conquered the World (1956) 34, 113, 114

It Happened One Night (1934) 105
It Lives Again (1978) 54, 143
It's a Wonderful Life (1946) 106, 107
It's Alive (1974) 53, 54, 143, 147

Jack's Wife (1970) 124
James, Henry 10
Janowitz, Hans 10
Jaws (1975) 33, 68, 69, 71, 133
Jensen, Paul 13
John Carpenter's Vampires (1998) 131, 139

Kaczynski, Ted 138
Kael, Pauline 60, 77
Karloff, Boris 13, 16, 17, 18, 19, 39, 40, 120
Kaufman, Philip 69
Kawin, Bruce 2, 31
Kelly, Grace 109, 110
Kemper, Edmund 90
Kennedy, Jamie 86
Key Largo (1948) 131
Kidder, Margot 72
King, Stephen 1, 2, 30, 60, 71, 73, 74, 75, 127, 128, 136, 148
King Kong (1933) 16, 23, 33
Kingdom of the Spiders (1976) 33
Kiss Me Deadly (1955) 29, 159
Knight, Tracey 70
Knightriders (1981) 127
Kohner, Paul 11
Kracauer, Siegfried 1, 8, 10, 101
Krauss, Werner 9
Kubrick, Stanley 73, 74, 75, 118

Laemmle, Carl 14, 100
Landon, Michael 36
Langella, Frank 88
Langenkamp, Heather 84, 85, 169, 170
The Last House on the Left (1972) 48, 51, 52, 56, 162–164
Laura (1944) 111
Lee, Rowland V. 19
Leigh, Janet 62
Leni, Paul 100, 101
Leone, Sergio 132, 134, 135
The Leopard Man (1943) 27
Let's Scare Jessica to Death (1971) 10
Levin, Ira 49
Lewis, Herschell Gordon 62

Lewton, Val 5, 23, 27, 28, 31, 133
Lifeboat (1944) 107
Lillard, Matthew 86
Little Caesar (1931) 142
The Little Shop of Horrors (1960) 41, 115, 116
Lloyd, Danny 74
LoBianco, Tony 145
London After Midnight (1927) 100, 101
Loomis, Nancy 63
Lorre, Peter 18, 39
The Lost Boys (1987) 90
Lost Highway (1997) 157, 158, 159, 160
Love at First Bite (1979) 88
Lovecraft, H.P. 118
Lugosi, Bela 10, 11, 12, 13, 16, 17, 18, 23, 39, 101
Lust for a Vampire (1971) 88
Lynch, David 76, 77, 91, 151–161

Macabre (1958) 39
Machine-Gun Kelly (1958) 112, 114, 115
Mad Love (1935) 18
The Man Who Shot Liberty Valance (1962) 132
Maniac Cop (1988) 144, 149
Mankiewicz, Joseph 112
March, Fredric 14
Mark of the Vampire (1935) 101, 102
Marnie (1964) 104, 109, 110, 111
Martin (1978) 78, 79
The Masque of the Red Death (1964) 45, 46, 47, 118
Matheson, Richard 117, 127
Maturin, C.R. 3
McCarthy, Joseph 147
McCarthy, Kevin 35, 81
McLachlan, Kyle 76, 154, 155
McLuhan, Marshall 82
McMahon, Ed 147
Melmoth the Wanderer 3
Merrick, John 154
Milland, Ray 29
Miller, Dick 40, 81, 115
Mind Ripper (1995) 170
Mr. and Mrs. Smith (1941) 105
Mr. Smith Goes to Washington (1939) 107
Monkey Shines: An Experiment in Fear (1988) 129
Monster from the Ocean Floor (1954) 113

The Monster Show: A Cultural History of Horror 9
Moriarty, Michael 146, 147, 148
Morricone, Ennio 135
Morrison, Jim 90
The Most Dangerous Game (1932) 16
Motel Hell (1981) 81
Ms. 45: Angel of Vengeance (1981) 65
Muir, John Kenneth 85
Mulholland Drive (2001) 159, 160
Mulvey, Laura 109
The Mummy (1932) 5, 13
"The Mummy's Pool" 31
Murnau, F.W. 10, 87, 94
My Bloody Valentine (1980) 62
My Darling Clementine (1946) 132
The Mysterious Doctor (1943) 23
Mystery of the Wax Museum (1933) 15, 16, 40

Nadja (1994) 91
Near Dark (1987) 90
Neill, Sam 85
Ngai, Sianne 84
Nicholson, Jack 74, 119
Nicholson, James 42
Nietzsche, Friedrich 92
Night and the City (1950) 158
Night of the Lepus (1972) 33
Night of the Living Dead (1968) 6, 49, 50, 51, 52, 70, 122–126, 129, 132
Night of the Living Dead (1990) 71
Night School (1981) 62
A Nightmare on Elm Street (1984) 82, 165–169
A Nightmare on Elm Street Part 2: Freddy's Revenge (1985) 82
A Nightmare on Elm Street Part 3: Dream Warriors (1987) 82, 83, 167–169
North by Northwest (1959) 106
Nosferatu: A Symphony of Horror (1922) 10, 11, 87, 94
Not of This Earth (1957) 34, 114, 118

O'Bannon, Dan 81, 129
The Oblong Box (1969) 118
Obsession (1976) 111
O'Connor, Flannery 5
Ohmart, Carol 41
The Oklahoma Woman (1956) 112

Index

The Old Dark House (1932) 18
Outside the Law (1920) 98

Peckinpah, Sam 132
The People Under the Stairs (1991) 168, 169
Perfect Strangers (1984) 144, 147
Perkins, Anthony 43
Phantom of the Paradise (1974) 111
Phase IV (1974) 33
Pickens, Slim 81
Piercing the Darkness: Undercover with Vampires in America Today 92
Piper, Roddy 137
Piranha (1978) 81, 120
Pirie, David 88
Pit and the Pendulum (1961) 45, 117, 118
Pitt, Brad 91
Pleasence, Donald 135
Poe, Edgar Allan 4, 7, 17, 41, 45, 47, 118, 119, 120
Polanski, Roman 49, 58
Poltergeist (1982) 72, 73
Poltergeist II: The Other Side (1986) 73
Pratt, William Henry (a.k.a. Boris Karloff) 13
The Premature Burial (1962) 45, 117, 118
Preminger, Otto 111
Price, Vincent 40, 41, 42, 46, 47, 116, 117, 118
Prince of Darkness (1987) 131, 136
Prom Night (1980) 62
Prophecy (1979) 34
The Prowler (1980) 62
Psycho (1960) 43, 44, 45, 48, 49, 58, 62, 79, 104, 107, 109

Q: The Winged Serpent (1981) 81, 144, 146, 147
Quatermass II (1956) 41
The Quatermass Xperiment (1954) 41
Queen of the Damned (2002) 92

Raines, Claude 13
Ramsland, Katherine 90, 92
The Raven (1935) 18
The Raven (1963) 45, 118
Re-Animator (1985) 81
Rear Window (1954) 107, 108, 109
Rebecca (1940) 20, 105
Rebel Without a Cause (1955) 36

Red Dragon (novel) 90
Red River (1948) 132
Repulsion (1965) 49, 58, 152
Ressler, Robert 90, 92
The Return of Dracula (1958) 78, 88
Return of the Jedi (1983) 154
Return of the Living Dead (1985) 78, 81, 129
The Return of the Vampire (1943) 23
A Return to Salem's Lot (1987) 148
Revenge of the Zombies (1943) 23
Rice, Anne 90, 91
Richter, W.D. 69
Rio Bravo (1959) 131, 132, 139
Rio Lobo (1970) 132
Robbins, Tod 98
Robinson, Edward G. 142
Rock All Night (1957) 112
Romero, George A. 50, 51, 70, 71, 75, 78, 79, 81, 90, 111, 122, 123–130, 132
Rope (1948) 107
Rosemary's Baby (1968) 47, 48, 50, 58
Rothman, Stephanie 120
Ruben, Joseph 75
Russell, Kurt 133, 135, 136

Saboteur (1942) 106
The St. Valentine's Day Massacre (1967) 112, 118
'Salem's Lot (1979) 75
'Salem's Lot (novel) 74, 148
"The Sandman" 7
Sarris, Andrew 95, 97, 112
Sartre, Jean-Paul 92
Savada, Elias 97
Savini, Tom 71
Saxon, John 84
Sayles, John 80, 81, 120
Scheider, Roy 69
Schrader, Paul 27, 29
Schreck, Max 10, 94
Scorsese, Martin 120
Scott, Tony 88
Scream (1996) 86, 162, 170
Scream Blacula Scream (1973) 88
The Search for Bridey Murphy (novel) 114
The Searchers (1956) 132
Season of the Witch (1970) (a.k.a. *Jack's Wife*) 124
Seizure (1974) 10

Selznick, David O. 23, 105
Sennett, Mack 98
The Serpent and the Rainbow (1988) 168
The Seventh Victim (1943) 28
Shadow of a Doubt (1943) 26, 27, 104, 106, 107
Shadow of the Vampire (2000) 94
Shaft (1971) 142
Sharrett, Christopher 54
Shatner, William 117
Shaye, Robert 83, 84
Shelley, Mary 8, 14, 167
The Shining (1982) 73, 74
The Shining (novel) 73, 74
Shocker (1989) 168
Siegel, Don 35
The Silence of the Lambs (1991) 91, 92, 93
The Silence of the Lambs (novel) 90
Silver, Alain 87, 91
Simon, Simone 24, 25
Siodmak, Robert 111
Sisters (1973) 58, 59, 62, 66, 111
Skal, David J. 1, 2, 9, 11, 12, 22, 97, 100, 101
Smith, Perry 163
Son of Dracula (1944) 20, 28, 78
Son of Frankenstein (1939) 19, 53
Sorority Girl (1957) 112
Spacek, Sissy 61
Special Effects (1984) 144, 147, 150
Spielberg, Steven 68, 69, 72
The Spiral Staircase (1946) 111
Spoto, Donald 50, 106
Squirm (1976) 33
Stagecoach (1939) 132
Stallone, Sylvester 120
The Stand (novel) 75, 127
Starman (1984) 136
Stefano, Joseph 44
The Stepfather (1987) 75
The Stepford Wives (1975) 6, 59, 60
Stevenson, Robert Louis 14
Stewart, Jimmy 107, 108, 109, 132
Stoker, Bram 10, 11, 87
Stone, Oliver 10
Strait-Jacket (1964) 39, 47
Strangers on a Train (1951) 107
The Student Nurses (1970) 120
The Student of Prague (1913) 7, 8, 14

The Stuff (1985) 147
Subspecies (1991) 91
Summer of Fear (1978) 163
Superfly (1972) 142
Suspicion (1941) 106
Swamp Thing (1982) 165
The Swarm (1978) 34

Tales from the Darkside (television series) 127
Tales of Terror (1962) 45, 118
Tarantula (1955) 33
Targets (1968) 120
Teague, Lewis 75
Teen Wolf (1985) 81
Teenage Doll (1957) 112
The Terror (1963) 120
Terror Train (1980) 62
The Texas Chain Saw Massacre (1974) 54, 55, 65, 68, 81
The Texas Chain Saw Massacre Part 2 (1986) 65, 66, 84
Thalberg, Irving 98
Them! (1954) 33, 34, 41
There's Always Vanilla (1970) 124
Thesiger, Ernest 18, 19
They Live (1988) 136, 137
The Thing (1982) 81, 131, 135
The Thing from Another World (1951) 30, 31, 35, 36
The Thirty-Nine Steps (1935) 104, 105, 106
Thompson, Hunter S. 119
To Have and Have Not (1944) 131
To Sleep with a Vampire (1993) 91
Tobey, Kenneth 81
The Tomb of Ligeia (1964) 45, 118
Tourneur, Jacques 24
Towne, Robert 120
The Trip (1967) 118, 119
Truffaut, Francois 95, 104
Twice-Told Tales (1963) 118
Twilight Zone: The Movie (1983) 81
Twin Peaks (1990) 152, 155
Twin Peaks (television series) 156
Twin Peaks: Fire Walk with Me (1992) 157
Twins of Evil (1971) 88
Twitch of the Death Nerve (1972) 62
2001: A Space Odyssey (1967) 118, 132, 153

Index

Ulrich, Skeet 86
"The Uncanny" 7
Uncle Sam (1997) 149
The Undead (1957) 114
The Understudy: Graveyard Shift 2 (1988) 87
The Unholy Three (1925) 98, 99, 101, 103
The Uninvited (1944) 29
The Unknown (1927) 99, 100, 101
Ursini, James 87, 91

Vampire in Brooklyn (1995) 169
The Vampire Lestat (novel) 90
The Vampire Lovers (1970) 88
Vampyr (1932) 11
Vampyros Lesbos (1970) 88
Van Cleef, Lee 113, 114, 135
Veidt, Conrad 9
Vertigo (1958) 109
Videodrome (1983) 81, 82
The Virgin Spring (1960) 51, 162, 163
Von Richtofen and Brown (1971) 118

Wallace, Dee 80
Waller, Gregory 2
Walpole, Horace 3
War-Gods of the Deep (1965) 118
War of the Satellites (1958) 114
The War of the Worlds (1953) 31, 32
The Wasp Woman (1960) 115
The Waste Land (poem) 124, 125, 126
Waxworks (1924) 101
Wayne, John 131, 132, 133, 136
Weaver, Sigourney 66
Webling, Peggy 12
Wegener, Paul 7, 8, 14
Weird Woman (1944) 57
Weldon, Joan 34
Wells, H.G. 13
Wells, Paul 3, 9, 17, 48, 66, 77, 86
Wes Craven Presents Carnival of Souls (1998) 170
Wes Craven Presents Dracula 2000 (2000) 170

Wes Craven Presents They (2002) 170
Wes Craven Presents Wishmaster (1997) 170
Wes Craven's New Nightmare (1994) 84, 85, 169, 170
West, Nathanael 5
Whale, James 5, 12, 13, 18, 97
What Ever Happened to Baby Jane? (1962) 45
White Zombie (1932) 11
Whitworth, James 55, 56
Whoever Fights Monsters 90
The Wicked Darling (1919) 97
Wicked Stepmother (1989) 149
Wiene, Robert 10, 18
The Wild Angels (1966) 118
Wild at Heart (1990) 156, 157
The Wild Bunch (1969) 132
Wilder, Billy 5
"William Wilson" 4, 7
Williams, Linda 64
Williams, Tony 2, 53, 54
Williamson, Fred 142
Williamson, Kevin 86
Wise, Robert 31, 112
The Wizard of Oz (1939) 156, 157
The Wolf Man (1941) 22, 24, 81
Women in Cages (1972) 120
Wood, Robin 2, 52, 54, 57, 65, 71, 79, 94, 106, 110, 141
Woods, James 139
Worsley, Wallace 98
Wray, Fay 16
Wright, Teresa 26
The Wrong Man (1956) 108
Wyler, William 112
Wynter, Dana 35

X: The Man with the X-Ray Eyes (1963) 118
X The Unknown (1956) 41

Zombie (1979) 126